Getting Over the Color Green

Getting

Over

the

Color

Green

Contemporary

Environmental Literature

of the Southwest

EDITED BY SCOTT SLOVIC

The University of Arizona Press   Tucson

First Printing
The University of Arizona Press
© 2001 The Arizona Board of Regents

♾ This book is printed on acid-free, archival-quality paper.
Manufactured in the United States of America

06 05 04 03 02 01   6 5 4 3 2 1

Library of Congress Cataloging-in-Publication Data
Getting over the color green : contemporary environmental literature of the
Southwest / edited by Scott Slovic.
        p. cm.
Includes bibliographical references (p.   ) and index.
ISBN 0-8165-1664-2 (alk. paper)
ISBN 0-8165-1665-0 (pbk. : alk. paper)
        1. American literature—Southwestern States. 2. Environmental protection—
Literary collections. 3. Environmental literature—Southwestern States.
4. Southwestern States—Literary collections. 5. Wilderness areas—Literary
collections. 6. Nature—Literary collections. I. Slovic, Scott, 1960–
PS566.G47 2001
810.8'0355—dc21

                                                        00-010458

British Library Cataloguing-in-Publication Data
A catalogue record for this book is available from the British Library.

This book is dedicated to my son, Jacinto, and my nephews Spencer, Cameron, and Oblio in the hope that you will all enjoy the beauty of the desert Southwest for many years to come in a condition not much diminished from today's.

And to the Camacho family, especially Amelia and Eduardo, my closest ties to the Southwest from 1983 to 1999—thank you!

And to the Center for the Study of the Southwest at Southwest Texas State University in San Marcos, directed by Professor Mark Busby. This book began as a special issue of the journal *Southwestern American Literature* (Fall 1995), published by the Center.

I would also like to express my gratitude to Jimmy Guignard, Tere Linde, and Barbara "Barney" Nelson for research assistance and help in preparing the manuscript of this book at the University of Nevada, Reno. A grant from the Office of the Vice President for Research at Nevada also proved invaluable in making the book possible.

Contents

You have to get over the color green; you have to quit associating beauty with gardens and lawns; you have to get used to an inhuman scale; you have to understand geological time.

—WALLACE STEGNER, "THOUGHTS IN A DRY LAND" (1972)

Introduction

Getting Over the Color Green provides, for the first time, a collection of excellent contemporary writing about nature from the greater Southwest, spanning several genres (nonfiction, field notes, fiction, and poetry) and more than half a dozen states. Many readers have enjoyed the eloquent and cantankerous voices of Joseph Wood Krutch and Edward Abbey and other southwestern authors who rose to prominence during the latter half of the twentieth century, but fewer have had the opportunity to encounter new voices from the region. Focusing largely, though not exclusively, on these new, emerging, and innovative voices, this anthology celebrates and illuminates the unique vitality and complexity of southwestern environmental literature during the final decade of the twentieth century: its treatment of places often deemed vacant, inhospitable wastelands; its response to the region's pyrotechnic colors and Gothic shapes that both incite and overwhelm the artist's imagination; its demonstration that nature writing is not a collective, pastoral fantasy for white, male, middle-class, urban writers and readers, but rather a genre to which male and female artists of diverse backgrounds have contributed trenchant explorations of real places. In many ways the contemporary environmental literature of the Southwest exemplifies the future of such writing nationwide. The purpose here is not to be encyclopedic and exhaustive but to provide a stimulating sample of the literary explorations of southwestern places that have appeared since 1990.

During the final decades of the twentieth century, there was a

flowering of important writing about the relationship between human
beings and the natural world, a virtual renaissance in the branch of
American literature that scholars refer to as "nature writing" or "environmental literature." The scholar and anthologist John A. Murray,
introducing the "Nature-Writing Symposium" in the Fall 1992 issue of
the Hawaiian journal *Manoa,* writes, "Since the first Earth Day on
April 22, 1970, a once obscure prose genre—nature writing—has steadily grown in stature and popularity, attracting more and more of the
best writers and larger and larger portions of the reading public until, in
1992, it is arguably *the* major genre in American literature." Murray's
claim continued to hold true as we neared and passed the landmark year
2000. What has also become increasingly clear is the extraordinary
richness of environmental writing from particular geographical regions,
from coastal Alaska to the Florida Everglades, but none more so than
that from the arid Southwest.

One could argue that powerful literature about the American
landscape began not with Henry David Thoreau's *Walden* in the Boston
suburbs of the mid-nineteenth century but with Álvar Núñez Cabeza
de Vaca's *La Relación y Comentarios* (often translated as *Adventures in the
Unknown Interior of America*), an account of the author's journey across
Florida, Texas, New Mexico, Arizona, and northern Mexico between
1527 and 1537, which was published in 1542 in Spain. Anglo explorers,
including Clarence Dutton and John Wesley Powell, produced splendid
accounts of their adventures in the Southwest during the nineteenth
century, perhaps offering the first inkling of genuine aesthetic appreciation for the unaccommodating landscapes of the Southwest, this region
of too little water, too many thorny plants, a surreal gaudiness of clouds
and land—purples, oranges, reds, and browns—and downright weird-
ness of rock formations. The Rutgers University art historian John C.
Van Dyke, with the publication of *The Desert* in 1901, further appropri-
ated the Southwest for mainstream American readers. In the middle of
this century, such writers as Roy Bedichek in Texas, Frank Waters in
New Mexico, Aldo Leopold in New Mexico and Arizona, Joseph
Wood Krutch, also in Arizona, and Walter Van Tilburg Clark in Nevada elevated the images and narratives of the Southwest, as presented

in written English, to a high art. Much of this writing, from Cabeza de Vaca through Edward Abbey and Wallace Stegner, was collected and contextualized in Peter Wild's 1991 anthology, *The Desert Reader.* The aim of this new anthology is, in a sense, to pick up where *The Desert Reader* leaves off, focusing on the special emergence of significant and diverse southwestern environmental writers during the final decade of the twentieth century. One could argue, in fact, that the abundance of outstanding women writers and writers of diverse cultural backgrounds is the hallmark of today's environmental writing from the desert Southwest—and perhaps the distinctive feature of this collection, too.

Wallace Stegner exclaims in an essay called "Thoughts in a Dry Land" (1972) that to appreciate nature in the arid West, "You have to get over the color green; you have to quit associating beauty with gardens and lawns; you have to get used to an inhuman scale; you have to understand geological time." It's taken American literature a long time to "get over the color green," to recognize the value of vast sprawls of land devoid of human forms and lacking in the verdant, accommodating color green—and its many variants—so appealing to cultures that have evolved in the earth's temperate zones. David Teague argues in *The Southwest in American Literature and Art: The Rise of a Desert Aesthetic,* "Until about the mid-1890s, deserts were powerful icons of howling wilderness for citizens of the United States. They were incomprehensible to the collective imagination of the 'civilized' portion of the country because they were places where accustomed modes of geography, agriculture, industry, and commerce did not obtain. But by 1910 deserts had become associated with the very height of American culture."

Despite the rapid rise of a desert aesthetic between 1890 and 1910, it has actually taken much longer for the general public in the United States to embrace the arid and apparently empty landscapes of the Southwest as beautiful and meaningful places. Deserts, for many people, remain simply blank areas on the map—wasted paper, wasted land. Terry Tempest Williams powerfully articulates the implications of this attitude in her book *Refuge: An Unnatural History of Family and Place* (1991):

A blank spot on the map translates into empty space, space devoid of people, a wasteland perfect for nerve gas, weteye bombs, and toxic waste.

The army believes that the Great Salt Lake Desert is an ideal place to experiment with biological warfare.

An official from the Atomic Energy Commission had one comment regarding the desert between St. George, Utah, and Las Vegas, Nevada: "It's a good place to throw used razor blades."

A woman from the Department of Energy, who had mapped the proposed nuclear-waste repository in Lavender Canyon, adjacent to Canyonlands National Park, flew into Moab, Utah, from Washington, D.C., to check her calculations and witness this "blank spot." She was greeted by a local, who drove her directly to the site. Once there, she got out of the vehicle, stared into the vast, redrock wilderness and shook her head slowly, delivering four words:

"I had no idea."

One of the goals of environmental writing in the Southwest, sometimes tacit and other times fully explicit, is to help readers attend to the reality of this special region, to see beyond the map's blankness. This constitutes an extension of the desert aesthetic that began to percolate in American culture a century ago, thanks to the efforts of Frederic Remington, Albert Bierstadt, Thomas Moran, John C. Van Dyke, Stephen Crane, Mary Austin, and various other visual and literary artists. Some would claim that this is an uphill battle. In the tradition of Paul Shepard's classic study *Man in the Landscape: A Historic View of the Esthetics of Nature* (1967), Michael Pollan attempts to account for Americans' love of green grass in their yards, wondering if "the allure of the lawn is in the genes." Sociobiologists, he writes, have "gone so far as to propose a 'Savanna Syndrome' to explain our fondness for grass. Encoded in our DNA is a preference for an open grassy landscape resembling the shortgrass savannas of Africa on which we evolved and spent our first few thousand years. A grassy plain dotted with trees provides safety from predators and a suitable environment for grazing animals; this is said to explain why we have remade the wooded landscapes of Europe and North America in the image of East Africa."

However, as Yi-Fu Tuan explains in *Topophilia* (1974), "no environment is devoid of the power to command the allegiance of at least some people. Wherever we can point to human beings, there we point to somebody's *home*—with all the kindly meaning of that word." Increasingly, as native peoples from the American Southwest have gained access to mainstream outlets of cultural expression and as artists descended from immigrants to this continent have settled in the Southwest, this region, with its exposed rock and subtly dazzling red, brown, yellow, gray, and black animals and plants, has come to be "home" for some of the country's most articulate writers. Visitors to the region, like Edward Abbey's tourist from Cleveland, Ohio, might still be inclined to take one look at the red rock of southern Utah and opine, "This would be good country . . . if only you had some water," but the wealth of new literature celebrating the austerities of this dry region attests to the steadfast evolution of a new aesthetic, notwithstanding the air-conditioned subdivisions and grassy yards that sprawl across Phoenix and Las Vegas, Albuquerque and El Paso.

Nevada author Ann Ronald, herself a native of the Pacific Northwest, has picked up Stegner's cause after thirty years in Reno: "Stegner is right, of course. Almost all of us have been taught a worldview that prefers green and blue to ocher and beige, that values redwoods and oceans more than rabbitbrush and sinks. Stegner concludes by saying that we inherently lack appreciation for such things as sagebrush and raw earth and alkali flats. These, he suggests, are acquired tastes, ones not easily adopted by conventional sensibilities." Sensitivity to the ecological and aesthetic dimensions of the arid West may require something other than the sensibilities evident in environmental literature from the rest of the country—readers may, in fact, detect a common tendency to "appreciate the unappreciated" in the poems and stories and essays collected in this volume.

Stegner called the apprehension of arid landscapes "the process of westernization of the perceptions that has to happen before the West is beautiful to us." And not "beautiful" in aesthetic terms alone, I might add, but also understood and valued from an ecological perspective. Although deserts are difficult places to live, human population growth and the corresponding need for places to live and grow food have resulted in a steady population influx in desert regions throughout the world. As Gregory McNamee notes, "The deserts now sustain about a sixth of the human population; in the next century, it may be half, and desert ecosystems—fragile for all their seeming fierceness—will suffer accordingly." All of the arts have contributed to this "westernization of the perceptions," but literature has played a central role. Among the arts, literature has offered an especially nuanced and effective presentation of ecological and social information, in addition to aesthetic appreciation.

In recent decades we have also witnessed—and increasingly welcomed into the canon—the emergence of important indigenous literary voices from the Southwest, including authors who use Spanish, O'odham, Nahuatl, and other languages. Apart from "Legends and Lore of the Papago and Pima Indians," compiled by two Anglo scholars, all the writings included in Wild's *The Desert Reader* are by authors of European descent. In assembling this new collection, I have tried to suggest the exceptional diversity of contemporary southwestern cultures—this is, indeed, one of the defining features of the "human landscape" of the region. As Thomas D. Hall puts it in his definitive study *Social Change in the Southwest, 1350–1880,* "The physical diversity of the region is matched by its linguistic and cultural diversity." Contributors include Gloria Bird, Joy Harjo, Linda Hogan, Pat Mora, Simon J. Ortiz, Alberto Rios, and Luci Tapahonso. Readers will glean a sense of richly diverse ways of experiencing the world from the poems of Ray Gonzalez and Ofelia Zepeda; and from the stories of Rudolfo Anaya and Benjamin Alire Sáenz and the poem by Jimmy Santiago Baca, they will become sensitized to issues of "environmental justice," to the ways that technology and economics impact the lives of particular groups of people living in the region.

Working in the immediate wake of Rachel Carson's *Silent Spring,* the early years of the modern environmental movement in the United States, and the experimental merging of fictional narrative techniques with journalistic research that Tom Wolfe called "The New Journalism," Edward Abbey published in 1968 the cornerstone work of modern American nature writing, a paean to southern Utah's canyon lands: *Desert Solitaire: A Season in the Wilderness.* More than three decades have now passed since *Desert Solitaire* launched the renaissance of modern nature writing in this country. This collection places the spotlight on Edward Abbey's contemporary heirs, ranging from his peers and old friends (including Charles Bowden, Edward Lueders, Richard Shelton, Peter Wild, and Ann Haymond Zwinger) to the new generation of southwestern environmental writers, led by Alison Hawthorne Deming, Stephen Harrigan, Ken Lamberton, Kent Nelson, Naomi Shihab Nye, Sharman Apt Russell, Terry Tempest Williams, and many other impressive artists.

Some readers may wonder what I mean by "southwestern." This anthology began as a special issue of the journal *Southwestern American Literature,* and it may be the obligatory gesture of every guest editor of that publication to offer a definition of "the Southwest." Admittedly, it is more difficult to define such a region than it is simply to point to a state's borders on the map and say, "This is Texas nature writing" or "This is environmental literature from Arizona." As someone who grew up in the damp, green forests of Oregon's Willamette Valley, in a place the locals like to call "The Emerald Empire," I think of the Southwest as anywhere in the United States (and perhaps Mexico) where the general hue of the land is more brown than green, where one's lips crack from dryness and sweat dries almost instantly, and where cactus or tumbleweed or sagebrush abound. Or where it's so dry, or the drop-offs so sheer, that nothing grows at all. When Stegner writes about the West, he means in particular those states, or the portions thereof, where water is scarce; "aridity, and aridity alone, makes the various Wests one," he states in a 1987 piece called "Living Dry." We're talking, then, about Arizona, New Mexico, Utah, Nevada, and parts of Texas, Oklahoma, Kansas, Nebraska, the Dakotas, Wyoming, Idaho, Montana, Washington, Oregon, and California. This may seem an overly loose and encompassing way of circumscribing the region, but it's a loose and encompassing definition that can be traced all the way back to John Wesley Powell's *Report on the Lands of the Arid Region of the United States* (1878). In other words, people have been struggling to define "the West" and "the Southwest" for quite a long time.

Some scholars would claim that we must come to terms with such definitions before we can begin to appreciate the social and cultural implications of literature that emerges from the region. Reed Way Dasenbrock, for instance, makes the following powerful argument:

> To ask what Southwestern literature is, one must first ask, What is the Southwest? For whom is it the Southwest? What is the Southwest southwest of? These are not questions we ask very often, even though—or perhaps because—the answer is so obvious. The Southwest wasn't the Southwest for its original inhabitants, Native Americans of whatever nation or people. It was the center of their world. Just as clearly, it was not the Southwest for the successive waves of Spanish (and Mexican) travelers and settlers. It was the north. . . .
>
> So for whom is it the Southwest? For the Anglo, whose first penetration into the area was down the Santa Fe Trail, heading southwest. And it is easy enough to see how the term *the Southwest,* in naming a region according to its direction away from the centers of power and population, is a perfect representation of the dependent status of the whole area. Once an area to which statehood was long denied, and now an area whose economy is dependent on the military who love having big open spaces to blow things up in, the Southwest has been treated virtually as a colonial possession by those it is southwest of.

Most of the selections in this book do not overtly express the defiance toward northern and eastern centers of political and cultural power evident in Dasenbrock's comments. Nonetheless, perhaps in a somewhat subtler and gentler way, these literary texts aim to demonstrate that there is grace and beauty in this long-disparaged, long-neglected part of the world—beauty in the human traditions that have developed in the desert and in the natural features of the desert itself. Dasenbrock points out that "traditional Southwestern literature is . . . the discourse of an outsider, not a celebration of the local but a celebration of the exotic." Times have changed, though: much of the work collected here has been produced by long-term (sometimes lifelong) residents of the region.

There are still other approaches to characterizing the Southwest.

Thomas D. Hall, in his chapter "The Southwest: The Region, the Peoples and Prehistory," offers a map that includes San Francisco, California, in the far northwest; southwestern Missouri in the far northeast; all of Baja California; and a good part of the Mexican mainland, down through the southern reaches of the Sierra Madre Occidental and the Sierra Madre Oriental, the country's major northern mountain ranges. Leslie Fiedler, in defining "the Western," once commented: "Never mind the geographical setting. The West is a metaphor for, a mythic name of, the Unexplored wherever it may be: the retreating horizon, the territory that always lies just ahead of where we happen to be, waiting to be penetrated by anyone willing to light out ahead of the rest." I like this idea, too—perhaps it would do to say that, for me, the Southwest is a realm of heat and aridity and "the retreating horizon," both physical and psychological. More concretely, any writing about landscape, about natural phenomena, within the boundaries of America's southwestern desert regions—the Chihuahuan, the Sonoran, the Mojave, and the Great Basin—constitutes, to my mind, indisputable southwestern environmental literature. But allow for some slippage to include such places as the scrub country of south-central Texas and the dry mountains of Colorado. Hall, in *Social Change in the Southwest*, quotes geographer Donald Meinig on the difficulty of defining the Southwest: "The Southwest is a distinctive place to the American mind but a somewhat blurred place on American maps, which is to say that everyone knows that there is a Southwest but there is little agreement as to just where it is. . . . The term 'Southwest' is of course an ethnocentric one: what is south and west to the Anglo-American was long the north of the Hispanic-American."

Rather than splitting more hairs in pursuit of an ultimate definition of the American Southwest, I'll count on the specific selections in this anthology to help concretize notions of this region particular to the mind of each reader. Some of the "settings" of individual texts are imprecise or multiple, but I have tried to identify the particular locations represented by the various readings—and this may help to clarify the geographical range of the anthology. These settings are listed in the index.

The book is organized according to four thematic categories: "Watching Closely: Forays in Natural History"; "Risking Experience: Adventures in the Wild"; "Living Close to the Land"; and "Taking a Stand: Voices of Conservation and Restoration." The first of these sections emphasizes the effort, not only in traditional natural history essays but also in attentive and knowledgeable poetry and fiction, to observe the workings of the physical world and its inhabitants. Many of the natural history contributors, such as John Alcock and Robert Michael Pyle, are trained scientists, while others have, as Robert Finch once put it, "slip[ped] in through the back door of the humanities." One of the unique traits of environmental writers is their frequent willingness to risk discomfort—or worse—in an effort to experience something vivid and authentic, something meaningful. Of course, such adventures need not occur only in traditional wild places, removed from human traffic, but often such places—from tumbling whitewater to chilly mountaintops—are indeed the loci of revelations. Some of the narratives in the second section emphasize the lone explorer's daring encounter with reality—this is the case with Leslie Ryan and Reg Saner. Others, though, such as Karen Brennan and Stephen Trimble, show that powerful experience often occurs as a result of contact with other people. While some of the contributors to the anthology point to the value of venturing away from home into "the wilds," others explore various notions of being at home—this is, of course, one of the crucial aspects of the process by which the desert Southwest is achieving recognition in mainstream American culture as a beautiful and fragile region. Contributors to the third section of the book range from exiled Southwesterners such as Rick Bass to such lifelong natives as Simon J. Ortiz and Ofelia Zepeda. As many environmentalists have noted, attachment to place (to home) typically leads to a sense of responsibility, a desire to protect particular places and the inhabitants, human and nonhuman alike, of those places. The fourth and final section of the book highlights the protective, hortatory mode of contemporary southwestern environmental writing, ranging from the strident social critiques of Rudolfo Anaya and Gregory McNamee to the more philosophical approaches of Linda Hogan and T. H. Watkins. My goal has been to illuminate several of the key dimensions of this rich body of literature, if not to exhaust its richness and complexity. From this starting point, readers should have a set of landmarks to aid in their further explorations of the field.

Five years ago, in June, I spent three days in a U-HAUL truck with my mother and two dogs, a silver Hyundai in tow, traversing what some might consider the entire span of the desert Southwest. We began our drive in San Marcos, Texas, turning our backs on north-south Interstate 35 and the rolling green hills, muggy air, and bayous down east toward Houston. As we entered the hill country, just minutes west of San Marcos, already we recognized southwestern landscape icons: abrupt, flat-topped mesas; prickly pear cactus, mesquite, and scraggly live oaks; and rocky, brown-and-yellow soil. Had we turned off Highway 290 for half an hour north of Fredericksburg, we could have stretched our legs on Enchanted Rock, the enormous yellow bulb of stone reminiscent of Australia's Ayers Rock. Instead, we pushed on toward the intersection with I-10, past Sonora and Ozona, after which the vegetation shrivels for hundreds of miles to the west and, as Roy Bedicheck groans in *Adventures with a Texas Naturalist* (1947), "peering into the mirage shimmering down long stretches of overheated pavement, [the tourist's] eyes will welcome anything to lean upon." We passed Van Horn as the sun began to set, our eyes savoring the first curtain of western mountains. Having put in 600 miles for the day, we reached our overnight stop in El Paso at about midnight—still in Texas. The vastness of the Southwest. The next morning I felt a pinch in my armpit as I buttoned on a clean shirt in the bathroom. I shook the shirt a few times and glanced in the mirror, surprised to see a three-inch brown scorpion scamper across my shoulders, tail curved over its shoulders, and drop to the floor. I chose to view this assignation as a goodbye gesture from the state of Texas.

A day later we were on the road again: mom, son, dogs. Not long out of El Paso, as we hauled across southern New Mexico en route to Tucson, we enjoyed the white-and-yellow plumes of blooming yucca plants, yucca plants everywhere—wildflowers desert style. Yuccas yielded the terrain to saguaros as we approached Tucson, then saguaros became Joshua trees north of Phoenix. Such rapid travel across the region at ground level has the effect of time-lapse photography, the spatial equivalent of collapsing time, clarifying the unexpected isomorphisms of desert plants. After a second full day of driving, we camped out with the dogs in the Kingman Holiday Inn, dreaming of mad right-wing bombers and human-shaped cacti.

It was still dark when we roused the dogs and creaked onto the highway again, racing to beat rush hour in Las Vegas, pausing only for an ironic photo opportunity: environmentalists enjoying the sunrise at Hoover Dam. We took turns photographing each other in front of the sunlit dam complex. Then I held my breath and clenched the steering wheel as we trucked through the Vegas crowds till at last we were home free on Highway 95 North. It was eight in the morning, and the whole day, plus much of western Nevada, stretched before us. We passed Indian Springs, Amargosa Valley, Beatty, Scotty's Junction, Goldfield, Tonopah, Hawthorne, and lots of open desert with snowcapped mountains—the Sierras—to the west in California and sere Nevada hills to the right, the east. We passed a mysterious naval test site near Hawthorne, strange, sod-covered bunkers arrayed across a nondescript field. We passed beautiful, dying Walker Lake, a blue jewel in the desert, much like Pyramid Lake to the north. Finally, a sharp turn to the west at Fallon, where the miracle of massive irrigation makes the desert bloom into agriculture, and we were a mere hour's drive out of Reno, the object of our 1,800-mile trek.

Reno sits, casinos and all, at the cusp of several distinct regions, most prominently the Great Basin Desert to the east and the Sierra Nevada Range to the west. Annual precipitation here is approximately seven inches. One could say that Reno is the apotheosis of human existence in the arid West. Its brilliant neon lights burst forth each night, beautifully, from what were once the Truckee Meadows—the dark outlines of various mountain ranges are visible, but only faintly, in the background, and the stars above are even more faint. I find myself asking, "Do people belong in desert country?" Reflecting upon his family's history in the West, Wallace Stegner writes: "Pipedreams. Arrogant pipedreams. Why should deserts be asked to blossom? They have their own intricately interdependent plant and animal species, including the creosote-ring clones that are the oldest living things on earth.

The deserts were doing all right until we set out to reform them." Human interference in such intricate, delicate natural systems is an act of hubris, a risk—yes, a profound and probably foolhardy gamble. Stegner recalls that his own father, having failed at mining, "ran a gambling joint in Reno, an occupation symbolically right for him as for the West at large." From endangered species and overused aquifers in Texas to drying, dying lakes and ravaged rangelands and the prospect of irradiated mountainsides in Nevada, the environmental history of human presence in the Southwest—at least that of immigrant cultures—is not particularly proud, the future ambivalent. But the lyrical, exploratory, and sometimes defiant literature that documents our experience of this part of the world is undeniably worth celebrating. Thus this anthology.

Works Cited

Abbey, Edward. *Desert Solitaire: A Season in the Wilderness.* 1968. New York: Bantam, 1985.

Bedichek, Roy. *Adventures with a Texas Naturalist.* 1947. Austin: University of Texas Press, 1988.

Cabeza de Vaca, Álvar Núñez. *Adventures in the Unknown Interior of America.* 1542. Trans. and ed. Cyclone Covey. Albuquerque: University of New Mexico Press, 1988.

Dasenbrock, Reed Way. "Southwest of What?: Southwestern Literature as a Form of Frontier Literature." In *Desert, Garden, Margin, Range: Literature on the American Frontier,* edited by Eric Heyne. New York: Twayne, 1992.

Fiedler, Leslie. "Malamud's Travesty Western." *Novel: A Forum on Fiction* (Spring 1977): 212–19.

Finch, Robert. "Being at Two with Nature." In *The Norton Reader,* edited by Arthur M. Eastman et al. 8th ed. New York: Norton, 1992.

Hall, Thomas D. *Social Change in the Southwest, 1350–1880.* Lawrence: University Press of Kansas, 1989.

McNamee, Gregory, ed. *The Sierra Club Desert Reader: A Literary Companion.* San Francisco: Sierra Club Books, 1995.

Murray, John A. "Nature-Writing Symposium." *Manoa* (Fall 1992): 73–96.

Pollan, Michael. *Second Nature: A Gardener's Education.* New York: Dell, 1991.

Ronald, Ann. *Earthtones: A Nevada Album.* Reno: University of Nevada Press, 1995.

Shepard, Paul. *Man in the Landscape: A Historic View of the Esthetics of Nature.* New York: Ballantine, 1967.

Slovic, Scott, ed. Special issue of *Southwestern American Literature* (Fall 1995).

Stegner, Wallace. *Where the Bluebird Sings to the Lemonade Springs: Living and Writing in the West.* New York: Random House, 1992.

Teague, David W. *The Southwest in American Literature and Art: The Rise of a Desert Aesthetic.* Tucson: University of Arizona Press, 1997.

Tuan, Yi-Fu. *Topophilia: A Study of Environmental Perception, Attitudes, and Values.* 1974. New York: Columbia University Press, 1990.

Wild, Peter, ed. *The Desert Reader.* Salt Lake City: University of Utah Press, 1991.

Williams, Terry Tempest. *Refuge: An Unnatural History of Family and Place.* New York: Pantheon, 1991.

Getting Over the Color Green

PART I

Watching Closely

FORAYS IN NATURAL HISTORY

John Alcock

A NATURAL HISTORY

The dry wash that drains the gentle canyon to the southwest of Usery
Peak passes through a narrow, rocky throat before spreading out again
on its static journey toward the distant Salt River. At the pinched entrance to the canyon, several strategically placed boulders act as an impassable barrier to off-road vehicles. The dead end boulders regularly
confront four-wheel-drive Toyotas, Chevy trucks jacked up so far that
the front door handle is eight feet off the ground, and even motorcycles
with the air let out of their tires, which zoom up the pebbly avenue
swerving past the projecting limbs of ironwoods lining the wash. The
off-roaders stop when they can go no farther and turn their machines
around by the boulders. Most linger for a while, some to riddle assorted
targets with ten dollars' worth of Winchester .22 longs, PMC sidewind-
ers, or Remington thunderbolts, some to dispose of a twelve-pack of
Coors, some to construct a fire ring in the middle of the wash, fueled
with punky paloverde limbs hacked from a nearby tree. Sooner or later,
they are on their way again, lurching down the wash in their ORVs toward reassuringly firm pavement.

Almost no one scrambles over the boulders to walk up the wash,
surmounting the obstacles that continue to obstruct travel for a half
mile or so. At least I do not find many footprints today after having
hiked in by a circuitous route of my own. I do find a neatly carved
groove, nearly three feet long, traveling down the face of one of the big
gray stones that forms a dry waterfall in the middle of the streambed. It
is hard to believe, but water has flowed down the wash with sufficient
force a sufficient number of times to gouge out a silky smooth spout in
solid rock.

Overhead a great horned owl flaps slowly from one ledge to another on wings as broad as they are long. Back-lighted against the
morning sky, its calm, silent flight seems part of the undisturbed atmosphere of this delightfully uncivilized place.

Eventually, the drop-offs and rock walls give way to more open
terrain, completely inaccessible to off-road vehicles. Here the wash has
formed a broader, smoother trail that ascends at a comfortable angle. A
single dried desert mint, now reduced to a skeletal memory of the past
spring, still stands upright on a sandy shelf in the middle of the waterless
stream.

Teddy-bear cacti gather in groups on the shoulders of the wash. A
house finch settles gently on one of the cacti ignoring multitudes of
spines that seem to offer a hostile landing spot at best. Here and there,
towering well over the three- and four-foot teddy-bears, stand the
Sonoran Desert's most famous plant, saguaros ten, fifteen, and twenty
feet tall. A few of these immense cacti grow right in the wash itself,
having reached a size capable of withstanding the thunderstorm thrown
surges that come down the streambed at great and irregular intervals.
The saguaros hold their arms up in postcard poses.

Some fifty feet from the wash, a monster saguaro that has lost its
picture-perfect innocence occupies a small depression in the rocky soil.
This cactus's immense arms have drooped to touch the ground before
turning up again. A severe frost long ago weakened the tissue in the
saguaro's arms, causing them to bend but not break, and in the years
since the disaster, the plant's customary response to gravity has induced
an upward turn in the still living but fallen appendages.

Somewhere along the line, perhaps due to freeze damage, the top
half of the central trunk of the saguaro fell to the ground and decayed so
long ago that no sign of its existence remains on the gravel beneath the
decapitated cactus. Despite its mutilation, the saguaro seems reasonably
healthy except for its flower buds, which have attracted consumers,
perhaps small pocket mice, whose burrows riddle the ground around
the cactus. In any case, something small and agile has managed to clamber onto the arm tips and gnaw into the buds. The damaged specimens
soon turn black before falling from their perches onto the little bursages
squashed between the saguaro's elbows.

The mammoth saguaro, through the accidents that removed its upper trunk and lowered its arms, will have no surviving fruits at all this year. Without fruits, it will produce no seeds. Without seeds, it will produce no new offspring. But even if it misses the annual opportunity to leave a descendant or two, it seems to be in no danger of dying. It looks capable of living on forever, occupying its special patch of desert, gleaning water from the soil after a rare storm, propping up the dead ironwood that once grew near it.

There is a timeless aspect to desert landscapes populated with huge saguaros, leaving the viewer with a sensation of an immortal and unchanging world. Which just goes to show that sensations can be highly misleading. First, although saguaros are without dispute capable of living a long life, most do not survive for a great deal longer than the average American citizen. To hang on for 200 years, as the mammoth cactus may have done, requires an exceptional run of luck and the capacity to tolerate a great many indignities.

Moreover, although it was once thought that the Sonoran Desert's vegetation had occupied its modern geographic range for perhaps 20 million years, in reality there have been big changes here relatively recently in geological time. Had you or I been fortunate enough to visit the western flank of Usery Peak 13,000 years ago, we probably wouldn't have seen a single saguaro cactus. I can make this assertion thanks to long-deceased woodrats of various species whose ancient middens provide clues about the past, clues that were unknown until just a few decades ago.

Woodrats are mid-sized rodents that have occupied the western United States for thousands of years during which time they have created durable mementos of their lives in the form of piles of trash. These middens, as they are called, are the result of the excretory habits of woodrats, which use a special cranny or recess in their dry cave homes as a bathroom. The bathroom is also a trash heap that receives half-eaten plant fragments and other inedibles in addition to the animal's feces and urine. The combined debris eventually forms a lacquered, urine-impregnated package, which can become a fossilized testament to the meals and excretory capacity of woodrats that lived in a long-gone millennium.

Some early pioneers on their hard journey through the arid west hoped they had found manna when they came upon woodrat middens, and they actually ate some midden fragments, having been deceived by their supposedly candylike appearance and texture. No modern Westerner who has seen a woodrat midden can easily imagine how one could take the first bite, let alone persist in eating a midden candy bar. But then again, few modern Westerners have been as hungry as the midden munchers doubtless were.

The use of middens as food was a short-lived phenomenon, but in 1964 Phil Wells and Clive Jorgensen realized that these materials might serve another function for us all, namely as samples of vegetative life during the years when the middens were formed. Radiocarbon datings can be readily secured from the organic material in a midden. Once the plant fragments and fossil pollen that the rat collected 1,000 or 10,000 or 20,000 years earlier have been separated, identified, and dated, the result is a snapshot of the plant life from a world that no longer exists.

Arizona middens tell us that the Sonoran Desert some 11,000 to 15,000 years ago was dramatically different from the current desert world. For example, middens made more than 10,000 years in the past lack saguaro seeds and brittlebush remains and instead yield fragments of pinyon and juniper trees, Mojave sage and Joshua trees, as well as numerous grasses, all plants that now occur far away at elevations hundreds of meters higher. The landscape of this time, instead of being covered with Sonoran desertscrub, was reminiscent of habitats now found at elevations several thousand feet higher, where scattered junipers and pinyon pines grow on grassy slopes and meadows.

As recently as 11,000 years ago, southern Arizona was evidently cooler and wetter than it is currently, creating a climate suitable for plants that today survive only at higher elevations. Saguaros did not arrive until 10,500 to 9,000 years ago. They are believed to have come up from an arid refugium in Mexico, as the weather turned slowly drier and warmer throughout the Southwest.

The transformation of the region took place gradually. The first saguaros to reach Usery Peak probably coexisted with junipers, and perhaps shrub live oaks, for hundreds or even thousands of years. The continued drift toward extreme aridity and higher temperatures resulted in the eventual disappearance of these trees from lower elevations in the Sonoran Desert and their replacement with paloverdes and iron-woods. But it was not until around 4,000 years ago that the Sonoran Desert of Arizona adopted its current aspect in which paloverdes, bur-sage, creosote, and a host of cacti, among them saguaros, dominate the land. Despite appearances to the contrary, the current desert environment is young in geological terms, barely formed, yet formed well enough to obscure a past that might have been lost forever were it not for the durable labors of desert rats.

Looking out across a vast bajada cloaked in eye-catching saguaros and a supporting cast of hundreds of paloverde trees, my fellow cactus-huggers and I might conclude that this is the way it has always been (and always should be). We are entitled to our opinion on how it always should be, but if the past is guide to the future, the woodrats occupying the Userys several thousand years from now may well be urinating on midden heaps laced with bits and fragments of novel plants that do not occur here today. Perhaps there will also be a few plant-huggers around to admire the new species that have replaced the diverse and wonderful vegetation of the present. But the persistence of humans is far from as-sured, and so we, the living, had better enjoy the present desert land-scape while we can.

SueEllen Campbell

THE ELEMENTS

Light

Western light, most days, is brilliant, palpable. It has body. Its particles
hit your skin with soft, firm thuds, its waves push and tug you like a
warm sea.

Midday in summer, at high altitudes, the light is laser-sharp, cutting razor edges for every grass blade, leaf, rock rim, every vivid petal,
stamen, seed, every tiny sliver and disk of shadow. From every surface
light flashes vivid, vibrant. It saturates every color, separates each shade,
tone, texture.

When I was little, I discovered that when strands of my hair pull
loose and blow in front of my eyes, they turn to filaments of colored
light. Indoor blondes and reds and browns and whites become outdoor
violets, greens, vermilions, golds. The colors of light. My own feathers,
iridescent.

Backlit, when the sun is aslant, flowers and leaves catch the light
like stained glass, hold it inside, glow.

Late afternoons and evenings, summer light turns red-gold, pools
in meadows and sandy arroyos, washes over rocky peaks, stains the
pinks of sandstones and granites a deep, soft, silky red. This is the Romantic light of Bierstadt's western paintings. Like the neon gaudiness of
desert sunsets, it looks unreal on canvas or postcards, intensely real on
the land.

If you stand just before it rains in a grove of aspens, the light will
be green and liquid. In the fall, when the sun is lower and the leaves
have changed color, the light, liquid still, will be gold. Through the
shifting stencil of leaves, the sky's deep autumn blue will seem even
deeper, more saturated. One September, after a watercolor class, I saw

why—blue and orange, opposites on a color wheel, complementary colors, intensify each other. Pigment and light: circles of red and gold on a cobalt ground.

Winter light sharpens again, mirrors summer's brilliance and heat with a narrower palette of colors, blacks and whites, deep greens, bright blues. Variation comes in surprising places. A meadowful of willows will flash russet and saffron and claret. Up close, the white of aspen bark will reveal itself as pale green or burnt orange. Shapes etch themselves in your head, stay with you into sleep. On fresh snow, light fractures into diamonds. Tree shadows are sharp, but blue light gathers softly in snow hollows, rabbit prints, the round beds of elk and moose, ski tracks. At twilight, space fills with blue and violet.

The effects of light are countless. "Look at the light," I'm always insisting, pointing to a bright bar shooting across the sky, to the gleam of a spider's web high in a tree, to the sweep of silver on a field of grass, to the glimmering ripples on a streambed. When I travel I note differences shaped by latitude, altitude, humidity, measure them always against the quality of light that marks home.

Many places seem dim, their shapes and colors dulled by thick air, blurred skies. One fall when I lived in Ohio, the sun did not appear for forty days. The local newscasters kept count. To read at noon by a window, I needed a lamp. In places like this I feel dim too, heavy, sluggish, full of murky shadow. "What can you do," the postmistress said. "It's like this everywhere." *No,* I wanted to shout, It isn't! Spoiled by western light, I'm particular, a connoisseur, a snob.

I live on light so bright I have to keep checking to see that I have my sunglasses on; on light so intense that at evening I feel sunblasted, exhausted and scoured by light as if I'd been scrubbed by blown sand; on light that rushes like fast water into my eyes, my pupils small and black against the flood, my irises wide and dark, the color of sunlit storm clouds on a July afternoon.

Rock

I know almost nothing about geology, but I love rocks. Smooth oval river rocks, painted like Easter eggs. Slabs of mica, layers of black translucence. Dark soft gray slate. Sandstone in pinks and reds and buffs, slightly rough against skin. Pink granite, every handful a hundred flat planes to catch the sun, a hundred rough edges to catch the shadow. A chunk of lapis lazuli from a secret mine, the midnight sky in my palm.

I've seen fossils of seashells and ferns on the top of a mountain nearly fourteen thousand feet high. I wander around old volcanoes, trace the errant paths of ash and lava, aa and pahoehoe, study chimneys and plugs, play with light puffs of pumice. At home I sit outside and try to grasp the story of the rock underneath me. It's very old, compacted red dust from an eroded mountain range, the Ancestral Rockies. I can barely begin to picture it, how they grew from the vanished traces of still earlier peaks until they were as tall as the Himalayas, then wore away into lush, dinosaury plains. The familiar Rockies rose later, just a short walk to the west, shoving the old plains out of their way into a fringe of hogbacks, narrow red ridges with gentle slopes on the east, cliffs on the west. Our house sits among these small ridges.

When Thoreau climbed Maine's Mount Katahdin, he found himself stunned by the raw power of exposed rock. He wrote about it with a mixture of terror and wonder, in language that reveals both the continuity in the concept of the marvelous and one fault-line in the concept of the sublime, one place where its structure has shifted in the years since. Mountaintops are hostile, he felt, no place for humans: "Only daring and insolent men, perchance, go there." But he also felt the powerful appeal of such places: "What is it to be admitted to a museum, to see a myriad of particular things, compared with being shown some star's surface, some hard matter in its home! I stand in awe of my body, this matter to which I am bound has become so strange to me. . . . Talk of mysteries!—Think of our life in nature,—daily to be shown matter, to come in contact with it,—rocks, trees, wind on our cheeks! the *solid* earth! the *actual* world! the *common sense! Contact! Contact! Who* are we? *where* are we?"

I climb another familiar ridge not far from Skyland, this one tall, among tall mountains, the trace of another massive event deep in the past. Along the top are level patches of fine gravel, purple, green, black. I choose purple and lie on my side with my head propped on my hand. Before me is space and rock, high peaks as far as I can see, white, gray, maroon, rose, several shades of each, shifting with moving shadow: the fascination of pure structure. The gravel beneath me is warmer than the air or the light. It presses hard against my hip, my ribs, my upper arm, sharp and solid. It writes on my skin. My body, earth body, ridgelines.

Space

Space, in the West, enters your body through eyes and the skin's pores, carried by light and wind, and flows through you like air, like blood, like the electricity of nerves.

For me it marks home. A dozen years in Virginia and Ohio, and I never felt quite comfortable: the space was the wrong kind. Clear around the world, in western China, in Mongolia, in Kenya, it was right, and I felt instantly at home.

Home space, huge and open, lets me see a long way. The air is dry and clear. The land can be flat or precipitous, I can stand on a mountaintop or at the bottom of a canyon, and still I feel the presence of space. Space is empty and full; it is not there, it is here.

A certain slant of light reveals how space is filled—with gleams of cobweb, insects like flecks of silver, golden dust motes, floating seeds, waves and particles from the sun's distant fire, the swoop and waver of swallows. Light pools in space, poured in and stirred by wind. At the ends of the day or in mist or with distance, space blues and blurs, turns soft between canyon walls. If you practice, you can learn to see space everywhere, between the edges of aspen leaves and pine needles, in the hollows of columbine spurs.

In the night sky in a dark place, space is insistent, intangible but substantial, invisible but embodied. A friend tells me how she once learned to lie still on a summer night, her back firmly held by gravity to rock, and perceive herself as looking *down* into the sky. I imagine floating on my stomach on the still surface of deep space.

"Breathing in," says a Buddhist exercise for mindfulness, "I see myself as space. Breathing out, I feel free."

Water

In my life, water has had the character of punctuation. I amuse myself by pairing memories with punctuation marks.

An exclamation point: One evening we drive north toward Laramie. We're in shadow, but the valley is full of light. Suddenly water splashes on the windshield and we look up. A fine thick curtain of rain fills the sky to the west, each drop catching the sun as it falls straight to the ground, each drop a tiny shining sphere. Brightness falls from the air.

A question mark: It's an October night, but the water in the Gulf of Mexico is still warm enough to stand in. I'm shoulder deep, unsteady in the push and tug of the waves, waving my limbs around like an anemone or a squid. I hold my arms out to my sides and pull them together. They glow pale green and flicker. I stand still and the water darkens. I lift one knee to my chest, straighten it, sweep a slow circle. Pale green, shimmer, darkness. I float loose of the sand, tread water, gild my whole body. I know the words—phosphorescent algae—but only the words.

A comma, tying sequences together: spring melt. Quick rivulets circle my tent, one every few feet all across this meadow, zipping down the hillsides to the icy creek just below, then, miles later, into the slow silty Colorado. At sunset black clouds drop torrents. Cocooned in blue nylon, I imagine the life of an ouzel, a water dipper, tucked in a moss nest on the edge of a cascade. Water rushes by like wind.

A dash—a pause, continuation: This island, Dominica, is one of the wettest places on earth, and the rainy season is starting right now. We eat breakfast on an open-sided terrace and gaze into a green tangle. While we sit, it rains five separate times, silently, air turning to water.

A semicolon, making connections between different but related things: If you stare at a waterfall, even a very small one, and then shift your eyes to the framing rock, the rock will move. Illusion; reality.

A colon, introducing what will follow: The lake at Skyland is still. I drift in a canoe, the soft waves of my own motion slapping lightly against aluminum, waxy yellow lilies and deep green leaf disks all around. The glassy surface doubles aspens, sage, mountains, sky. I lean over and trail my hand in the cold water. My face floats over clouds.

Wind

The wind will make you sick, they told me in China when I opened the window in the train. It will blow your body out of balance.

But I keep my balance against the wind. I lean into it and let it hold me, push me firmly upright. Wind blows sickness away from me, out of my head and lungs, scours my skin, empties that thick darkness between cells, fills it with cool, moving space.

The wind blows cloud shadows across rock fields and prairies. It whistles and roars and murmurs in my ears. With blades of grass it writes circles on desert sand. It sweeps over meadows in silver washes, turning to the sun the shining bottoms of grasses and willow leaves and aspens. In even the softest breeze, everything moves. The hairs on my arms sway lightly with spruce tops and reeds. Around my eyes and mouth and on my neck strands wander and whip and drift. The wind moves storms through, hail, lightning, snow coming hard and horizontal. It scrubs the earth clean, washes everything.

When the wind is soft or still, it fills with scents you can't describe but recognize with every cell. Dry sage and hot dust. The musty lilac of lupine at high altitudes in the sun. Pine sap. The metallic smell of rust-colored rock at old mine holes. Stock and wild roses. Ozone, summer rain, wet sage. When I breathe in, scent pools in my lungs, flows in my arteries.

I scramble through an explosion of sage and up a short cliff. I nestle into the rock where I'll be out of the strongest gusts, lean on a juniper, rest my head against its flat needles. Gazing at the slow green river, I dream, then drowse. A sudden tug at my pony tail wakes me up. Wind in the juniper, nudging me to attention.

Light, Rock, Space, Water, Wind

I'm standing on the rim of the Black Canyon of the Gunnison. It's late afternoon, so bright that even with sunglasses I have to squint a bit to see. The wind blows hair into my eyes and presses my shirt against my skin. I lean into it for balance.

Under my feet and before me across a deep chasm of space is hard Precambrian rock, well over a billion years old, some of the oldest rock on the surface of the planet. It's nearly black, matte and mysterious in shadow, gleaming and brilliant in light, shot through everywhere with broad bands of pink. Two thousand feet below I can see white water, its speed and power faintly audible in a soft, insistent roar.

Just below me a small flock of birds materializes, made, it seems, from wind and space. Pinyon jays, a soft, light, slightly gray blue, robin-sized, flipping and turning in synchronized unity, a score or so, sunlight flashing shades of blue on their backs, the tops of their wings, the color of the sky at dawn, of water under light cloud, of washed silk, the palest of juniper berries. Water on wing, wind-tossed space-shards, light moving on rock.

Elated, alive, I stand on the prow of the planet, my face into the wind, arms flung out, flying through space.

John Daniel

THE CANYON

Here below as the sun slides past its zenith
in the pale October sky, below
the crumbling basalt of the canyon rim
that spewed in fire when it was young,
now water-stained and streaked with lichen,
tumbling slow down dry grass slopes,
below the deeper layers of sand and chalk
containing lives that flourished once
when a warm sea lapped and pounded here,
below the bright crowns of ponderosa pines
and homely junipers, finding our way
on the canyon floor among silvered snags,
alongside the stream with its quiet song
discovering deeper and deeper ages,
here we walk with our good years together,
plucking juniper berries and sprigs of sage,
crushing them to breathe their savor,
to stain ourselves with this place we love—
this gorge time lets us wander in
as if all time were ours, as if our hearts
beat to the rhythm of volcanic storms
and we breathed to rising and falling seas,
as if time itself weren't scouring the canyon
of every sign of our two lives, as if
it weren't drowning us, each from the other,
from ourselves and all our places—my love,

there is no snag for us to cling to,
no ledge where we might rest and watch
our own spent bodies wash away,
yet we're the luckiest of all time's fools
to be alive together exactly here,
so lost in where we are and will not be
that we wander wholly, helplessly free,
following the canyon at our own pace
as it shows us down, with water song
and the odor of sage, through the long
unfolding of the afternoon,
our faces glowing with the same cool warmth
that lights the pines and junipers,
that brightens the dry bottom of an ancient sea,
and fires far above us the rimrock cliffs,
cracked and stained, crusted with age,
all flaws revealed to the deepening light—
faces, my love, such as we too must wear
and are wearing this day, beautiful
for all time brings and bears away.

THE CANYON WREN

for Bruce Bowerman

All afternoon as we hiked up the canyon
with our echoing talk, we heard that bright
long-winded whistle stepping down the scale.
We never saw the bird—only a shadow,
a twitch of limb, as slight and quickly gone

as the lizards flicking across hot stones.
Where the streambed steepened to dry waterfall
we almost quit, our packs absurdly heavy,
the rocks we jarred loose clattering below,
that sky-filled notch of canyon drawing us on.

We camped by a few scummed pools, loud with frogs,
and climbing on in the morning we didn't find
the big surprise we'd talked of: no bighorn sheep,
no petroglyphs, no monster waterfall,
just more and more of tumbled boulders, clumps

of prickly pear, dry sand with fool's gold glint,
the same heat shimmer in the same still air,
and once in a while, from somewhere close, the wren's
clear song. And then, that evening, something more.
We walked into the canyon's trick of quiet,

into the ease of being just where we were,
the great walls shouldering high, flooded with moon,
and down the gorge, Death Valley in pale haze.
As we sat late by crumbling coals, the wind
came glancing, grazing our faces, alive

in the limbs of the junipers, dying down now
and rising, returning its song. Across
cool stones, along the canyon's shadowed curves,
through all the secret slickrock passages
the wind came softly, and its voice spoke for our own.

David Darlington

FROM "DESERT OF DEFINITION"

The desert is evil. It is deadly and barren and lonely and foreboding and oppressive and godforsaken. Its silence and emptiness breed madness. Its plant forms are strangely twisted, as are its citizens, who live there because they can't get along anywhere else. Charlie Manson. Brigham Young. Bugsy Siegel. Carlos Castañeda and Don Juan's demons. Moses. In history and myth, the desert is the barrier to the Promised Land—our realm of trial and exile, the place where people go to be punished, seeking wisdom born of misery. Since modern transportation has compromised this relationship, reducing the desert's danger by abbreviating the time required to cross it, about the best thing you can say about the place is that it is boring. Aside from random deposits of minerals, it is valuable mainly as a zone in which to shed the shackles of civilization, race cars on infinitely straight highways, bask naked in unending sun, shoot guns at rocks and road signs, careen across sand hills on dirt bikes and dune buggies. In the desert, one is liberated from all restraint because nobody's around to notice. That's why we explode atom bombs there. Or dump things that might create problems elsewhere. They can't do any damage in the desert; there's nothing out there to damage.

Or so it was thought until rather recently, when the blinders were somehow removed and a new view was revealed to civilization: *the desert is beautiful!* It has limitless stretches of space, awesome landforms that loom up like monoliths, carpets of wildflowers that proliferate after rains. The crystalline air is inflamed twice daily, at dawn and dusk, when the landscape is washed in mauve and ocher and scarlet and vermilion. Far from oppressive, the desert is refreshingly free of clutter and contagion—"clean," in T. E. Lawrence's phrase—which is perhaps why Europeans in particular seem to be drawn to it (aside from the fact that they don't have anything like it at home). As for its supposed desolation, the desert is in fact full of life: hardy flora, resourceful fauna, a panoply of human artifacts no less stimulating than they are unsettling—dinosaur statues, opera houses in the middle of nowhere, buildings made entirely of bottles, rocks painted to resemble fish. The character of the place once considered so barren is now redefined as "austere." In the same way that Alaska has risen to an exalted place in the national consciousness after long being considered a wasteland fit only for polar bears and Eskimos, the desert—purportedly the exclusive province of rattlesnakes and prospectors—is now recognized as a fragile and fascinating environment. Indeed, in pristineness, population, precipitation, orneriness, and vulnerability to abuse, the desert has more in common with the Arctic than any other place on the North American continent. Deeply and utterly profound in its silence, it possesses inexhaustible mystery. Here, as nowhere else, one feels free.

This "new" view really isn't. The desert has always had its adherents—people who valued it for its beauty, its solitude, its science. The recent ascendancy of the New View of the desert owes its existence to the popular rise of environmental consciousness, to the American migration to the Sunbelt, and in no small measure to Madison Avenue's expedient embrace of "Santa Fe style." I don't suppose it would be honest to claim that I was converted to the New View by any influences other than these. I made my first trip through the desert soon after Earth Day in 1970, albeit for the same reason that most Americans did and do: to get from one coast to the other. Having spent my whole life up to that point within the humid purview of the Atlantic Ocean, I still recall how bleak Interstate 10 seemed east of Palm Springs, how alienating the dehydrated rockscape, how unnatural the absence of noise. The monumental emptiness of the place seemed a frightening weight to bear. The desert struck me as an enormous vacuum—a void, like outer space.

I later discussed these notions with a native Coloradan, who told me that she considered the East prettier than the West but found herself frustrated there because "you can't walk anywhere—there's *green* stuff all over the place." It took me several subsequent years of living on the West Coast, backpacking in the Sierra Nevada, skirting the edges of the Great Basin, and learning about arid-land ecology to develop the same sort of feeling. After a decade of such education, I finally acquired the wherewithal to mount an intentional fact-finding expedition into the California desert.

Not incidentally, I did it in the company of a friend with whom I had also spent time in the Arctic. Our destination, inevitably, was Death Valley—the place that has probably experienced the greatest reversal of reputation as a result of the New View. We arranged to meet at a trailer park near the town of Mojave, from which we made a classic drive along the northeasterly route commonly followed by people coming from the coast: Past the weird limestone pinnacles near Trona, where the Kerr-McGee Corporation mined chemicals from a dry lake bed, the air smelled putrid and stores were painted green, apparently to impart some impression of photosynthesis. Through the town of Ridgecrest, where we got lost inside the China Lake Naval Air Weapons Testing Center (I have no idea how we got in), and upon leaving saw a sign that said: WHAT YOU DO HERE, WHAT YOU SEE HERE, LET IT STAY HERE. Across the expanse of Panamint Valley, Death Valley's enormous sibling, where Manson & Company lived in an abandoned ranch house up an all but impassable canyon while awaiting Helter Skelter. Into storied Death Valley itself, where at midday we rested in the shade and swam in the pool but at dawn and dusk exposed great quantities of celluloid to the effects of light on a landscape devoid of cover, a veritable multiring circus of unexpurgated geology.

The most provocative place was a remote basin three hours by car from any telephones, utilities, or asphalt—an ancient lake bed strewn with greasewood and volcanic debris, ascending into alluvial fans that resembled earthen glaciers thousands of feet deep. The valley's western wall, a range of eleven-thousand-foot-high mountains, concealed astounding year-round streams that stay cool even when the air temperature reaches 120 degrees. Where these streams merged on the valley floor, they formed a salt marsh that serves as a haven for invertebrates and migrating birds. North of the marsh were sand dunes—the beach at the edge of the vanished Pleistocene lake—and beyond the dunes was the magnet that had drawn us, the *pièce de résistance:* a pair of hot springs that sat in the baking sand of the basin like imperturbable Arabian mullahs.

To reach this obscure and isolated place, my friend and I traversed two mountain ranges, guessing our way along an unsigned route, passing occasional water bottles set out to aid drivers in distress, winding through high passes of piñon and juniper, bouncing over washboarded dirt roads that destroyed our car's air conditioner. As we descended into the basin, the late sun threw the naked hills into sweeping relief, their brick- and chocolate-colored bands glowing a surreal orange. Gradually the granite mountainsides gave way to glimpses of the valley floor, its alkaline surface shining like a dream—and not necessarily a nice one. More than one person has disappeared without a trace in this area, prompting the *Los Angeles Times* to tag the place the Bermuda Triangle of California.

We turned off for the springs at a rock that was painted like a bat. After driving eight more miles up a sandy track, we made out some cars and trailers—even an airplane—arranged around a low stand of mesquite. We assumed we'd arrived when we saw a naked man walking down the road. As we passed the lower of the two springs, we encountered that indefatigable camel of the California desert—a Volkswagen bus—backing up while its driver, a guy with a gray beard and a head band, yelled something out his window at a Doberman loping alongside. A few minutes later, this bus pulled in behind us at the upper spring, unloading a half-dozen time travelers from the sixties. While we were walking around looking for a campsite, the group's dogs got into a fight. When I glanced over, I heard a fat guy comment: "I don't like the way that asshole's looking at me."

When the sun went down, we made our way to one of the hot pools, where somebody handed me a pair of binoculars and showed me Halley's comet. Bats swooped low over the tubs as we soaked in 105 degree water beneath a billion stars. Unfortunately the Doberman party proceeded to keep us awake all night, with one of their number yelling, *"I feel good!"* at regular intervals. At dawn he was accompanied by a wild burro braying off in the bush, which encouraged the dogs to join in.

Morning revealed our whereabouts: an oasis in the middle of an enormous saline bowl, surrounded by striated mountains, with creosote and burro brush dotting the desert as far as the eye could see. Mesquite, arrow weed, and fan palms grew around the spring; the hot water from the source, a natural well surrounded by grass, trickled down to two bathing pools—one a raised oval, the other a sunken hexagon. A pair of giant peace signs had been scraped onto nearby cinder cones, and an outhouse stood off in the scrub, wittily equipped with a seat belt and a sign that said: PATROLLED BY LOW-FLYING AIRCRAFT. Sure enough, as the sun began to climb, fighter jets appeared over the horizon, passing a hundred feet over the springs, well in advance of their engines' own roar.

While my friend and I were eating breakfast, the fat guy wandered over. He was wearing an olive-drab army jacket and a black wool watch cap. "Hi!" he said, staring at us intently.

"Hi."

"Real free country out here, huh?"

We nodded.

"We really love it out here," he said. "We're from Darwin [a mining town to the south]. My name's John."

Tentatively, we shook his hand. "What do you do in Darwin, John?"

"Whatever I want."

We chewed our granola; John kept staring. I wondered if maybe he wanted something to eat.

"I used to live here," he finally said. "People called me Dirty John because I never took a bath. We come out here to get away from the telephone poles and power lines. If we do anything that offends you, just let us know."

"Well," I volunteered, "I guess I thought you could have been a little quieter last night."

John shrugged. "We're working on it," he said. He started to turn away but then thought better of it. "You know," he said, "we come out here to be by ourselves and do what we want."

"With all these other people around?"

"Listen," he said. "I can show you lots of beautiful places where you can go to be by yourself. If you try to control people here, you're gonna get in trouble."

"Right," I said, and turned to my companion to ask if he thought it was all right to use soap in the dishwashing pool.

"You can do whatever you want," said Dirty John. "It's your place."

That afternoon, we hiked up a canyon in the nearby mountains. We found a rope at the top of a beautiful perennial waterfall that fed a fecund microenvironment of willows, ferns, and angel hair. At sunset we chased the light across the dunes, but it kept disappearing from the next ridge as we slogged doggedly along, barefoot. Finally we gave up, sat down, and listened to the quiet (the flyboys had called it a day) while the lowering sun turned the distant alluvial fans into giant root systems. A warm wind was blowing across the dunes, and as we sat there, we knew the intoxication—the giddy, unfettered freedom—of the desert.

We had no plans to revisit the hot spring—extended relations with Dirty John and the Dobermans weren't what we'd come here for—but those plans changed (as did our sense of freedom) when we returned to the car and heard a hiss coming from our left front tire. The infamous roads had taken their toll. We made our way back to the campground, which contained the only congregation of people within three hours' drive.

This time, however, we went to the lower spring. As we pulled in, we encountered a couple of septuagenarians wearing nothing but straw hats. When we announced our predicament, one of them said, "Bring the tire over by the pool; we'll spray some water on it and find the leak." The other one went and got his truck, which came equipped with a compressor. He used it to fill the tire after a third guy plugged it with rubber and glue. Pretty soon, we were relaxing in the pool with no worries.

The situation was completely different from that at the upper spring. There were several pools, a lot of shade, a dishwashing sink, a goldfish pond, a circle of couches, a lawn with a sign that said BERMUDA GRASS TRIANGLE, and a paperback library divided into sections ("Action," "Mystery," "Lust"). The person who'd plugged my tire turned out to be "Major Tom" Ganner, the official campground host. As an unpaid volunteer for the U.S. Bureau of Land Management (BLM), which controlled the property, Ganner lived at the spring year round— even in summer, when he said the main problem was sleeping on sheets that were hotter than the air. As we reclined in the tub, he told us that the upper spring tended to attract transient visitors; this one had a more committed clientele. Nevertheless, the BLM had a six-month limit on the length of any stay.

"There is no law here," Ganner proclaimed. "There are just varying degrees of common courtesy and consideration. For example, people have to put up with John, as long as he doesn't do anything too outrageous. We've had Manson people pass through here, but they're really more of a pain in the ass than anything else. People *have* been asked to leave; if somebody brandishes a gun, I get on the radio and the county sheriff comes over from Independence. But the percentage of problem people is real small. It seems to work out that the people we like to have around are the ones that come back."

It was a decidedly nonlinear universe, this terrestrial outer space. Though nowhere near as removed as the Arctic, which after all remains innocent of roads, it was still a largely anarchic kingdom where one was expected to get along without being ordered or nursed—a kind of lawless commons where people had to find their way with few directions of any kind. The hot springs were maintained solely by the people who visited them; the pools had been built by volunteers. The place was a free zone in the middle of nowhere, an antibureaucratic Eden. As such, it seemed the epitome of the American desert: a decidedly eccentric environment whose overarching quality is *openness,* established and encouraged by the landscape itself.

Alison Hawthorne Deming

THE ROCK FIG

Drenched in the cascading
song of canyon wrens, its gray
wood spills out of rock
in the driest, most remote
arroyos, like plastic extruded
from a seam in the tuff,
like cables spooling from
a cave, like sheeting drapes
of liquid stone, like tentacles
the tendrils stuck to stone—
inadequate, all the words
and equations one might draw
to describe something as simple
as a kind of wood that has
responded to the circumstances
of day after day in one place.

Some say that its presence
describes the discipline
of water—floods ripping out
all vegetation in their
bouldering path—so that
meeting a rock fig means
understanding the interval
between such events. Some
say its tea can cure

snakebite in mules and cattle.
Some carve their passion
in its bark and decades later
others find it, a new testament
that echoes with the locating
calls of evening bats
off the rosy canyon walls.

DRIVING THROUGH NATURE

Past the canyon's rosy gouge and spires,
past the whack of copter blades and overbooked rooms,

past ponderosa and piñon scrub, the shacks begin.
Dirt lot, brush fence, nomad shelters built for shade.

American flags snap on the scrapwood stalls
where the Navajo sell rugs and beads,

behind them, the planet's skin
stretched out bare and raw so that it seems

the land will tell its story to anyone—
rifts, upheavals, wear and rest.

I'm tired of trying to find a place
where history hasn't left its scars and wounded.

There is only one earth and its laws
are a mystery we're here to solve.

Susan Hanson

WHY WRITE ABOUT NATURE?

Lilac and gold, the flowers of autumn rise resplendent from the brittle grass. Gayfeather and goldenrod, frostweed and sunflower golden-eye— they shine against the backdrop of a gray, soft-focus sky.

It is just after first light on this stretch of Texas highway, and the spray from the whooshing tires sings against the bottom of the car. Rising from bed at 6:00 A.M. on a Saturday morning, I had grumbled about getting such an early start. But here on the empty road now I'm content, glad for the taste of solitude.

This drive toward the coast is one I've made at least a hundred times or more. And because I once saw a patch of Michaelmas daisies in bloom beside the porch of a weathered house, I find myself glancing in that direction each time I pass. Today, though, the yard is empty, save for a rusty pickup parked beneath the branches of an ample oak.

What can be said for such a landscape? What can be made of the simple fact that where liatris blooms this fall huisache will blossom in the spring?

"Change is a measure of time and, in the autumn, time seems speeded up," Edwin Way Teale writes in *October*. "What was, is not, and never again will be; what is, is change."

Why write about nature? a friend asked me not long ago. *Why say what seems so obvious to the eye?* It is not for lack of imagination that she finds this habit odd, or for lack of appreciation of the earth. It is the weight of words that puts her off, I suspect, the burden of language on what should be known by sense alone.

Why write about nature? The question occurs to me again as I drive through the fog of an autumn morning. Is it not enough to see the marsh hawk perched atop the telephone pole, to feel the touch of velvet-leaf mallow soft against my skin, to smell the dampness of the pungent earth? Must I write of these things as well?

I must.

"It makes them more real," I told my friend, ineptly, when she asked. That is part of the answer, I suppose, but only part.

Physical being that I am, I know the world primarily as it comes to me through my fingertips. I know it through the polished surface of a snail's shell, the nubby cap of an acorn, the density of clay. Piece by piece, I collect the parts, assembling it as I go.

But what of that hidden life, that life that exists beyond my grasp? It is no less real, I suspect, and yet when I try to give it form or weight or color, it disappears, ethereal as sunlight.

Holding just the memory of its brilliance, I am rendered mute and blind, senseless in the face of a mystery I can't name.

Shall I call it Transience? Mutability? Loss? If so, what is its shape? How will I know it when it looks me in the eye?

Creature of sinew and soul, I feel my life go deeper underground, potato-like, spreading out beneath me in a web of roots. Sightless, I can only sense what this other self must know.

Along an empty highway, an hour south of my home, a stand of Maximilian daisies blazes out against a hedgerow of elm and oak. All the more beautiful for their unexpectedness, they will bloom for a week or two and fade, turning brittle in the first November chill.

How does the intellect perceive impermanence and change? How does it comprehend the fact that a life can flourish for a season, die, and vanish like the morning fog?

Fragility, evanescence, the delicacy of beauty brought too swiftly to an end—what the mind rejects, the body surely knows.

Why write about nature? Spirit and flesh, I am nonetheless part of the earth. And earth it is that teaches me the mysteries of love and loss.

How can I understand that what is absent is not gone, that what has ended is not finished, that what is taken is returned as more than memory?

I can't.

What I *can* do, though, is listen for the sound of the sandhill cranes flying high above my house this fall, feel the supple shoots of next spring's phlox, memorize the curve and hue of Michaelmas daisies in full bloom—and in them, I can *know*.

for Pablo
SEPTEMBER 8, 1994—OCTOBER 18, 1994

Stephen Harrigan

SWAMP THING

I was at an impressionable age when I saw my first snapping turtle. I was ten, standing on a low earthen dam in central Oklahoma and casting with a child-size Zebco into a gloomy lake not much bigger than a stock pond. The lake had a prehistoric feel to it. Dead trees rose from the water, the bare limbs swaying and creaking. The water itself was muddy and still. It looked as if it had been sitting there, immune to evaporation, since the beginning of time.

I had fouled my line on enough of those trees to begin feeling cranky and put-upon. And on the occasions when my plastic lure did reach the water—disappearing like a space probe into the toxic brown clouds of an inhospitable planet—it reported no signs of life. I was about to reel in the line when some unseen force gave a brutal tug that pulled my cork deep below the surface. The pressure from the bottom of the lake kept the fishing line as taut a bowstring.

I was scared. This thing did not feel like a fish at all. I knew, as I cranked on the reel, that I had hooked something powerful and hostile, something that did not wish to be disturbed. The muscles in my arms were quivering with exhaustion by the time the creature finally appeared. I saw its head first, and then a neck so long I thought it was a snake, and finally the undersized shell, so small when compared with the thrashing mass of the body itself that it looked like a saddle on the back of a dragon.

Not knowing what else to do, I continued to reel in the line. The turtle was hooked in the mouth, and in its anger it kept flinging out its neck and snapping its jaws. It was the most ferocious, the most un-worldly thing I had ever seen. The back of its head bristled with spiky warts, its shell was covered with algae and slime, and the skin of its front legs dragged the ground in loose, grotesque folds. As I hauled the turtle up the dam, it grasped the dirt with its sharp claws and contested every inch. But then, sensing a little slack in the line, it lunged forward with such force that its front legs cleared the ground. Paralyzed with awe, I stood and watched as it lumbered hissing toward me, its reptile eyes fixed on mine, its neck coiling and striking. I remember thinking, *It's coming to get me!*

My uncle, who was chopping firewood nearby, came trotting down the slope of the dam with an ax. Of course, I realized, this thing would have to be killed. It was an evil that must be vanquished. My uncle tried to cut off its head, but the turtle was quick and could retract its neck faster than the ax could fall. It died instead from a blow to the shell. After it stopped moving we scooped it up with the blade of the ax and tossed it back into the lake. Watching it sink, I began to cry. It was not pity I felt, but disgrace. That such a savage, primeval beast could be destroyed by a thoughtless child seemed to me a mistake, a cruel imbalance of nature. Until I encountered that snapping turtle, it had never occurred to me that the existence of another creature could be a greater wonder than my own.

I see them all the time now. When I'm strolling across the Congress Avenue bridge in Austin, I can often spot snapping turtles in the lake below as they paddle along the banks just beneath the surface. Snappers are immediately distinguishable from the other turtles that inhabit the lake—the red-ears, cooters, and stinkpots. For one thing, you never see snapping turtles basking on tree limbs or swimming companionably alongside your canoe. They prefer to linger in the dark ooze, now and then extending their necks like snorkels to take a breath from the surface. Their tails are thick, long, serrated, semi-prehensile. (Snappers in fast-moving water have been known to grasp a submerged branch with their tails to keep from being swept downstream.) Their bodies are squat, and the forward edges of their shells ride high above their necks like the collar of an ill-fitting coat. Except for the eerie parchment-yellow color of their eyes, they are dark all over.

In the early summer the females crawl out of the water to lay their eggs, their carapaces thick with drying mud. Hiked up on their stubby legs, their necks extended, their long tails dragging in the dirt, they look more like dinosaurs than turtles. The females are on their way to build a nest somewhere nearby. They will dig a hole in the dirt and deposit twenty or thirty eggs, guiding each one into position with the hind feet like fussy hostesses arranging canapés on a tray. When all the eggs are laid, they will fill in the hole with dirt and then tamp it down by crawling back and forth. Their trip to the nest site and back will probably add up to less than half a mile, but for these awkward aquatic turtles it is an epic journey through an alien world.

Last summer, driving with my family to Houston, I saw one stalled with fright on the highway in the pine country just outside of Bastrop. I pulled the car over and we all got out to look at it. I told the kids to stand back, half afraid this low-lying reptile would leap up and grab one of them by the throat. But the turtle kept still, its neck tucked into its shell. It looked craven and terrified. A car roared by in the opposite lane and the turtle hugged the asphalt with its claws.

I wanted to get the turtle off the road, but that childhood encounter had made me a coward, and I was unwilling to reach down and touch it. I had read that the only safe way to pick up a snapping turtle is by the rear legs, or by the rear edge of the shell, "holding him well away from your body." An agitated snapper has an extensive biting range. It can fling its neck to the side like a whip and strike a target far back on its flank. This turtle was placid, but I didn't expect it to stay that way if I put my hands on it. It would, I thought, explode with rage. It would wriggle violently, release a gaseous cloud of musk, and lunge with its bony beak at my fingers.

I scooted the turtle forward with my foot, and it began to crawl across the highway. Seeing no cars coming from either direction, I decided that the turtle would probably make it without my intervention, and gathered the family back into the car. Driving away, I watched in the rear view mirror as it lumbered forward with excruciating slowness.

"Oh, no!" my wife called out as a car suddenly bore down upon the snapping turtle. The children cringed and hid their eyes. But the car passed harmlessly over the snapper, which continued on its journey, a dark slouching shape older than any human thought.

It surprised me how much we all had feared for the turtle in its moment of peril. Over the years, I had managed to conquer my atavistic revulsion to certain animals. It was nothing to me now to handle a snake or to brush with my finger the silken fur of a living bat, but a snapping turtle was still a kind of nightmare creature, and a part of me did not want to accept the idea that it was as vulnerable as the rest of creation. I knew that characterizing nature in this way was an ageless human fallacy, but I still could not quite get over the sensation that snapping turtles were the enemy. Their outward appearance was the manifestation of their grim consciousness. Snapping turtles lived, it seemed to me, in a constant state of wrathful agitation. They were like the souls of the damned—irredeemable, and loathsome even to themselves.

"A savage, cross-tempered brute." That's the way one biologist, in an otherwise unemotional volume on reptiles and amphibians, describes snapping turtles. "The general aspect," another authority queasily reports, "is so sinister that it imparts more of the feeling inspired by a thick-bodied, poisonous serpent than that of a turtle."

Snappers are ferocious, but it's important to remember that they are that way for a reason. They are not simply dyspeptic. Snapping turtles are underwater predators; they are attack vehicles. They lie in wait and strike at passing fish, or they paddle up to the surface and seize ducklings by the feet. Their strike has to be fast, the grip of their jaws tenacious.

Out of the water, a snapping turtle's small shell is an imperfect refuge, and so its best defense is to attack. "I have seen it snapping," a nineteenth-century naturalist wrote, "in the same fierce manner as it does when full grown, at a time when it was still a pale, almost colorless embryo, wrapped up in its foetal envelopes, with a yolk larger than itself hanging from its sternum, three months before hatching."

Folklore says that when snappers bite they will not let go until it thunders. Not true, but they do like to hold on to their claim. They are also very efficient scavengers. This trait was supposedly once used by an Indian in northern Indiana, who exploited a snapping turtle, tethered to a long wire, to locate the bodies of drowning victims. And one of the worst practical jokes I ever heard of was perpetrated by a friend of mine when he was a rowdy adolescent. He put a baby snapping turtle into the purse of his friend's mother.

There are two kinds of snapping turtles, both of which are native to Texas. The common snapping turtle—*Chelydra serpentina*—is the smaller and more aggressive species. Its range extends throughout the entire eastern half of the continent, all the way from Canada (where it has been observed walking on the bottom of frozen streams beneath the ice) to Central America. It lives everywhere—lakes, rivers, swamps, even brackish tidal streams—but its prime habitat is sluggish, muddy water. Common snappers are not behemoths. The largest one ever caught in the wild weighed slightly less than seventy pounds, though one captive turtle that was kept in a swill barrel for two months ate its way up to eighty-six pounds.

Those figures are nothing compared with the mighty *Macroclemys temmincki,* the alligator snapping turtle. Alligator snappers can grow as large as sea turtles, up to 250 pounds or even more. Their heads are massive and blunt, their eyes lower on their heads than those of common snappers, their shells crowned with three high longitudinal ridges that look like miniature mountain ranges. Common snappers are common, but alligator snappers are increasingly rare. Alligator snapper meat has long been a steady seller in the fish markets of Louisiana, and the turtle population took a nose dive when Campbell's came out with a snapper soup in the early seventies. In Texas, alligator snappers are classified as a threatened species by the Parks and Wildlife Department. They tend to inhabit coastal drainages in East Texas, though they have made appearances as far west as Burleson County.

Unlike common snapping turtles, alligator snappers do not stalk their prey or seize it with serpentine strikes of their necks. They lie in wait, settled motionlessly in the cloudy water like boulders or stumps, their mouths hinged open to reveal a fluttering gob of tissue rooted to the lower jaw. When a fish spots the lure and enters the cavern of the turtle's mouth, it is either swallowed whole or neatly sliced. With this leisurely feeding strategy at their disposal, alligator snappers tend to have a less urgent temperament than their cousins. Though they look even more hideous than common snappers, they are comparatively docile.

Alligator snappers are strong and, in strange ways, agile. There is a report of a three-legged specimen climbing an eight-foot-high cyclone fence. The turtles have been known to shear off human fingers. All sorts of things—small alligators, entire beaver heads—have been found in their stomachs. For years it was a commonplace observation that an alligator snapping turtle was capable of biting a broom handle in two. Peter Pritchard, a Florida biologist who has written extensively on *Macroclemys temmincki,* decided to test this hypothesis. He waved a broom handle in front of a 165-pound alligator snapper to see if it really could bite it in half. It could.

"If common snapping turtles were as big as alligator snapping turtles," an East Texas herpetologist named William W. Lamar told me, "they would take bathers regularly."

Several years ago, when Lamar was the curator of herpetology at the Caldwell Zoo in Tyler, I dropped in to see his alligator snapper collection. The zoo had three specimens, including a baby that was kept in an aquarium tank in the reptile house. The first time I saw it I wasn't sure it was even a living thing. It was settled down at the bottom of the tank, eerily still, its jaws hinged open as if in some epic yawn and its right foreleg raised like a pointer's. The only things moving were the lure inside its mouth and a doomed fish that swam near the surface. Lamar remarked that the snapper looked like a log with a worm on it.

We left the baby still angling for the fish and went outside to look at the larger specimens. Another curator climbed over a fence and waded into a pond. He looked around on the bottom a bit, then reached down with both hands and hauled up a forty-five-pound turtle, lifting it by either end of the shell. The alligator snapper's name was Eugenia. She was dark and mucky and immense, a ghastly apparition from the dawn of time.

Lamar looked down at this strange beast admiringly. Eugenia seemed to me not an animal but an entity—a moving, moss-covered rock. I asked Lamar if alligator snappers were intelligent. What I wondered was: Do they think?

"If one looks at intelligence as the ability to learn functions that are nontraditional," he said, "I don't know. Nobody's ever trained one of these things to dance. A common snapper is lacking in personality to me. They do what they do with a lot of aggressive verve, but they're boring. They're like somebody you'd expect to meet in a casino in Vegas. But my opinion of alligator snappers is they're a lot more receptive to stimuli than most people think. A lot more goes on in their lives than most people imagine."

Some months later I acquired a snapping turtle. It was a baby, a common snapper, hatched from a clutch of eggs that a reptile fancier had discovered on the banks of the San Marcos River. A mutual friend delivered the turtle to me one day in a bucket.

I went to the pet shop and bought a twenty-gallon aquarium, a filter, and a pile of decorative rocks. When the aquarium was all set up and running, I put on a pair of gloves and picked the turtle up from behind. To my surprise, it didn't thrash about and try to bite my hand. It merely kept its head retracted into its shell as far as it would go.

The turtle was only a few inches long, no more than several months old. When I put it in the water, it sank to the bottom like a piece of lead and then began to scramble frantically upward without success. It didn't seem to be able to swim. I reached into the water and set it on one of the rocks, and it craned its neck up, up, up until its nostrils were above the surface. And there the turtle stayed.

"Let's call him Sam," my oldest daughter said, and that became his name, though we never used it. He was always just "the snapping turtle." He would lie there on the rock all day and all night, blinking, breathing. I dropped little pellets of turtle food on top of the water, but the turtle would not eat with me in the room. After I left, the food disappeared.

The little aquarium filter chugged along diligently, and I changed the water once a day, but the moment I put the turtle into the clean water it immediately turned into a fetid bog. I was tired of the maintenance, but I grew oddly fond of the snapping turtle. I found him more interesting than odious. His silent, patient, undemanding presence was somehow restful to me.

Nevertheless, after a few months I had had enough. The whole house was beginning to stink. I decided to take the turtle and release him back into the San Marcos.

The night before I let him go, however, I dropped a few pellets of turtle food into the tank and hid behind the door, watching. I saw the turtle track the food with his eyes as it sank slowly down to him. When a pellet was several inches away he shot his neck out with a startling and unnecessary motion, snapped his dinner savagely in half, then gulped it down with urgent, gagging movements of his throat.

The kids and I took him down to a murky little eddy cut into a bank of the river. I put on my gloves, set him into the water, and he was gone in an instant in a swirl of mud. I suddenly felt an unexpected pang, of what I cannot imagine.

We walked along the bank looking for him. We wanted to say good-bye to this creature that had never had any need or cognizance of us—that just was. I wondered if he would survive. If he did, if he was not eaten by another snapping turtle, if he was not caught on a boy's fishing line, he might live ten or twenty years, spending the winters denned up under cutbanks, the summers loitering in the mud. He would grow up to replace the turtle whose death I had caused so many years ago, and whose savage, unappeasable spirit was still alive, still snapping at me in my dreams.

Ken Lamberton

OF PINACATE BEETLES AND BEACHES

Near the end of Mexican Highway 8 the first thing we notice is the smell. It is a pungent odor that grows warm and wet and tastes like brine. In the distance the sky pales at the horizon and shimmers audibly in the sun. A fine white sand, reluctantly driven into dunes by the wind, hems the road. These surging crystalline waves, ragged with stunted gray vegetation, seem to emerge from a range of black volcanic mountains and plunge toward the horizon where the whole swelling landscape suddenly erupts into a brilliant blue expanse. Here, the desert has surrendered to the sea.

Less than sixty-five miles from the border town of Lukeville, Arizona, the Sonoran Desert meets the Gulf of California, also called the Sea of Cortés. I first visited "Arizona's Coast" in Sonora, Mexico, while a student at the University of Arizona. Although the secluded beaches offered a favorite party location for students on spring break (a condition that is rapidly changing today with the free trade agreement and tourism), I had another reason for venturing here—a fascination with tide pools and mud flats. So, while my friends packed volleyballs, swimsuits, and suntan lotion, I packed dip nets, flashlights, and field guides. In later excursions my wife joined me, and together, as now, we would explore this unique transition zone of desert and sea.

Some distance before Highway 8 disappears into the Mexican fishing town of Puerto Peñasco, a rough, sandy jeep trail breaks away from the asphalt and meanders westward toward the coast among low dunes. In places, drifting sand swallows the road. Withered brittle-bushes mention their waterless condition by rasping against the metal of our truck. Traveling is slow and uncertain with the likelihood of getting stuck a continuous threat. Both Karen and I consider the hazard of finding ourselves on foot many leagues from civilization, but we keep these thoughts unvocalized. It's March and already temperatures are in the high eighties.

Ahead the horizon suddenly solidifies into a dark wall, barring further progress. Like an iron-hued curtain, the barrier rises more than fifteen feet and stretches toward the coast from a dominant peak in the north. Afraid to turn the truck around in the deep sand, I get out to look around. The rock wall is lava.

Recent, at least in geologic terms, volcanic activity at the head of the Gulf of California has created one of the most inhospitable regions on the continent. The late Edward Abbey described this place as "[t]he bleakest, flattest, hottest, grittiest, grimmest, dreariest, ugliest, most useless, most senseless desert of them all." Perhaps desert sojourner John Van Dyke was thinking of this area when, at the turn of the century, he wrote, "Volcanoes have left their traces everywhere. You can still see the streams of lava that have chilled as they ran . . . there are great lakes and streams of reddish-black lava, frozen in swirls and pools, cracked like glass, broken into blocks like a ruined pavement." This is the Pinacate Desert, a 750-square-mile wasteland named for a diminutive black insect also known as a darkling or eleodes beetle but most commonly called a stink bug. It is the region's mascot. At the center of this place of cinder cones, craters, fumaroles, collapsed calderas, and lava fields, a dome-shaped volcano named Pinacate Peak rises 3,957 feet above sea level. To the south and west of the peak, salt marshes and sand dunes border the Sea of Cortés; on the north and east, low granite mountains, smudged with cacti and creosote, poke up through the desert floor. Only a stink bug, it seems, would choose to live here.

Local Mexicans refer to the Pinacate as *mal pais* ("bad land") and avoid it. It is part of the Sonoran Desert but the typical numbers of plants and animals seem curtailed. Only those adapted to the most severe conditions survive here, where sunlight strips the landscape clean of even shadow. Near the peak where basalt rock has crumbled, teddy-bear cholla have gained a foothold. A few spindly ocotillo and thin saguaro cacti are scattered about on the lower broken slopes. Where sand has reclaimed the lava field, pockets of mesquite trees, smoke trees, and brittlebush rest in a kind of fugue state, waiting, mostly in vain, for rain among the locoweed, sand verbena, and buffalo gourd. Here, life is narrowed to pockets, and only Italic imprints in the sand betray the presence of a few brave animals.

When sufficient winter rains arrive at the proper times, however, perhaps every few years or so, flowers like brittlebush, fairy duster, Mexican poppy, and globe mallow spatter the desert with seasonal color. But even in a good year the bloom is short-lived. Water and shade become scarce as summer approaches. Only two or three widely dispersed pools retain any moisture at all. Some people call them *tinajas,* Spanish for "earthen jars."

The road turns sharply at the edge of the lava flow and follows its contours. Soon, we come to a place where the black wall is less sheer and the road meets an incline that takes us above the sand. A broad, flat pavement, like hardened resin, spreads out before us. I stop the truck and we step out onto the surface of Venus. Silence envelops us. Nothing moves. Not even the air, which has gotten hotter, more stifling, offers a breeze as an apology. The sun bakes this basaltic altar and waits patiently for its next sacrifice. I pick up a rock and toss it a few feet in front of me. Its impact cracks the silence like the sound of breaking porcelain.

We drive on. From this elevated bench over the sand the overall dimensions of the flow become clear. Its source is obvious in the north as a tarlike discharge spilling from one side of Pinacate Peak. From there, the lava slips toward the sea with black fingers escaping the main body to explore alternate pathways over the uneven terrain. It covers many square miles. Typical of shield volcanoes, the lava contains iron and magnesium which was originally mixed with gas allowing it to flow easily and spread out in flat sheets. The effect is dramatic, dead serious.

One of the first scientists to describe this lava flow, more than two centuries after Father Eusebio Francisco Kino ventured here in 1689, was zoologist William T. Hornaday, who came to the Pinacate with an expedition early this century. At the time he was director of the New York Zoological Park, previously having been chief taxidermist with the U.S. National Museum. Two members of his team, Daniel T. Mac-Dougal, the botanist who convinced Hornaday to make the trip, and Godfrey Sykes, both worked for the newly established Carnegie Desert Botanical Laboratory in Tucson, Arizona; MacDougal was its director.

After leaving Tucson in the fall of 1907 the expedition traveled west through Papagueria (the reservation of the Tohono O'odham or "Stony Place People") to the tiny Mexican village of Sonoyta. From the spring at Quitobaquito, a "lonesome, stagnant, out-of-the-way-place," as Hornaday described its two-inch stream and small pond, the group took a circuitous route into the Pinacate Desert, first following the Sonoyta River south then heading northward into the infamous boneyard of El Camino del Diablo. Finally entering the lava field itself from the northwest, they located and named two volcanic craters and camped at a *tinaja* known as Papago Tanks. The group hunted and collected pronghorn and bighorn sheep, but all along Hornaday seemed most impressed with the plants that lived on the stark lava. He noted elephant trees or "torote," ironwood and smoke trees, small barrel cacti he called "bisnagas," tree cholla, and saguaro that "on account of the scarcity of water and total lack of soil, the straggling specimens of it were very small and limbless." His encounter with one plant on the lava, a small, hemispherical, white-leaved bush, common in the Southwest (but Hornaday first noticed it here), compelled him to give it a good English name. He called it white brittlebush.

On November 20, 1907, after traveling farther south to camp at Tule Tank, the expedition at last climbed Pinacate Peak. From its summit Hornaday wrote: "This huge basin between the three peaks once was the crater of this culminating volcano; and the peaks themselves when united formed the rim. First a notch was blown out toward the west, through which we came. Later on another one, much deeper, was blown out toward the south. Through these two notches ran great rivers of molten lava, and the congealed mass is there today, almost the same as when it came hot from the kettles of Pluto. . . ."

Although plants and animals are nearly absent from the surface of this "congealed mass," this is not the case at its margins. Here, where sand and lava battle and brittlebush takes the advantage, Karen finds a small, black lizard wedged into a cleft of rock. Dark blue markings

behind its front legs on either side identify it as a melanistic version of
the side-blotched lizard. Ubiquitous in the Southwest and throughout
the North American deserts, these lizards reach their greatest abundance in rocky areas, living off of beetles, flies, and scorpions—water
being unnecessary. The reptile's special physiology epitomizes adapta-
tion to the desert. A parietal eye on the center top of its head measures
light intensity, helping the lizard adjust its activities when sunlight is too
strong or too weak. In this way the side-blotched lizard keeps a relatively constant body temperature, knowing when to seek sunlight or
shelter from sunlight. Also, the side-blotched lizard escapes dehydration
at the cellular level as its cells produce energy by breaking down car-
bohydrates into wastes including carbon dioxide and water. All animals
make water this way, a process called oxidative respiration, but this lizard is extremely efficient at conserving it. Furthermore, the reptile saves
water in its excretory processes. Urination accounts for huge water
losses in most mammals, but reptiles excrete uric acid rather than urea.
The advantage of this crystalline waste is its water-stingy, paste-like
droppings.

Karen sets the lizard on the sand, and it shuttles back to its shady
cleft near a scrawny, hardly recognizable brittlebush. The plant favors
the outwash slopes of these volcanic hills and the lava-sand borders
where runoff sometimes collects. Smoke tree, ironwood, and creosote
are present, but brittlebush is most conspicuous, although without
much recent moisture the low shrubs with their cornflake leaves look
more dead than alive. But brittlebush likes it here. Its variable leaves,
large and fleshy after winter and summer rains or small and furry in
drought, enable the plant to adjust to a whimsical desert. And, as a self-
preserving tactic, it leaches a toxin into the soil that prevents other
plants from germinating close by where they might preempt essential
resources such as light and water.

We leave behind the lava flow and travel toward the Sea of Cortés.
Waves of sand, bullied by the wind, gradually become more suggestive,
voluptuous, and soon great shadowed dunes, double-stitched together
by the tracks of foraging pinacate beetles, surround us. We arrive at the
sandy beaches of Cholla Bay as the sun sinks into the sea. A red, bloated

moon rises soon after, promising an exceptionally low tide. After setting up camp we decide to postpone dinner, and with flashlights,
buckets, and dip nets in hand, we follow the ebbing tidewater out into
the mud flats of the bay.

From our campsite on the beach the coastline arcs wide to the
south where the sand disappears beneath a salt marsh. The coastline
then swings around northward into a rocky peninsula known as Pelican
Point. Straight across the mud flats several miles away we can see the
lights of a small *Gringo* community wavering along the peninsula like
unfamiliar constellations low in a darkening sky. Shallow, silted rivulets,
eddies, and pools are the only physical barriers between us and the
town of Cholla Bay. Time, however, could be a problem, especially for
nonswimmers.

The bay itself, a southernmost pocket of *Bahía Adair* named for
the cholla cactus forest just beyond the marsh, is one of the few places
in the world where low tides expose vast tracts of naked shoreline.
Spring tides, caused by the combined gravitational influences of the sun
and moon (which happens twice a month during the full and new
moon), in conjunction with the bay's geography, produce the greatest
effect, both high and low tides. The lowest tides (−6 foot ebb tides) un-
cover places normally hidden beneath deep water and provide perfect
opportunities for observing a wonderful array of creatures inhabiting
underwater plains of mud and silt.

Understanding the cycles of the tides is essential here. Ignorance
can be costly. A friend of ours once got his new jeep stuck out on these
mud flats. After trying unsuccessfully to free it himself, he decided to
walk the ten miles to Puerto Peñasco to get help. When he returned in
the evening he was shocked to find an ocean where his vehicle had
been. I've also had disturbing experiences with these huge tidal fluctua-
tions but not as expensive. I've never risked driving a vehicle out into
the bay, even though the Mexicans now have a tractor-like contraption
with an elevated chassis that keeps the engine and driver above water
for rescuing trapped cars (for a price). Instead, I walk. And this is where
I've gotten into trouble with the tides.

Stingrays tend to migrate into deeper water as the bay drains, returning with the next cycle six hours later. There is little danger of

stepping on one if you stay behind the ebb and ahead of the flow. But one morning I was so preoccupied with exploring a deep sponge reef, netting creatures and taking notes, that I forgot about the time. When I finally did notice the surging water I was more than a mile from shore. I ran where I could, but had to wade the last few hundred yards. It was summer, the sea was like foamy bathwater, and stingrays were massing. It seemed like every three or four steps one would rise up from its hiding place from under the mud and shuffle away. I was lucky that time. On another trip a friend of mine wasn't as fortunate. Under similar circumstances he planted his foot on a buried ray that showed its displeasure by slapping its four-inch, bony stinger into his ankle. Bruce said it was the worst pain he had ever felt. The wound, a small but penetrating gash, refused to close and oozed all that night, saturating his sleeping bag with blood. It took a week to begin healing.

Karen and I, stepping carefully, unavoidably crunch over carpets of mud snails—mostly tower shells and basket whelks—feeding on smelly, black detritus mixed with the sand in spots. It reminds me of raw sewage. Other snails we find include *Aplesia,* a sweet-potato-shaped, shell-less sea hare, deadly, fish-eating cone shells, and a fist-sized *Murex.* Far out on the mud flats our flashlights find beds of half-buried, scavenging sand dollars—not the white skeletons found on beaches, but the bristled, wine-colored, living relatives of sea urchins. An arrowhead-shaped sand dollar, *Encope grandis,* stains my hands Tyrian purple in protest to being disturbed. At more than a mile from our campsite on the beach, the backwater is knee deep. Two edible swimming crabs threaten us when we cut off their escape, snapping at the surface with giant, chitinous claws. I scoop them up in my net and dump them into a bucket of clams Karen has been collecting. They'll make a wonderful addition to our dinner.

In deep water we locate exotic tube anemones, christened "sloppy guts" by Tiny Colleto, a Mexican seaman and crew member of the 1940 Ricketts and Steinbeck expedition to the gulf, because its "encased body is very ugly, like rotting gray cloth." The silt and mucus tubes of these cerianthid anemones may extend three feet into the mud. Their delicate magenta and purple tentacles create an exquisite bouquet against a carbon background. Resembling thread-petalled flowers, they use their tentacles to capture tiny crustaceans and fish. Special stinging cells called nematocysts line each tentacle. When a small animal like a shrimp, drifting on the tidal current, comes in contact with the anemone, the stinging cells discharge, gripping and paralyzing the prey. The anemone then draws its victim into its mouth.

As the tide begins to return, bright orange tunicates float by us like waterlogged Nerf balls. Karen lifts a scarlet gorgonian coral out of the water and shines her light through it. It looks like a miniature, fan-shaped tree but is actually a colony of animals related to sea anemones. One slender branch is home to thousands of individual polyps, each armed with tiny tentacles that feed on the bay's rich plankton. Both the coral and the tunicates have broken away from a nearby reef, but the tide won't give us time to find it. We must quickly retreat from the mud flats to remain dry.

After dinner, Karen and I sit together by a campfire of incandescent mesquite coals (from wood gathered back in Arizona) and bathe in moonlight. The absence of wind means the surf is completely still; the sea silently creeps toward us, frothy fingers reaching for the high tide line of sea-refuse. The only sound comes from our fire, the occasional flatulent staccato of burning sapwood. When the temperature drops, we slip into our sleeping bags, feeling cradled by sand and protected by a clear dome of stars.

Dew coats everything by morning. We struggle to work off the chill, fixing breakfast, packing gear, inflating a small yellow raft (the same kind of one-man, drugstore river-runner made popular by Edward Abbey). With the high tide at mid-morning, I plan on dragging a baited fishing line across the stingray infested depths. On a previous visit to Cholla Bay, Karen and I had watched several Mexican fishermen unload their catch from their flat wooden boats. Using long poles with barbed points the *pescaderos* had speared more than a dozen rays, some of them a yard in diameter. The men had the meat filleted and cut into steaks within half an hour of landing. Stingray tastes like shark and is sometimes sold in fish markets or *pescaderías* by that name. My intention was to catch a small stingray to preserve as a specimen for my junior high science class.

I launch the raft and use a single plastic oar to steer a course 500 yards into the bay. Raw clam works well as bait, and I get several strikes almost immediately. Setting the hook in the small, ventrally located mouth proves to be a problem, however, and I decide to let the ray swallow the bait. This is a mistake. I can't remove the thrashing animal from the hook, and I'm afraid it might puncture the raft (or me) with its serrated stinger. I finally stuff the ray into my canvas creel, cut the line, and tie the now hopelessly lacerated bag overboard. One specimen, I assure myself, is enough.

We decide to spend our last night at Sandy Beach near Pelican Point. Here, the tide retreats leaving surprised boulders scattered around flat shelves of soft limestone called coquina. Low tide at Pelican Point provides an entirely different kind of exploration—tidepooling. Tide pools form in rocky basins and catchments as the tide recedes, placing invertebrates and fish within easy access of curious naturalists with flashlights. Tide pools are microhabitats, destroyed and recreated twice a day with every tide cycle. In them, various phyla of animals—sponges, coelenterates, worms, mollusks, arthropods, echinoderms, and chordates—struggle to survive the changes. A single tide pool, like a classroom aquarium, offers a miniature living world to the casual observer. No special tools or knowledge necessary.

In her definitive book about the Cape Region of Baja California, Ann Zwinger describes tide pools as "so still, in muted rose, coral, and olive, neutral tans and beiges. No bright colors at all. Tiny waterfalls between pools adjust the levels until there is no more adjustment to be done. The sound of the ocean diminishes and the landward sounds emerge, quiet poppings and clickings, tiny smackings as drying begins." On the northeast coast of the same gulf and a hundred yards from shore, Karen and I stand on the rim of a similar world less than two feet deep. The water is perfectly still and clear, invisible; our flashlights illuminate the whole pool as though the rock and sand and water were glowing themselves.

Movement is everywhere. Slender bristled arms of brittle stars poke out along the perimeter of the pool, sweeping, groping, entwining, the animals' vulnerable disks secured in crevices. Pencil urchins also hide in these crevices, using their stubby spines to wedge themselves between the rock. Scores of hermit crabs scuttle over one another, their shells the dispossessed homes of common snails, mostly *Acanthina* and *Turbo*. Shoals of fishes, like the bottom-dwelling speckled blennies and striped sergeant majors, patrol every liquid recess, searching for food.

Karen turns over a rock and uncovers a hidden zoo. A thumb-sized octopus jets away, leaving a black button of ink hanging in its place. The remains of its meal, a half-empty carapace of a crab, settles on the sand, legs pointing to the sky. Variegated brittle stars, suddenly in the open, scramble for cover in three different directions. A poly-chaete "fireworm," a segmented ribbon armed with a coat of poisonous glass spicules, double-coils and then retreats again under the rock. Sed-entary creatures encrust the rock's exposed underside. Patches of orange and yellow sponges like spilled paint feel slimy when touched. Eight-plated chitons, primitive relatives of snails, defy the most dexterous at-tempts to pry them loose. One member of a congregation of dark green sea cucumbers squirts a fine stream of seawater that ripples the surface of the pool. Karen replaces the rock while a pavement of colo-nial anemones watches her with a hundred, bulging, half-closed eyes.

We walk the length of Sandy Beach at midnight to express a voiceless farewell to this region of desert and sea. Under the lamp of a pale, wafer-like moon, we contemplate lava and sand, mud flats and tide pools. The gentle susurration of *El Mar de Cortés* whispers content-ment; its talismanic message draws us. Soon, however, we will return to another reality: congested city traffic, blue smoke, and fast food. We leave behind a region in transition, an in-between place, a wilderness open to sea and sky, simple, perfect, yet vulnerable.

Edward Lueders

NOTES OF A NATURE WRITER:
BIG BEND NATIONAL PARK

March 3: Sunny morning. Cool to warm to hot day. Drove the River
Road, a rough, rocky, occasionally rutted and washed, primitive road,
fifty-five slow miles to Rio Grande Village on the southeast border of
the park. After recent rain and subsequent warming, the road dry but
not dusty. Delighted to find the plant life beginning to emerge in spring
flowering, which usually begins later in March, depending on weather
and moisture, both favorable this year.

Cactus already blooming or on the verge of it, buds swelling as if
ready to burst. A great variety of cholla, prickly pear (these in a surprising array of colors—green, purple, brick red, and a strange deep brown
I'd never seen before). Ocotillo, with small, bright red blossoming at
the tips of their long, spindly arms. Here and there, spectacular large,
cream-colored blossoms in laddered flowering on the tall stalks of
yucca. Some of these growing in clusters and clumps of four or five
stalks, all flowering profusely into the brightness of their arid setting, up
from the splayed green spikes of the base plant. The strong sun emphasized their intense but soft off-whiteness.

Followed deep side ruts down to some of the primitive riverside
campsites designated by the Park Service. These were simply clearings
cut into the dense riparian brush of giant reeds, low-growing feathery
tamarisk, and tangles of mesquite. The Rio Grande itself slow-moving
and unspectacular as it winds through most of the Big Bend. The water
an opaque chocolate brown. Milk chocolate, to be more exact, with
here and there a small swirl of lighter hue and flecks of foam. The current steady but sluggish. Ripples where the shores are uneven, but no
boils. At the east and west ends of the park, though, it becomes a can-

yon river. Along the southwestern shore, a sheer cliff rises on the Mexican side, where the persistent river has cut deep into the rock face, obstructing its course. It soars 1,000 feet or so above the river at the Santa Elena location, with the Sierra de Santa Elena rising in progressively darker hues behind the cliffs. To the right, viewed from the U.S. side, the steep side canyon with the same name slices down and through the rock to join its drainage with the tumbling Rio Grande. At the far southeastern end of the Big Bend, the river funnels between sheer walls on both sides through Boquillas Canyon. A half-mile hike from the dirt road leads to the sand and cobbled mouth of that chasm.

Along the slow stretches of river between these rock-walled passages, flood plains prevail. At moderate levels, the river flows between modest cutbanks, steep-sided at one point, flat-sided at another, with layered deposits of silt everywhere, too fine to be called sand.

In the middle of the park are the jagged Chisos Mountains. Leaving the somnolent banks and quiet, sliding current of the Rio Grande from time to time, the River Road wanders up onto the stony flats and mounds of their foothills, providing an irregular, roller-coaster ride with steadily changing views and configurations of their rugged, emaciated forms against the horizon to the north. What countless seasons, years, eons of implacable time have eaten away the rock face of the Chisos, carrying them grain by grain to compact and wash into these same lumps and creases the road traverses! And eventually to join in the incessant flushing of the Rio Grande on to the Gulf of Mexico—and beyond. . . .

Notes

*Check geology of the Chisos and the canyons mentioned.

*Political implications of the Rio Grande? Consider U.S. Park Service policies and cultural attitudes together with Mexican life and land just across the Rio.

*Local animal life and insect relationship to plant life in the area. Animal and insect life as a controlling metaphor for human interaction with the land and its "development."

*Probable prehistory habitation.

*Cloud and sky and atmospheric conditions overhead. Bird life.

Kent Nelson

IRREGULAR FLIGHT

Claire had heard about the vagrant Thursday afternoon on the bird tape in L.A. and called me in Tucson. She couldn't get away from an early meeting at her lab, but met me at five at the post office in Indio. When I arrived she was sitting in the shade of her Land Rover, dressed in shorts and a loose khaki shirt and hiking boots. She'd cut her hair since I'd last seen her, and she looked slimmer too, as if she'd been exercising. Yet my initial impression as she got up was not of her appearance so much as something else less tangible. The slow way she lifted her body, the way she tilted her head and shielded her eyes from the sun made her seem younger and patient and more threatening. "We'll take my car," she said. "The light's going fast, so we'd better hurry."

I got my binoculars and my scope and my overnight bag from the trunk of my Corolla. Claire opened the well of the Rover, and I threw my stuff in beside the cooler and her camping gear. "Who found the bird?" I asked.

"Strachen Donelly."

"You think the sighting is reliable?"

"One hundred percent."

"And you got directions?"

"They were on the tape. North shore, Salton Sea."

"A petrel could be anywhere."

"It could already be gone."

We got into the Rover and Claire started the engine, revved it, and we took off to the south. I rolled down the window and let the breeze blow in.

It was hard to pin down my history with Claire. When I knew her in Tucson she was married to a man I never met. She was a biologist, a lit-

tle overweight, with dark hair. For more than a year we shared a ride to
the research institute where we worked—twenty minutes each way. We
spoke mostly about the ongoing project, which was to study the effects
of radiation on flora and fauna in the zones of government nuclear testing in the Southwest. Our relationship was professional: she never asked
me a personal question and never confessed anything about herself. At
the same time, perhaps in the absence of anyone else, I thought she was
my friend. I sensed things about her—how much more alert she was in
the afternoons when we drove home, how on a particular day she was
aware of the wind from the north; sometimes I felt a distant anger from
her, as if she knew she wasn't happy.

But she knew nothing about me. I lived alone. My father had died
when I was a child, and my mother, who was slightly disturbed, lived
back East in New England. I was not a social person. I had been to college, of course, and to graduate school in chemistry and had simply
never had the need to be with people. I had no expectations or desires.
And yet I was perfectly at ease in this solitariness. I didn't want company. I liked my work, was enthralled by birds, and fascinated by what
was happening in the wider world.

I had terrible insomnia, and often to appease the demons I stayed
up all night and watched the international news. That I saw the slaughter in Rwanda or a man walking on the moon, or watched a bomb as it
was falling into a building in Iraq was thrilling to me, not for the occur-
rences themselves, but for their comprehension—that I could know all
at once everything everywhere.

It was by accident I discovered Claire's love for birds. One day on a
group fact-finding excursion to a missile range—there were six of us; I
was driving—I spotted a bird flying low over brush along a streambank.
I didn't see it well—just a gray blur—but I knew it was a bird of prey
larger than a kestrel, smaller than a buteo. I slowed down and followed
its flight, and from the backseat Claire said, "Mississippi Kite."

I pulled off the road and stopped. "Are you sure?"

"It's a kite, not hovering, and it has a black tail."

I trained my binoculars out the window and saw the long, pointed
wings of a kite, the black, flared tail Claire had noticed. I was shocked
at her precision, how she had seen so much in so brief a moment, how
she had kept such a secret as bird love from me all that time.

"Come on, Slater, keep driving," one my colleagues said. "We want to get there someday and home again."

After that, we talked birds on our daily commute. Claire had traveled in quest of rarities—to Alaska, South Texas, the offshore islands of both coasts. Her knowledge was more extensive than mine. She knew biology and courtship rituals, field marks, food sources, habitat, and range overlaps. Compared to her, I was an amateur.

As the days went by, the commute seemed shorter. What I learned of birds, the places Claire had been, the details of her life startled me. I discovered, for example, she had once spent a week on an island in the Bering Sea, alone, studying the nesting behavior of Arctic foxes and kittiwakes. The foxes had been introduced to kill rodents that plagued the Aleuts, but once the rodents became hard to find, the foxes preyed on birds. The birds had evolved a way to protect their young. When a fox appeared, the birds flew off their cliffside nests, and the fox, finding the abandoned fledglings, was lured down the steep terrain. When he had gone far enough, the birds swooped in and knocked him from the cliff into the water a hundred feet below. It was not so much the kittiwake behavior that interested me as that Claire had viewed it. She had the desire to be there, the patience and stamina to endure the cold sea breezes, the rugged terrain, and still to speak of the experience with wonder.

My life changed gradually. I slept better at night, and because of that, though I was still mesmerized by world events, I didn't follow them so assiduously. On weekends I drove to the mountain canyons south of the city where the year-round streams made such perfect habitat for birds. I camped and woke early and listened to Sulphur-bellied Flycatchers and Grace's Warblers and, higher up, Hepatic Tanagers singing in the morning air.

Then one day in the spring on our way home, when we were stopped at a traffic light, she looked over at me behind the wheel. It was hot out, and neither of us liked air-conditioning, so the windows were open. My left arm hung loosely over the window ledge. Her expression was soft in a way I had never seen before—forlorn, maybe. "My husband got promoted," she said. "We're moving to Los Angeles."

I heard these words, but did not believe them. The light changed.

I accelerated through the intersection. Colors bled in the air around me. I smelled exhaust. It was the first glimpse I had of her personal life, and I thought of questions to ask—What about your job? How can you leave the desert? Is this what you want? But I asked nothing.

The bird we were after was Cook's Petrel, a *Pterodroma* that nested on the islands off New Zealand. It was smallish—thirteen inches from head to tail—and had a black M pattern across its gray wings and back. Except for its breeding period, the Cook's, like other gadfly petrels, spent its life at sea. It fed on the wing, rarely alit on the water, wandered erratically throughout the Pacific. Its status off the California coast was uncertain. Several individuals had been photographed on pelagic trips over the years, but none had ever been seen inland, none ever before at the Salton Sea.

We drove the main road from Indio to Mecca, passed a dozen migrant workers in red and yellow and blue shirts and dresses hoeing lettuce, slid by groves of date palms and orange trees. To the west, ten miles distant, were the treeless, sun-weary Santa Rosa Mountains, and southeastward, the Orocopias and the Chocolates, which framed the valley with a jagged horizon. I didn't know what to say to Claire. Her abandoning me—that's how it felt—had made me afraid of her.

We slowed through Mecca, a few run-down pastel buildings—a general store, a gas station, a cafe. The houses and trailers had trellises covered with bougainvillea, and in the dirt yards were empty fruit crates stacked high. At the south end of town, Claire turned onto an unmarked dirt road, and we crossed an irrigation canal. She handed me a piece of paper. "You navigate," she said.

I read the directions aloud. "We stay on this road to the next bridge. Then it's one mile to an adobe house. Turn left there toward the sea." I looked out through the windshield to the fading light over the mountains. There was no sea—just the absence of trees where the water must have been and the wide sky.

"How is work?" Claire asked.

"All right."

"No new discoveries?"

"We found contaminants on the Cabeza Prieta Refuge," I said.

"You always knew they were there."

"Even with the evidence, there's no way the government will let us publish it. They pay for the research, then hide the results."

"You can't be so cynical," Claire said.

"Why not?"

The Land Rover raised dust behind us on the dirt track. Ahead, the small steel bridge appeared. We clanked across it, then ran along a broken fence line. The smell of orange blossoms was thick on the breeze. We passed a broken-down Ford on the berm, then came to the adobe house where, on the left, a narrow lane opened up. Claire threaded the Land Rover through the mesquite on either side.

We proceeded past a nearly dry alkaline pond where four Black-necked Stilts dipped their long bills into the scum. A few peeps flew up and swerved over the canal, and as we neared the end of the pond, the stilts flew too and wheeled away to the west where the mountains were a dark blue haze. We climbed a low rise—maybe ten feet—and there before us was the sea, a great blue-gray sheen without wind or sunlight. High white cirrus above the mountains were reflected in the water.

When Claire left Tucson, I had been lonely in the lab. I retreated into my research with a vengeance, and yet I knew my work suffered. I was like a musician who, despite his talent, cannot bring himself to the emotional risk that let the music live. Who cared whether the chromatic patterns of genes had been altered years before by A-tests in the desert? Or that groundwater was radioactive enough to make lizards sick?

On weekends I went to the desert instead of the mountains. I camped on creosote flats or on the edge of a dry wash in the cover of palo verde. I sat in the sun as if to let the desert erode my whole body and mind. At night I listened to the high-pitched laughter of Elf Owls that derided my arrogance and the soft calls of Poor-wills that made me weep.

The Salton Sea lay in a sink created eons ago by the uplifting of the mountains. The Colorado River had silted in the south end of the basin at the Gulf of California, and then had changed its course east-

ward, leaving a valley without water. At the turn of the last century, the
U.S. Army Corps of Engineers decided to construct a canal to irrigate
the Imperial Valley, but typical of the government (as they had done in
all those missile test sites), they miscalculated. During a spring run-off,
the river cut a new channel into the canal before the canal was ready,
and for eighteen months the whole river flooded into the Salton Basin.
A sea was born.

"This is where the bird was seen," Claire said. "From the beach
here."

She drove ahead to the collar of gray sand bordered on either side
by thick saltillos. We got out and scanned the sea quickly with binoculars. Ducks and grebes floated on the near water, and a few gulls
whirled in the air above us. A dark line of cormorants filed eastward toward the distant shore.

"What's farther out?" I asked.

"Terns, mostly. Forster's Terns. And a Black Skimmer. Let's look
with the scopes."

We set up the tripods and scopes on the rise behind the beach. My
scope was a Nikon that gave good resolution to 40 power, and through
it the indistinguishable birds far out over the water became what Claire
said they were: Forster's Terns, two Black Skimmers, a flock of Cinnamon Teal. Three White-faced Ibises flew as silhouettes against the pal-
ing hills.

"I don't see anything unusual," Claire said. "Do you?"

"Now there are other birds farther out."

"But you could make out the bounding arcs of the way the petrel
flies."

I saw no bounding arcs. The sun vanished from the high clouds,
and without that refracted whiteness, the sea light diminished to a
heavy gray. I gave up scanning and walked down to the shoreline,
where the smell of brine rose acrid to my nostrils. I kneeled and put my
hand into the water. It was warm as the air. I took off my shoes and
socks—I had on shorts already—and waded around the saltillo at the
edge of the beach.

On the other side where the canal fed in was a brackish cove filled with drowned trees. It must have been a riparian woodland once, before the land had been converted to orange groves, before the canal brought wasted chemicals, before the inundation. The water was shallow, slick with algae, unmoving. The bare black branches of the trees spidered into the air, and on them herons and egrets perched like huge, grotesque, faintly colored leaves. I felt as if I had stepped into a world already destroyed.

It was Claire who made me see this place in that way, though I blamed myself. I had created the person I was at that moment, the lonely soul. I had let myself be affected by the tenuous moments of conversation driving to and from work, by her knowledge of birds I wanted to make mine, by my thinking foolishly I knew something about her. And then to be so weak as to meet her again . . .

I thought of the earthquake that must be happening at that moment in Malaysia, the train wreck in France, the man in Guatemala being killed by his countrymen. But all I knew was this world before me—the cove and the far shore, the dark beach, and beyond it the date palms waving their spiky fronds against the barren hills.

"Slater?"

"I'm right here," I said. I turned, but I could not see her through the saltillos.

"Look west, flying low."

"Where?"

"About three o'clock."

I waded out into the shallows to be clear of the brush and lifted my glasses. Dark birds winged over the water.

"Do you see the bird I see?" Claire asked.

"I don't know."

I stepped around the brush to where she was, and she stood up from her scope. "He was a possible possible," she said, "but the light's not good enough to be positive."

"But it might have been?"

"Anything might be," she said. She lifted her scope and collapsed the legs of the tripod and leaned it against the fender of the Land Rover. "Are you hungry?"

I was surprised by her tone, by the casual way she let the bird go.

She went around to the back of the Rover and lifted the gate. "I have ham-and-cheese sandwiches, potato salad, and beer."

It had not occurred to me to be hungry, but I was. I took a sandwich and a beer.

Claire went off to urinate up in the higher brush, and I climbed onto the hood of the Land Rover and rested my back against the windshield. The beer was cold. The pale sea, the rising breeze, the soft lapping of the waves made me lethargic, almost sleepy. I closed my eyes and listened to the drone of insects in the saltillo.

I must have dozed for a few minutes because when I opened my eyes it was night. I saw the red blinking light from an airplane far away among the stars. Claire was beside me, leaning into the fender, but I could not see her well in the darkness.

"Do you love me?" she asked.

Her voice surprised me. "You're married," I said.

"Is that an answer?"

"Isn't it?"

"After all that time together, you never called me."

"You never called me."

"Today I did. I tried to think of something you would meet me for." She paused a moment. "What do you feel, Slater? Do you ever feel anything?"

I didn't know how to answer, and I turned away toward the sea where faraway lights of the small towns glimmered along the black shore.

"You don't have to look away," she said.

She walked around to the front of the Land Rover and stood up on the bumper so I had to see her. She unbuttoned her shirt and held out the corners like wings. Her skin was pale in the warm air, luminous. I do not know what gave her the courage to risk herself in this way. She must have been tired from working all day, driving from L.A., delving through the heat to the beach where we were, and yet she was able to summon a desire I had never imagined. She took off her shirt and knelt down on the hood near me.

"Can you see me?" she asked.

"Yes."

"And?"

I did not answer, and she bent forward and slid her hand under my shorts and touched me.

"Is this all right?" she asked.

Everything around me dissipated into one sensation. I was on the side of a cliff, petrified of falling and at the same time wanting to fall. I reached for her hand and pushed it away.

"Let me," she said.

She unsnapped my shorts and pulled them down. I felt the moist moving air, the touch of her hand again, and for the first time in my life, the eerie helplessness of desire. We spent the night on the hood of the Land Rover, the feathery air moving over us like water. In the morning at dawn, we dressed and heated water on the campstove for coffee and took up our vigil on the beach. We scanned through the scopes back and forth, back and forth, for the irregular flight of the petrel that may never have been there.

Robert Michael Pyle

FIELD NOTES FROM THE SOUTHWEST: 1992–1997

February 28, 1992. Desert Botanical Gardens, Phoenix. Wow! Saguaros! I've never seen them in the wild before. How such a comic-book plant, first seen for real, can *still* affect me, after all the cliché cartoons and pre-conceptions, is remarkable. Among yellow composites and pink penstemons and bottlebrushes they thrust, poking this hot air. By the buildings, a "Texas laurel" (docent) or mescal of the Mescalero Apache (Gary) is in fulsome bloom. Huge black xylocopid bees (Roger), like Wallace's bee of Borneo, nectars on the dense, purple, wisteria-like flowers. The fruit is hallucinatory; the scent cloying. It reminds the docent of grape Kool-Aid; Hannah, of grape popsicle. Not at all grapy to me but rapy, with the sweet reek of mustard-seed rape or concentrated wisteria. Color rather than scent association? A big, brilliant hummer at red penstemon, a pair of gilded flickers in a framework of rotted saguaro, mockers and wrens loud in the cactus tops, and the arid heat. Wow.

February 29, 1992. Tontozona, Arizona. A walk in the Tonto Creek Canyon. Pink Mogollon Mountain granite, pools & falls & pine & oak hillsides—like the Front Range of Colorado but for the white and live oaks. A California tortoiseshell basking where Gary & Nels are napping. In a cleft in granite above the stream, a mob of wasps is milling—long, narrow mud daubers with long, brown, blue-flashing wings; one dead below, thrown out? Coming awake, attacking prey? No attack pheromones, happily. Carla and Susan come down the canyon; we watch the river and the wasps and share nature-awakenings and rodeo-tales (theirs). This is way up out of the saguaro, but there's a desiccated prickly pear and a clump of *Echinocereus* (Susan) near the wasp nest. It's *not* Colorado—agaves poke up from weathering logs.

March 1, 1992. Tontozona to Phoenix. In the afternoon, we leave Tontozona Camp and go for a walk in saguaro country, along a wash with a little water and a lot of sand, among palo verde and mesquite brush. *Rain* on the way down the mountain, and here it smells *so good*— spice/mint smells, rain/sand smells, rabbitbrush/*Baccharis* smells. We cluster by a pillow-saguaro for group photos, one straight, one in saguaro-arm positions. Warm sun coming through cloud: it's all as green as it gets here, and exceedingly pleasant. I catch a male Sara orange-tip by hand on the wing—it's flight is so feeble—and am able to show it around and place it on Hannah's nose before it flies on.

January 29, 1993. Arizona-Sonora Desert Museum, among the pumas, jaguarundis, otters, and others; the beaver, lying *so* flat, its meaty paddle over a bubbling filter stream as if the gentle jet were titillating or sooth- ing. In the hummingbird house, our own backyard rufous and calliope in breeding plumage; and a gorgeous male Lucifer, its spotty gorget the neon violet of *Graphium weiskii* (the butterfly known as the purple mountain emperor) in New Guinea. A big broad-bill flies back and forth (as the wolves had paced; perhaps neurotic as well, from the cage?), with its long red bill and black fanned tail looking most un-hummerlike. No one else has binos, and though the hummers up close present an ig- nition flash, the merely eye-equipped cannot fully appreciate their feathered brilliance. (When people carry binoculars and hand lenses in- stead of Walkmans and cellular phones, we'll be getting somewhere.)

February 1, 1993. Saguaro National Monument, east section. Big buteos atop saguaros on our way from the cactus store and greenhouses to the monument. At Mica Springs picnic area, phainopeplas flash blue-black, fling whiplash calls; cactus wren and gilded flicker sound off from saguaros. Thea and I take off on the Cactus Forest Trail, noon; at one, take a shade stop. But not too hot, 70F, with refresca breeze. This place is so close to town that we can hear airplanes and sirens, see smog and hill homes; but all that is muted and not too obtrusive. The net of trails crosses level land and dry washes, damp near the surface of the banks; and a plain of pain if you didn't watch your step. I think this would have been the worst territory to be caught in by angry Indians. So many kinds of spined and stickered plants! We joke about hugging a saguaro, finally come upon one you can: so old, weathered, and smooth, there are no spines on much of the trunk. I hug it. I'm so overcome by saguaro that I find little to say. Just taking them in.

We're hearing and spotting crissal thrashers with their rusty underbutts, and one bright male spring azure basking in the arroyo—a surprise. Three more lifers: black-throated sparrows in small flocks on the ground beneath mesquite and palo verde, a handsome, crisp bird; verdin, which Thea spotted and I called without quite knowing what it was—just one, yellow head, smart rust shoulder patch, chippy voice; and, with little wheezes, coming right up to us, a tiny, pert, black-tailed gnatcatcher.

4:30. Now, in the cool, thrasher songs ring about us, phainopepla issues whistled little questions like a Swainson's thrush back home in June. A lone cactus wren, almost absent today. White-throated swift overhead, white-crowned sparrows all about. Now the Mica View grove is really coming alive, and a cryptic bird is working the area in small ground-and-bush flocks: brown towhees, with rusty crissums like the undertail coverts of the thrashers.

Cacti seen today: jumping cholla *(Opuntia fulgida)*, teddy-bear cholla *(O. bigelovii)*, desert Christmas cholla *(O. leptocaulis)*, staghorn cholla *(O. versicolor)*, prickly pear *(Opuntia* spp.), pencil cholla *(O. arbuscula)*, saguaro *(Carnegiea gigantea)*, hedgehog cactus *(Echinocereus fasciculatus)*, yellow-flowered hedgehog cactus *(E. pectinatus)*, fishhook barrel cactus *(Ferocactus wislizenii)*.

We saw no orange-tips at Saguaro, though we did see one on a pink-flowered shrub at the Arizona-Sonora Desert Museum, and T. photographed it. It might have been a male or female *pima* or a female *sara*, but we shall never know, as there was no film in the camera—and that befell our Saguaro Nat'l Monument photographs as well. So many images . . . but no matter. They are firmly recorded in our neurons, if not on celluloid.

July 27, 1994. Phoenix to Tucson by bus. Arizona time is the same as Washington time because they don't go on Daylight Savings: "We don't need another hour of daylight," says the Arizona Stagecoach woman. I can see why—it's *hot*. Bring on the night. (People actually *live* here, I am amazed to remind myself.) A violet light suffuses the hills as we head toward Tucson. The windows are so tinted it's almost dark inside; a protection from the heat, I guess, like the almost ineffectual air-conditioning; but still another way to block out the world. I look forward to the saguaros. So far, I prefer January here.

July 30, 1994. Garden Canyon, Huachuca Mountains. The array of new biomes and creatures has left my head in a stew of color and life and movement, so that I have watched instead of written. A dozen butterflies, several birds and herps, and many plants I have never met before. Among the butterflies: gold-spotted, hoary-edged, and long-tailed skippers, a parade of roadside skippers, and a two complete mimicry pairs: southern viceroys and queens, red-spotted purples and pipevine swallowtails. I netted all but the pipevine and released them, but not before I photographed the russet viceroy and queen and the blue admiral against Sande's red hair and blue top. A thunderstorm comes on, bringing the monsoon. Soon the butterflies will really be out.

April 2, 1995. Evening, Gary and Caroline's house, outside Tucson. Hooded orioles and cactus wrens in the desert garden, a crescent moon setting beneath Orion.

April 4, 1995. Canyon across road from Arizona-Sonora Desert Museum. Up a gravelly wash, over CCC dams and natural-step waterfalls without the water. A butterfly gridlock, at least compared to home. Several skippers, blues, checkers and crescents, sulfurs, queens, satyrs, anglewings, orange-tips, a Hunter's butterfly, a pipevine swallowtail, and a lot of black buckeyes (=dark southern buckeye)—the first I've seen, almost as deep in their pitchy darkness as the Magdalena alpines of the alpine talus. We watch ash-throated flycatchers and black-throated sparrows; yellow daisies and purple verbenas in abundant bloom. Almost hidden among some California poppies, a brilliant orange mariposa lily *(Calicortis)* leaps out and surprises me. Then Simon points out a whole hillside of them. If the poppies are Union Pacific gold, these are the orange of overripe papaya. All of this, fine pictographs too, among saguaros, a plant I could never tire of consorting with. How we'd all fled to this canyon, how we'd needed it, after all the words indoors.

Afternoon, Arizona-Sonora Desert Museum. In the hummingbird aviary, a brilliant male Lucifer hummer, probably the same one we saw in 1993, along with female broad-billed, male black-chinned, and Costa's, a violet-goitered male of which I'd seen outside. They visit people's jeans, pulling at threads. A woman docent on hummingbird interpretation duty approaches us and says: "The jiz of the Costa's is rather butch."

April 5, 1995. Gary and Caroline's house, early morning. A place of crested birds with wonderful names: cardinal, pyrrhuloxia, phainopepla.

April 7, 1995. North from Prescott. We cross a straw & olive landscape of juniper grasslands after Flagstaff, then some forty miles short of Tuba city, the infinite pinkness of the Colorado Plateau appears on the northern rim like a scum of tomato soup on the saucepan of the world. All of a sudden we cross into red rock gravel, gulley, and vista-land. A jewelry stand by the roadside with a person in a tan pickup; others, deserted, and a sign in tall white letters on black: "Welcome to the Navajo Rez." The first slickrock as we cross the Little Colorado, hogans and trailers like ascomycetes on the dustfields. The tidy little breast-mounds of the Mancos shales, gray and bare, their few plants mostly endemic. A fresh cool spring coming straight out of the base of a big cottonwood. East toward Kayenta, past muddy hoodoos, to Tuba City. On the walls of the Navahopi Cafe, photos of country music and Indian rodeo stars who have stopped in; among them, a clipping about the visit of Bruce Springsteen and friends on motorcycles. "They looked like guys who'd been on the road a while," said the reporter. When a trio of Mormon women arrive in fancy dresses and nametags, the manager says that they are thick on the reservation, as if he's commenting on a feature of natural history. "Also the Witnesses," he said. "Yeah, they're everywhere . . . them and the Amway salesmen."

7 P.M. . . . all silenced by the late sun on the vast redstone mantelpiece of the land as we enter Monument Valley.

April 8, 1995. At dawn Gary insists we go horseback riding with Navajos. Harold, the albino trail boss, meets us at the stable. Ron and Alex, the wranglers, take half an hour to lasso and saddle the tough and matty little Indian ponies. We ride into the silence of the red rocks, the tall stone towers rolling past. A little way on, Harold says, "Now you guys got to take your imagination out of your back pocket." He says, "Now let's gallop!" My pony is named Edge, and I name my bruises the Edge Effect. At the end of how far we can go, Harold says, "Now you guys get to hear a prayer." He and Alex sing to the rocks and Raven, looping a slow ink scrawl overhead.

Canyonlands National Park, Utah. A plant, encountered among scarlet paintbrush and salmon-flesh stone: beak-pod nippletwist *(Streptanthus longirostrus)*.

April 9, 1995. Arches National Park, Utah. Into the Fiery Furnace. An inconceivably stilling place among the fins of sandstone. Up a canyon, arches roofed with raven lime, cool sun over pink and blue varnished stonewalls. Picking our way over boulders, up sand washes, through slots, farther and farther into the furnace . . . cool today, it's snowing at Pack Creek. Only a couple of hours with the rare lovage, the broomlike Mormon tea, the one-leafleted ash; the swifts and wrens that don't show or sing. Among these wonders we writers are wordless, so we babble.

March 27, 1998. Bluff, Utah. Under the slickrock, in shifting cloud and sun, cold and hot, out of doors among the cottonwoods, grow amazing thorn trees. The chink and clang of horseshoes being thrown and the soft expostulations of the throwers. The thorns are amazing because the trees look like "regular" locusts, with seed pods on the ground among last year's cottonwood leaves; but their thorns are two or three inches long, bone-break sharp, and clustered around the bases of branches like nails in a nail-claw in a hardware store nail barrel, like spikes in a Catherine's wheel.

Coming cold drives me south. Pinyon-juniper begins at Ganado south of Canyon de Chelly, after snow stripes on red rocks. At six, in Grease-wood, Arizona, the radio choices are two: Navajo girls' championship basketball or a Mormon sermon by a Scotsman. Into the pinkstone dimmit and the flocking snow.

March 28, 1998. In heavy snow, stop for a hitchhiker named Alton. He's been to see his Navajo girlfriend and is trying to get back through the blizzard to the Zuni Pueblo, eastward into New Mexico. In his family's mud-fronted, stuccoed house in the pueblo, one brother, Alvin, sweeps and another, Sam, makes silver, turquoise, and lapis lazuli jewelry. I leave with turtle earrings, a foot pin, a drawing, a bear carved in stone, and a flat tire. I have also been given a little cottonwood ka-china named Ola Maidan, carved and painted by Alton's nephew Jeffrey; an invitation to the Zuni Shalako in December; and a hand-drawn map of Dowane Yallane, the sacred mountain that looms over the pueblo: a great wedge of red, lime-blue, and white, lunging into the woolly sky.

Ravens and kestrels follow the road; pinyons give way to ponderosas, prickly pears, and finally palms in the snow; cottonwoods go from bare twigs to early leaf to full chartreuse foliage as I head south.

March 29, 1998. Below Palominos, Arizona. The blizzard changes into cottonwood fluff over the San Pedro River. Queens, sulfurs, and checkered skippers nectar and skitter along the riparian shore. Barn owl and black hawk ignore the border. Vermilion flycatchers (like red-and-black cinders come alive) and Lucy's warblers stand out among the chipping sparrows and yellow-rumped warblers that are legion in the mesquite.

Dusk, Coronado Nat'l Memorial. Their sweet-fetid stink leads me to a dozen-plus turkey vultures flapping in to roost low over Cave Creek. Javelinas snuffle down the creekbed beneath.

April 5, 1998. Window Rock, the heart of the Navajo Nation: a great oval hole gaping in a vermilion wall. Marion Skye shows me silver squash blossoms out of her van. "It's nicer to work here," she says. "At home, there's the TV, and dishes, and washing." Her friend's young daughter, Vanessa, sells me a purple butterfly necklace, not knowing until I tell her that she shares her name with bright butterflies otherwise known as Ladies.

Four resident ravens fly around Window Rock. Juniper berries are pink, as if they took up the tincture of the rock through their roots. I very much want to see a raven or a pair fly through the hole on the rock. Ask Marion if they ever do, and she says she supposes so, and that it is the birthing channel of the people. They do not fly through it now. But several times I see them soaring, diving, and playing *beyond* the window, framed by it. Against the blue; against the perpetual red.

Richard Shelton

FROM *GOING BACK TO BISBEE*

The clouds are developing dark centers now. It begins to look promising for a storm. And the temperature seems to have dropped a degree or two. The country gets greener and greener, positively lush by desert standards. The road here curves through low hills, following, and slightly above, a wash that runs between the Empire Mountains, just to the east, and the northern thrust of the Santa Ritas, to the west and south. This must be the upper reaches of Pantano Wash, a twisting ribbon of bright sand and stone ledges, dropping down to the desert floor where it passes under the freeway I have just turned off of and heads northwest toward Tucson. It is usually dry, but today, because of recent rains at higher elevations, it is running a thin sheet of water several feet across, often dividing into rivulets which leave small islands of sand and gravel between them.

The water looks inviting. Just as I'm considering whether or not to stop and go down for a cooling wade, I see a coyote who must have had the same idea. He—I assume it is a male because of its size—is standing on one of the little islands of sand, looking intently downstream. He seems oblivious to the highway and traffic just above him. He is magnificent, one of the subspecies I call big blondes, although I don't know its technical name. In the bright sun his coat glows golden amber, exactly the color I suspect many women try to duplicate at the hairdresser's, but seldom with total success. The amber, which is most prominent around his head and hindquarters, shades into lighter buff on his belly, with darker, almost black striations on his shoulders, back, and tail. He looks healthy and well fed, ears up, tail down, in an alert but casual posture, totally elegant.

There are at least nineteen subspecies of *Canis latrans,* and this has got to be one of the most beautiful. Since coyotes are noted for their ability to adapt to new habitats, this may be a subspecies which originated at a higher elevation where water and food are more plentiful, a subspecies that has spread or been driven to the edge of the lower desert, into the upper bajadas. The most commonly encountered coyote in the lower Sonoran Desert is the subspecies *mearnsi,* which is much smaller and scrawnier, surviving as it does in spite of little water, extremely high temperatures, and a more limited food supply. It is also paler, grayer, and has little of the vivid coloring of this glamorous creature in the wash.

The Navajo name for coyote translates "God's dog," and they give the coyote a place of prominence above that of the wolf, referring to the wolf as a big coyote, rather than the other way around. But the coyote's name comes to us from the Aztec *coyotl.* The Aztecs associated the coyote's name and character with several gods and goddesses, including *Heuheucoyotle,* the mischief maker, and *Coyolxauhqui,* the moon goddess. Early Anglo settlers called the coyote a prairie wolf, but the Aztec name prevailed.

The relationship between humans and canines, both domesticated and nondomesticated, is fascinating to me. I do not understand how the person who truly loves a dog, loves it enough sometimes to risk his or her life for it, can exterminate coyotes, the dog's cousin, in hideous and sadistic ways. The war against coyotes in the Southwest has been monumental and has gone on since the earliest settlers arrived. In many respects, here and elsewhere, it represents a kind of ethnic vendetta that has nothing to do with economics. Something very basic in humans resents the coyote, just as something very basic in humans domesticated certain canines at an early stage in our groping toward civilization and our own humanity. We love and cherish our dogs because they respond with loyalty and affection, and because they obey us. But the coyote, so much like the dog in appearance and even behavior, has refused to accept us as masters, has spurned us, and we can never forgive it.

I have lived with large dogs most of my life. Some of my earliest memories involve a large German Shepherd who would have fought to the death to protect my older brother and me, although we didn't al-

ways treat him as well as we should have. And I have lived in close prox-
imity to coyotes for the last thirty years, have observed them enough to
be able to distinguish between them and have come to have a strong admiration for them. But not one of them has ever shown me any defer-
ence, and only a couple of them have ever shown that they trusted me,
even a little and for a few minutes. Coyotes generally avoid us and make
us feel insignificant in the natural scheme of things. Dogs make us feel
loved and can break our hearts.

My first real awareness of coyotes came about because of one of
our large dogs, an oversized male Samoyed who had a brief but har-
rowing love affair with a big blonde coyote, a female version of the one
down in the wash, who is very much aware that I have stopped the van
and am watching him, although he is ignoring me.

Large dogs seem to run in some families like a tendency toward
insanity runs in some families. Or perhaps a penchant for large dogs is a
form of insanity. My wife and I consider any dog who weighs less than
70 pounds a runt. And there are some advantages to having large dogs.
If you should trip over one of them in the dark, as I have done, the dog
will cushion your fall. On the other hand, our Great Pyrenees once
knocked me unconscious while being playful. He weighs 165 pounds. I
think of our dogs as house-horses and don't expect anyone except another large-dog lover to be understanding about the condition our
house is in.

My first real awareness of coyotes came about because of one of
our large dogs, an oversized male Samoyed who had a brief but har-
rowing love affair with a big blonde coyote, a female version of the one
down in the wash, who is very much aware that I have stopped the van
and am watching him, although he is ignoring me.

The dog's name was Shushu, which we were told was the Navajo
word for bear, although we didn't name him and called him Shushy,
rhyming with bushy. A friend found Shushy wandering in a distracted
state along the highway near Tucson, where he was struck by a car but
not seriously injured. She took him home, but all her attempts to find
his owner failed, so she named him Shushu. Then, because she already
had a male dog who was jealous, she gave him to us.

After getting to know him, we realized that Shushy had been a
show dog, if not a movie star, and we surmised that he had been stolen
in Southern California and was being transported east for sale when he
escaped from his dognappers. He was the best-trained dog we have ever
had, primarily because we had nothing to do with his training. He
never walked anywhere—he pranced. Strangers on the street would

throw their arms around him without asking if he were gentle. One look at his grinning face was enough. Each of the long white hairs of his outer coat was tipped with silver. He glistened in the daylight and glowed in the dark. He could do all manner of tricks and loved to entertain. He could learn a new trick in ten minutes and never forget it. He mimicked human facial expressions with an audacity that was astonishing, and sometimes hilarious, especially after I taught him to wrinkle his nose as if he smelled something unpleasant. He was also a terrible ham. Once, in a shopping mall, we encountered a professional clown who was entertaining a large group of children. Shushy loved children, and he picked up on the idea at once. He stood up on his hind legs and began to dance in circles. The children immediately deserted the clown and gathered around Shushy, laughing and applauding. The poor clown stood at a distance, alone, dejected, and thoroughly upstaged.

Shushy and I often took long hikes in the desert. I had heard that there were packs of feral dogs in the Tucson Mountains, but I had never seen any and believed such stories were local folklore, like reports of flying saucers. According to the stories, abandoned or runaway dogs turned wild in the desert and roamed in packs that could be dangerous. But one evening Shushy and I were walking down a desert road, which had been cut over the brow of a hill so as to leave a bank about four feet high beside it, when suddenly I heard what sounded like horses galloping toward us. As I turned in the direction of the sound, two very large dogs, a German Shepherd and a Boxer, leaped from the bank and landed almost on top of us. Both were in terrible condition and must have been living off the land for some time. The Shepherd went for Shushy and the Boxer hurled himself at my throat. I was carrying Shushy's heavy chain leash. Using it like a whip, I struck the Boxer across the face as hard as I could, catching him in mid-leap. Shushy was totally occupied with the other dog in a wild melee. Acting out of pure panic, I continued to lash the Boxer with the leash until it ran off into the desert, yelping. By then, Shushy had the Shepherd down with a death grip on its neck. When I pulled Shushy off the Shepherd, it too fled, bleeding badly. The whole encounter probably lasted no more than two minutes, and when it was over and my adrenaline began to subside, my first thought was of rabies.

In the desert counties of Southern Arizona, we take the activities of the rabies control units of the County Health Departments very seriously. I sometimes make fun of the pretentious building at the edge of Tucson which houses the Pima County Rabies Control Center—it looks like a cross between a fake Moorish palace and the Taj Mahal—but I never make fun of the work done by the people there. And although they have made significant progress toward controlling the spread of rabies among wild and domestic animals in the desert in the last twenty years, the disease is still a continuing problem. It is generally believed that bats spread the disease to rodents and larger mammals, who then infect domestic dogs. I remember years in the early sixties when rabies reached epidemic proportions and it was foolhardy to take one's dogs into the desert at all.

After our encounter with the two feral dogs, as I began to get my wits together, I realized that neither Shushy nor I was in any real danger of being infected. He had had his rabies shots, and neither dog had actually broken my skin. So we were safe, and I learned to pay more attention to local folklore. I also learned that my pampered, movie-star companion was as tough as he was beautiful.

But I had not yet learned anything about the habits of coyotes, and it was a coyote who would prove to be the one menace Shushy could not handle. And what a beautiful menace she was, the big blonde coyote who began to hang around our house, even during the day, sitting beside the driveway and retreating only when we approached. I thought she had come to mate with Shushy, and congratulated her on her good taste. Later, when I found out more about the behavior of coyotes, I realized that she had probably already mated with him and was waiting for him to accompany her, help her dig a den in which to raise their pups, and help her later to feed and protect them, as any good male coyote would do. And as Shushy ultimately tried to do, not because he had the instincts of a coyote, but because he was a husky. Huskies are the only breed of domestic dogs whose males have a tendency to take responsibility for their offspring. All other male domestic dogs are merely lotharios, but a male husky, possibly because huskies are so closely related to the wolf, will sometimes attempt to assist his mate in the rearing of pups. The big blonde must have sensed that this handsome hunk of dog had all the right instincts to make him a fit companion and helpmeet.

Female coyotes seem to choose their mates, rather than being chosen. In most other matters they are subservient to the males, but in affairs of the heart, they seem to be dominant, and a female coyote will drive away any other female who tempts the male on whom she has fixed her attention. The pair-bond is extremely strong and is, in some observed cases at least, formed long before the pair mates. Once they have mated, the pair becomes the nucleus of an extended family unit whose primary function is the protection, feeding, and training of the pair's offspring. Coyotes are superb parents. It has not been scientifically determined that they mate for life, but many veteran coyote-watchers believe they do and have documented instances in which the pair-bond lasted several years during which the same couple raised several litters.

So it might not have been exactly the call of the wild Shushy heard; it might well have been the call of domesticity. At any rate, he ran off with her into the desert. But while his husky lineage made him willing to enter into such an arrangement, for a while at least, he was only a domestic dog, and a pampered one at that. And we did not know what was going on. We thought he would be back in an hour or two, when his immediate needs were satisfied, tired but happy. But he did not come back. We began to search for him, driving down desert roads and beating our way from ridge to ridge. We searched until dark. The next day we started again, this time carrying a photograph of him, canvassing every house in the sparsely settled area. Toward evening of that day we knocked on the door of a house where a woman recognized the photograph. She had seen Shushy—he wasn't exactly inconspicuous— running with several coyotes. She gave us a general direction in which to pursue the search, and renewed our hopes. But by sunset of the fourth day we were heartsick, trying to convince ourselves to give up, knowing he could not have survived so long in the desert without water. There had been no rain in months.

We turned the car around and started slowly for home, straining see in the growing darkness. Then we saw a patch of something white lying just off the road. It was Shushy, and he was almost dead, but he was able to lift his head a little and give us a ghastly version of his irresistible grin. It looked as if he had been trying to make it home, but had collapsed several miles short of his goal. We tried to give him water, but he was too weak to drink. He had several bad wounds from fighting, probably with male coyotes. His mouth, lips, and tongue were impaled with cactus spines. I lifted him into the car and broke every speed limit getting to the animal hospital, where they immediately began pumping liquids into him intravenously. The vet told us he was suffering from dehydration, malnutrition, and a raging fever caused by infection. But he survived, and after a prolonged stay in the hospital, recovered completely. The vet said it was probably his color that ultimately saved him. His silver-white coat had reflected more of the sun's rays than a darker dog's would have, retarding the dehydration which would otherwise have killed him before we were able to find him. And as it was, he could not have lasted more than a few hours.

Shushy never again showed any inclination to run off with a coyote. I guess, as far as he was concerned, one grand affair was enough for a lifetime—almost too much. Nor did I ever see any suspiciously light-colored young coyotes in that part of the desert, although I kept on the lookout for them. They probably did not survive. It is unlikely that coyote pups will survive in the wild when their mother has no mate to help her feed and protect them.

Terry Tempest Williams

DAYBOOK: BOSQUE DEL APACHE, NEW MEXICO

11.19.94
No need for binoculars
individual birds
become identified in flocks
long shadows
furrowed mountains
dark storm clouds
round sun like a mirror

———

Tour loop

———

bodies of water
maroon willows
cattails

———

area of yellow willows
waving in the wind
waist high flooded
black cottonwoods

The water is silver

coots, shovelers, gadwalls
flocks of gulls careening
toward the wind like
drunken sailors

salt cedar cleared

big sky blue sky
pintails
cranes snow goose

Ah, the snow goose
flapping hard against
the wind   salmon
colored willows   pink,
orange whispering

elegant light

wind launches the waterfowl

It is so beautiful

rippled water   hissing
cattails   bottom up ducks

a redtail sits calmly in a
golden cottonwood

waves of snow geese
undulating against the
mountains

everything is in motion

tamarisk nodding
harrier hovering, wings
quivering above the willow

seeds blowing   catch in my
hair—a scalp is not
good for sowing seeds

grebe—pied-billed

We are underneath
a long cloud bank as
though we are standing
beneath an island and
all life is swimming
below it . . . The sky as
ocean

wind cold against my face.
I am at home these are
the caresses I desire

Canada geese
near the grade

gadwalls rise and
fly south like arrows

a solitary sandpiper
stands in a pool

And here are the cranes
large deliberate—grey
in shoulder high grasses
we watch heads above
the banners

More fly in—they dip
down rise up hang
in the air—glide the
land

mts in background a
series or the angles on the
horizon

constant calligraphy
of birds   signatures in
flight   wings everywhere
above the hissing grasses

silver cranes four more

crisp mountain air—silver
tipped shrubbery

a flock of willets

cranes + snow geese
thousands flash
light

sound everywhere

coyote in the cornfield
of course   we can count
on him   prancing on the
periphery of the cranes
he tries to sneak up on them
he breaks over the knoll
grey birds against green
they fly   he appears to
be herding them like sheep
he is surrounded by them
red crowns   oh, its [sic] cold!
a group takes to the air
circles, blows back in the
wind   they move like
currents in the sea in the
corn—motion sound
that prehistoric sound
pecking in the cornfields
a few flutter up in a dance

flapping wings   touch
down feet first in an angle
grey when standing   black
when in flight

beyond white confetti—
snow geese
above blackbirds

19 snow geese   the symmetry
the asymmetry   can there
be anything more beautiful
than the migrations of birds

Pale wolfberry
Screw bean mesquite
New Mexico olive
Black willow

"bosques" riparian woodlands
along the rio grande
almost vanished now
being restored

young girls from Sorroca
Socorro come each year

a raven against juniper
berry sky

looking through this
screen of willows
and under the canopy of
cottonwoods   orange
we watch acres of cranes
grey   walking south
crying to each other

as they forage. The
cranes are the color of
the grey clouds above
only the orange cottonwoods
break the monocromatic [sic]
landscape of feathers and
clouds

I look down at my
feet and discover a small
clam   whiteshell   where
am I.

a blizzard of snow geese
They just keep coming
Brooke is holding me
There are thousands of
birds above us
what a homecoming

In 1941—only 17 greater
sandhills wintered at
Bosque del Apache
now combined with lesser
and Canadian sandhills
over 17,000 use the Refuge.

Greys Lake in summer
        spring

It is so cold   my head aches

School of fish
Flocks of birds
Swarms of gnats
        bats
these spectacles of nature

Brooke turns on the radio
to catch the tail end of
New Mexico and UTEP.

My hands are numb
knuckles ache
We are such lightweights

Everywhere we look
these elegant
configuration[s] of cranes
and geese—white bodies
           black tips.

The sun is soon to set
4:45 pm. We watch two
sandhills forage in the
field   nine more touch
down to join them. The
sun is hanging below the
cloud bank . . . full light
cranes backlit.

               strands of
angels behind us   pearls
against   navy blue sky

red wing blackbirds
streamers

It is so beautiful
I cannot take it all in

platinum grasses
   and the dried leaves
   of cottonwoods navy sky.

I do believe in God
these birds   outlining
the face of Creation

And the two cranes
we have been watching
remain

More flow flocks
shifting configurations
making allowances for
one another   what are
they thinking?

Theatre
Pure improvisational
    theatre

My eyes are blurred
as the sun disappears
behind the mountains

these flocks of birds
become constillations [sic]
against the night sky

The musicality of
the Bosque del Apache
a symphony of voices
and wings against the
wind *a crescendo*
        4:50 pm
        sunset
a stillness settles
    in—I see no
birds in the sky

The silver trees
have lost their magic
Now they are quiet
    and grey   everything
                is grey

VIVALDI cello concerto
            in D Major

5:03 pm

    It is all a watercolor
now   cranes silhouetted
against pink clouds
darkening sky   everything
is in soft focus   the
gift of aging vision

    A storm of geese
a tornado of wings   the
settling of down
"*settling down*" . . . the
resting place of souls
thousands of snow geese
falling from the sky to
roost. Four deer

HOMECOMING

It is a Japanese watercolor of yellow and maroon willows and the silhouettes of long-legged birds standing in the marsh. Brush strokes: water, wind, and wings.

Brooke and I have traveled to the Bosque del Apache National
Wildlife Refuge in southern New Mexico. The refuge stretches alongside nine miles of the Rio Grande, 57,000 acres in all. It is a holy place
stored in the minds of cranes.

Grus canadensis. Sandhill cranes are extraordinary birds, primitive
birds with a wingspread of six to seven feet. They stand four feet tall in
fields and wear their wings as capes. They are regal creatures that walk
the earth with great dignity, and when you hear their deep, resonant
call in the solitude of open country, you are stopped and held in place.

In place. In 1941, only seventeen greater sandhills wintered at
Bosque del Apache. Now, combined with lesser and Canadian sandhills, over 17,000 use the refuge, most migrating from their spring and
summer grounds in Gray's Lake, Idaho. Theirs is a long and ancient
journey. The restoration of these wetlands and bosques, or riparian
woodlands, in central New Mexico begins a necessary healing between
human beings and animals. Habitat once taken and destroyed is now
being returned.

And so, each year, the sandhill cranes return. Thousands of snow
geese, on their own pilgrimage, accompany them. We watch. Images
wash over us like waves.

The water is silver.

The sky is navy blue, dark with clouds.

Flocks of snow geese are flapping hard against the wind.
Willows are whispering.
Rippled water.
Hissing cattails.
The wind launches more waterfowl into the sky: pintails, gadwalls, mallards, and teals. Salt cedar is nodding.
A harrier is hovering, his wings quivering above willows.
Cotton-like seeds are cartwheeling across meadows.
Everything is in motion.
And here are the cranes—in flight, their long, wide wings flap down slowly, followed by a quick upstroke. Their legs extend way beyond their short tails. Their necks are outstretched. In the sun, I take note of their red caps and amber eyes. The light is elegant and flattering.
More fly in, dip down, rise up, hang in the air, then glide toward land. A constant calligraphy of birds, signatures of flight. Wings everywhere above the singing grasses.
We spot a coyote in the cornfield. Of course, we can count on him prancing on the periphery of the cranes. He tries to sneak up on them, catch them off guard. He breaks over the knoll. Gray birds against green, they fly, hundreds of cranes. He looks up; so do we. They circle, he runs, and they return to fields farther down. The coyote appears to be herding the cranes like sheep. In truth, he watches and waits for the weary, the nervous. Biologists tell us this animal thins the flocks of avian cholera, a devastating disease for the cranes. The health of this population is secured in the coyote's grin.
Another group of cranes takes flight, circle, blow back in the wind. They move like currents in the sea. In the corn, motion, sound, that prehistoric sound—more cranes pecking in the cornfield. A few flutter up and dance.
This is pure, improvisational theater. Everywhere we look in this circle of sky, we see exquisite configurations of cranes and geese. Constellations. My eyes blur as the sun disappears behind the blue furrowed mountains.[1]
Standing in the midst of these wetlands of the Rio Grande, I begin to glimpse the meaning of the sacred. Above us, it is a blizzard of wings.

Tens of thousands of snow geese and sandhills are returning home. A cacophony of voices in the desert. Angels are above us, below us, all around.

Only a few minutes of daylight remain. The sun is setting, creating a depth of light, pink and gold, that I have never before witnessed. Wherever the sacred is to be found, be it a person or a place, we recognize it as a homecoming. Brooke holds me in the Bosque as twilight approaches and we, too, are absorbed inside creation.

Editor's Note

1. The original version of this essay quotes a twenty-nine-line excerpt from the poem "The November Angels" from the book *The October Palace,* by Jane Hirshfield (New York: HarperCollins, 1994).

Ann Haymond Zwinger

FROM DOWNCANYON

In the waiting quiet of daybreak, the sound of a coffeepot lid being lifted and reset works better than an alarm clock. While it is still middling cool, I walk the perimeter of my territory. Yellow rayless daisy heads bedeck a big three-foot-high sweetbush, the involucral bracts (the cup that holds the individual flowers in the head) tipped with glands. Small bee flies with narrow cream-and-black striped abdomens wrap themselves around the half-inch flowers to feed. At water's edge yellow Hooker's evening primroses, accented by scarlet Indian paintbrushes, grow as tall as I. Bushes of dogbane with red stems nod over the water. The usual seep willow. The usual coyote willow. The eternal tamarisk, dripping strings of tiny flowers, soon to loose untold numbers of seeds upon an unsuspecting world.

Here, sixty miles from Glen Canyon Dam, it takes about nineteen hours for a release from the dam to reach us (the water travels about 4 mph). The river falls during the day and begins rising between midnight and 2:00 A.M., with highest water in early morning. At the moment, the river-edge apron of boulders lies uncovered and three, quarter-inch planarian worms wriggle in a small pool between the rocks, tiny snippets of wet, brown velvet ribbon. Photosensitive, they spend most of their time safely under rocks and are very vulnerable to predation in full daylight, probably saved by their slimy coatings, which gum up the mouthparts and antennae of insects that might otherwise feed on them. They live a hermaphroditic existence, a him/her searching for a him/her.

A handsome, iridescent dark green tiger beetle stalks the sand, its brilliance caused by innumerable, minute raised ridges striating the stiff elytra so that the surface works on the principle of a diffraction grating. Its common name comes from its voracious ways and lethal mandibles, its stealth, its ability to spurt up to three feet per second, enough speed to escape most predators. Tiger beetles withstand high sand temperatures by running on stilted legs, but when it's too hot, they survive by digging shallow burrows where females also deposit their single eggs.

On hatching, the S-shaped larva, often called a doodlebug, digs a tunnel in the bare, hot sand and latches itself in place with curved hooks on its back. It holds its flattened shieldlike head, usually colored to match its surroundings, at right angles to its body, blocking the opening. There it waits until a small insect blunders by, snapping it up without having to forgo the protection of its tube. A small wasp ingeniously parasitizes a doodlebug by decoying it into thinking it has a meal. The wasp allows herself to be seized, then stings the larva in its vulnerable extended neck. She enters the burrow, draws in the immobilized larva, lays a single egg on it, seals the opening, and departs.

By midmorning, the red line of the thermometer hung on my tent zipper can't go any higher. I repair to the river to pour water on an overheated head. I rinse, wait a second for the ice-cream headache to start, endure it until it stops, pour over another cupful, pause, endure. It helps.

Near my tent a beautiful boulder of limestone sits imbedded in the beach, sculpted with fluting that ranges from the most dainty channels to gouges an inch wide, carved in overlapping fans. A collared lizard, an exquisite creature with a double black color, bounds across the searing sand, launches itself into a series of grandiose jetés, and lands on this boulder in the filmy shade of a tamarisk. Fluorescent chartreuse washes its haunches and stamps it as a male. The black spots that dapple his legs diminish to dots on his back, spattered on a sulphur yellow ground. His tail, longer than his body proper, languishes over the rock. His dainty spidery toes flow into the fluted contours of the rock. He stilts himself up away from the heat-radiating rock, courting as much circulation as possible under his body. Watching him, I wonder what the lizards looked like that left footprints a yard apart in the sand of the Coconino Sandstone.

In the middle of this stultifying noontime heat, a canyon wren with a cinnamon brown tail and back and clean white bib searches cracks in a boulder close by. It chatters and tsks about the availability of insects, the vicissitudes of life, and the vagaries of a summer's day. I retreat to the river to slosh another bucket of water over my head, wait for the ice-cream headache to begin and abate. If I have to have one I'd prefer to get it eating ice cream, but it's the only alternative to boiling over like a radiator.

In this enervating heat, my brain turns to mush after lunch. I head for the shadiest place in town, which is the kitchen. As I settle under a tamarisk I dislodge a side-blotched lizard, named for the oval black spot on each side just behind the front leg. The smallest, most generalized of the canyon's riparian lizards, they are as numerous as house sparrows. Insectivorous, they prefer ants and flies and snag them either by aggressive stalking or by a sit-and-wait strategy, according to need.

Tiny two-inch young predominate among those that scamper around the kitchen. This noon I watch two that stay in the fragile shade of a snakeweed, fortuitously on the foraging path of some red ants. Oftentimes rodents burrow beneath bushes like this snakeweed, and lizards use them for a hasty retreat, and in some places side-blotched lizard numbers depend upon the frequency of rodent nests available for quick haven. They are a delight to watch, quick and wary tail flickers, always on the qui vive. While I sit sweaty and lethargic, they remind me that others thrive in this turgid heat.

In the sky antimacassar clouds avoid the sun like the plague. Cicadas heat up to band-saw intensity. I try to lose myself in reading *Don Quixote.* The don's housekeeper, curate, and niece are having a fine, righteous time heaving all of the don's "romances" out the window. Sweat trickles down my nose and dots the page. Even reading is too much exertion.

I switch to watching the resident yellow-backed spiny lizard, whose sit-and-wait technique more fits my state of stasis. Two desert spiny lizards habitually hang out around the kitchen. One has more bright yellow dotting its body and head plates, while the other is more orange, the deeper color that usually indicates a male. Today only the male is on duty. He remains on his elevated survey perch for minutes on end before scrambling off to scarf up a dozen red ants. A big healthy lizard, he looks as if he lifts weights in his spare time, a solid, portly sort that would not look out of place with a watch chain and spats, a sophisticated boulevardier. When he spots an ant carrying a kernel of corn, his pell-mell dash is so tempestuous that it tosses ant and burden into the air and they disappear in the sand. The lizard stands there for a moment, swings his head back and forth, then waddles with a certain insouciance back to his station.

On one of his periodic forays he patters close to my chair. As I shift to get a better look, he darts into a plastic milk crate turned on its side that I've been using as a footrest. He dashes back and forth, sticking his head through one after another of the one-inch-square openings on the now vertical bottom that faces his home tree and safety, never turning around to see the wide open freedom behind him. Finally he discovers one of the larger oval openings on the side and flees to his sandy perch under the tamarisk, turns around, raises himself so far up on his front legs that he resembles a sitting dog, probably having had more of an adventure than he bargained for on a simple trip to the market.

Another noontime a tiny tree lizard winds by my chair so slowly that I reach down and pick it up, a baby barely an inch long with a tail half that length. Despite the name, tree lizards are found not in trees but usually on rock walls right above the river. This one's an elegant little creature: two rows of enlarged scales stripe its back, divided by a line of smaller ones, and a narrow fold of skin extends along its flanks, an impervious skin that made possible its reptilian trip to dry land, the first vertebrate to invade a terrestrial habitat. On its eyelid are two vermillion mites, firmly attached. Mites are everywhere, in soil, moss, fungi, from tundra to tropics, on land and in water, and only one of many parasites that affect lizards. Under a hand lens this pinhead of red has body segments completely fused into a single unsegmented disk hung with eight legs, four forward, four back, its mouthparts adapted for sucking blood. Its brilliant red color may be a warning, for although spiders gobble them up, almost any other potential predator tends to avoid them.

Tree lizards, coming up from mainland Mexico, probably ranged much more widely in previous epochs. Now their present distribution is an odd one, restricted to the riparian habitats of the Southwest deserts and to rocky habitats on isolated mountains. Adults are small, under three inches in length, much the same size as side-blotched lizards, with which they avoid potential competition by exploiting different habitats. Here in the canyon tree lizards prefer water's edge with large rocks and overhead cover, while side-blotched lizards seek boulders with sandy spots between. Both tree and side-blotched lizards belong to that group of "annual" lizards that are short-lived, mature within a year, and produce multiple clutches.

When summertime temperatures become too high, lizards seek refuge in cooler places, for they have no sweat glands or other method of lowering their temperature other than panting, an expensive, last-resort way to cool because it expends so much precious water. They effectively conserve water by not excreting liquid urine and by metabolizing extremely efficiently. Their water conservation is ten times higher than that of desert rodents, and their energy requirements, 10 to 20 percent lower than that of mammals and birds, is impressive.

The tree lizard moves to the edge of a flat rock, smacking up tiny ants with its darting tongue. It saves energy by allowing the ants to come close by rather than chasing after them—any ant coming within two inches is a goner. Two ants appear on the scene from opposite directions. The lizard eyes each in turn as if deciding which to snatch first, then, thsp-thsp, it nails them both.

In the fascination of watching the lizard I have forgotten about the ten-ton heat, which now registers again. Cicadas sputter like a static-filled radio that I can't turn off. I have no idea what time it is. My heat-registering chromosomes may have melted like butter on a hot rock.

PART II

Risking Experience

ADVENTURES IN THE WILD

Bruce Berger

TRANSITION ZONE

As pavement climbs north from Phoenix, the expanse of cactus fractures like a shook jigsaw. Smooth desert suddenly rears into domes, palisades, crenellations and rockfalls, labyrinthine, crazed, a troll's nightmare. The phenomenon is known as exfoliation, literally, the losing of leaves. The substance is granite that cracks at roughly right angles. Once it has been cubed, the corners crumble faster than the faces, a geological way of rounding the square. What the square loses on the way to circlehood is what becomes desert sand. Solid granite? The desert's mother lode is sheer rot, rock on its way to becoming a million square miles of kitty litter.

The whole formation registers a bare mile on the odometer, two drainages splintered by assorted cracked ribs. I had driven through once too often, and one January afternoon, on a whim, I pulled off below and stopped to explore. That two-hour ramble took on the contour of an allegory.

Hiking up the first ridge and gazing into the stratum, I was struck by a 180-degree sweep of flesh-colored jumble, a single organism becoming many. Beehive formations barely held together; broken columns leaned against each other for support; boulders sprawled with no plan. Rain that had slid from the rocks filled pockets between them with sharp green—paloverdes, jojoba, and, because this was the topmost rung of the Upper Sonoran, the leathery beginnings of chaparral. This softening was punctuated by vegetation that seemed firmer than the rock itself, the shafts of great saguaros. A formation splintering apart, sending up numberless green lives—it was what theologians might call creation by division.

I made my way to the smooth sand at the drainage bottom, then started into the rocky panorama. There was no way to pick a route beforehand; one could only clamber from rock to rock, calculating two or three boulders ahead. The coarse granite easily held my boot treads, but granules pulverized into sand even as I climbed. My arms—atrophied as the arms of most hikers—got a workout as I hoisted myself through this stone jungle gym. Often boulders were too big, defied passage, and I had to descend here and try over there. Or I was funneled into vegetation between the rocks, where the serrated edges of barberry leaves and the spikes of yucca waited on point. Backtracking, zigzagging, I won my way to the next ridge, across a small drainage and onto the spine of the formation. The foreground of intricate granite suddenly gave way to vast distance. Low clouds hung over peaks luminous with fresh snow; far darkening relieved busy foreground. As I caught my breath, a clatter burst beneath me, and I spun in time to watch a four-point stag bound through the very rocks I'd been threading. I followed the ridge in a kind of exaltation, watching the stone labyrinth beneath me as hanging clouds heightened the far mountains. I came to a virtually boulder-free fold that escorted me back to the main drainage, over the ridge, and I was back to the car in two hours. As I say, the ramble was like an allegory, though fortunately there was no one around to tell me what it meant.

Once I had sampled the place on foot, I made time for exploration every time I passed. I hiked it from the top down as well as from the bottom up, at different times of day. I became familiar with topography that always sprang surprises. I saw clumps of hedgehog cactus whose tips had been eaten by javelinas, the pulp gone, the spines and skin strewn like fast food wrappers. A saguaro had a wraparound lower limb like a skater descending into a sit spin. There were cardinals, the relatively uncommon ladderback woodpecker, and one day I flushed a great horned owl. After a February storm I came upon a free-standing granite basin cupping melted snow, so symmetrical it could have been commissioned with tax dollars. I sat and drank: the water was cool, bland, sublime.

Sated with rocks, I became aware of the way moss and grasses filled their hollows, particularly on north slopes, and the way lichen covered the rocks themselves. Growth-coated rocks weren't flesh-colored at all; they were olive, baize, mustard, day-glo chartreuse, and, more interestingly, a perfectly unreflective, eye-resistant, matte black—one or more of the 120 species of *Andreaea,* commonly known as granite moss. Here and there were bright green shotgun shells and sometimes I heard shots, for no desert seems complete these days without the most dangerous predator. My winter explorations were well timed to avoid the second most dangerous predator, the rattlesnake, which is really only dangerous when it can't see you coming: in places like this. As the season warmed, only the open sand in the central wash would be secure from snakes, and I had already walked its length, back to the highway and underneath. The culvert was a cold plunge where dry air suddenly hung dank, my footsteps rang from all directions, and pupils tightened by bright granite were unmoored by concentric rings where corrugated iron caught the far sky.

Most of all, I liked to sit on the first ridge as day declined and rocks leapt forward as individuals from their shadows. I could rehearse the way granite cooled and hardened from magma beneath the surface. Tectonic forces lifted it, exposed it, relieved it of subterranean pressure. It cracked along perpendicular faults. The outer surface of the rock dried rapidly after rain and snow, but moisture that seeped inside was caught until decay set in. Layers peeled off in the unsheathing of exfoliation, also known as spalling and spheroidal weathering. Lichen, the first plant to colonize the land, clung to layers as they fell, perhaps even helped them go. Here, in this vegetal transition zone, where cactus mingled with chaparral, was a geological transition zone, rock released into sand. Just as a spring is a source for water, so is disbanded rock, for a desert, pure source.

Staring until I had only enough dusk to find my way out, I liked to imagine the whole formation disintegrating under the moon, in darkness, offering new soil at first light. No other corner I know of so merits some lines I remember from Robinson Jeffers:

> *I have seen the dust on a summer day*
> *Crying to be born as much as flesh*
> *Ever cried to be quiet.*

Janice Emily Bowers

FEAR FALLS AWAY

Throughout the wet November night I have been aware of the hard knot of fear that has been lodged in my throat for ten days now, ever since Renee invited me to accompany her and three others in climbing Baboquivari Peak.

"I'd love to," I said, whereupon my throat tied itself into a knot. The other major peaks in southeastern Arizona are accessible by trails, and anyone with strong legs and lungs can hike to the summits. Only Baboquivari requires more: ropes, harness, and carabiners if you have them, or better-than-average climbing skills and plenty of confidence if you do not. I have a harness, a carabiner, and not much else except Renee's assurance that I can make the climb. The route we will use is rated class four, so it is not a technical climb—the holds being large enough that ropes are not absolutely necessary. On the other hand, a class four rating also indicates enough exposure to kill or maim you if you fall. Renee promised that she and Gordon, her husband, would bring their climbing equipment. This would have set my mind at ease if she had not emphasized *bring,* leaving me with the impression that she would prefer not to use the equipment at all. For a whole week, I have been promising myself that if I just do this one climb, I will never have to climb again. I've lost track of the number of times I have asked Renee if she is absolutely positive that I can do it. Am I secretly hoping she will change her mind?

Of the five of us, only Kirk has no experience with rocks and ropes. Gordon has been climbing since he was a boy and could manipulate the equipment in his sleep. Renee is also a good and fearless climber. Gordon and Renee have ascended Baboquivari Peak several times by the Forbes route, the one we will use today. Laurie, strong and graceful on rocks, has enough confidence to climb anything. Knowing that I could hardly be in better hands brings no comfort. People have died on this route. People have also started and been turned back by incapacity or fear. I knew two women twenty years ago who began the climb with their husbands in expectation of an easy scramble. When the women became terrified and wanted to turn back, the men refused. My friends survived, no mean accomplishment, but what remained in their minds was the fear, not the triumph.

Even if I had never heard that particular story, I would still be scared. My fear of heights is exceeded in my experience only by my husband's fear: I am decidedly nervous when I am less than two feet away from a precipice; standing another two feet behind me, Steve will be outspokenly anxious on both our behalves, and only when we retreat to a safer distance will he relax. Like my friends of twenty years ago, I have experienced uncontrollable fear in the midst of a climb; like them, I have been unable to move and certain of death. I too survived, but it felt like failure.

Despite these and other truly excellent reasons for staying at home with a good book, or even a bad one, here I am. Years ago, when I half believed in astral travel and other occult nonsense, I read somewhere that not only is Baboquivari Peak sacred to the Tohono O'odham, it is also a "power point" such as Carlos Castañeda describes in his Don Juan books. Castañeda's work has been exposed as fictional, if not fraudulent, but the idea that Baboquivari Peak is a sacred and powerful place transcends scholarly criteria for verifiable truths. The desire to be on Baboquivari Peak, born at the moment I read those words, has never left me and is one reason I am here. Unlike other sacred peaks in our area, Baboquivari looks like a holy mountain. A 1,500-foot-tall granite dome rising from an otherwise unremarkable ridgeline, Baboquivari Peak resembles a bishop's miter tossed on a rumpled robe. It can be identified from a hundred miles away, and when I am high in the mountains, I never fail to look for it. Always I have looked, then shifted my glance, all too willing to accept Baboquivari Peak as my Impossible

Dream. Now the prospect of moving away, combined with Renee's fortuitous invitation, makes it clear that if I do not tilt at that windmill today, I never will.

Apparently no one slept very well last night. To call us *subdued* this morning would be to greatly overestimate the average level of cheeriness. The ground is still wet from rain, and the log where we sat at suppertime is sodden. Breakfast is a dismal meal eaten under dreary skies. Gordon and Renee talk quietly together in one part of camp, Laurie and Kirk in another. I sit on an uncomfortable rock by myself and sip coffee from a plastic mug. My free hand, shoved into a jacket pocket, fingers a metal bottle cap that I have brought on purpose. Long ago someone told me that if you throw a bottle cap off the peak, the cap falls up instead of down because wind currents snatch it away. Dubious but hopeful, I am prepared. Maybe that is the real reason I have come— to fling a bottle cap from Baboquivari Peak.

Eventually, a spattering of rain stirs us to pack our belongings. There is some laconic talk of what to do in case it really rains. Wait out the storm in a rock shelter? Cancel the climb? In my head I am shouting, "Cancel! Cancel!" but I suspect that only a hurricane could allow me to back out at this point without losing face. Immersed in my own pitiful misery, I nearly miss Gordon's quiet statement that everyone will use ropes for the entire climb. My heart lifts. I might fall, but at least I will not die, probably will not even be maimed. Bless the man. I will love him forever.

We camped last night within easy striking distance of the peak, so we have only a short hike this morning. This side of the Baboquivari Mountains—the west side—belongs to the Tohono O'odham Nation. Renee and Gordon obtained permission for our climb ahead of time; most people use the eastern approach to save themselves the bother of getting a permit. As we walk, a blue umbrella unfurls overhead, rolling the clouds to the perimeter of the sky. We talk of this and that, including how the Forbes route was established. Georgie Scott, the young woman who eventually became Mrs. Forbes, had so many suitors that she could not decide among them. ("Oh, poor thing," Renee interjects.) Like a princess in a fairy tale, Georgie set a challenge: the first

suitor to climb to the top of Baboquivari Peak, something no Anglo
had ever done, would be the one she married. Robert Forbes made
three attempts before he finally discovered a feasible route in 1898. It
required creeping up the Great Ramp, a vast granite slab, then scaling
an eighty-foot vertical pitch that had decent holds unless you strayed off
line. Above that pitch, you had an easy scramble to the top. It was
nightfall by the time Forbes completed his first successful ascent.
Elated, he lit a bonfire that could be seen as far away as Tucson.
Georgie might have been the only person to know the fire for what it
was. Everyone else thought that Baboquivari Peak was erupting.

Our trail parallels the crest of the range, ducking under small,
gnarled oaks and skirting boldly colored outcrops shaped like prehistoric beasts. These rocks are not the smooth, hard granite of the peak
itself but a crumbly volcanic tuff in hues of tan, rusty orange, and maroon. Gray twists of coyote scat are plentiful on the trail, crumbled bear
dung not uncommon. The abundance of wild animal sign suggests a
place not much used by humans or, better still, one used in ways that
create little disruption.

Much sooner than I like, we arrive at the Great Ramp. It tilts upward at just enough of an angle to make my palms sweat. We step into
our climbing harnesses, which basically comprise two adjustable thigh
loops connected front and back to an adjustable waist loop. My harness,
garishly striped with pink and yellow, elicits the usual comments—"if
the rope breaks, at least you'll be easy to see at the bottom of the cliff,"
and so forth. Gordon and Renee snake out the ropes, feeding them
length by length from neat coils into loose, lazy loops on the ground. I
pick up a rope and, about three feet from the end, tie a knot that looks
like the number eight. I thread the end of the rope through my harness,
leaving the knot dangling, then loop the end back to the knot. Next, by
coaxing the end of the rope through the knot, following every twist
and turn, I create an identical figure eight that hangs the original knot.
This ingenious two phase device links my harness (and therefore me) to
the climbing system so securely that it will be hard to untie when the
climb is over. Finally, I secure the loose end with half a double fisherman, which is a double fisherman tied once. Don't ask me why it is not
simply called *a fisherman.*

I check to make sure that my knots are properly tied. Renee checks my knots, and I check hers. Gordon checks my knots and double-checks his own. Laurie checks my knots and Kirk's. Kirk and Renee check one another's knots, then I check Kirk's, and he checks mine. All of them look fine. Clearly, none of our lives will be jeopardized by a badly tied knot today.

At last we are ready to ascend the Great Ramp. Gordon and Renee go first, then Gordon belays me, and Renee belays Kirk. Laurie is gloriously on her own. After a minute or two of scrambling apelike with hands and feet, I realize that I could actually walk up the slab, so I do, legs a little rubbery at first, then fully in control. Midway, l look back down the slab. The base appears to drop into infinity, an unnerving illusion; I am glad for the rope even though I do not really need it.

Above the Great Ramp, we follow a well-worn path to the vertical pitch I have been dreading. Gordon climbs first. I probably should watch every move, trying to memorize exactly where he places his hands and feet, but getting the route by rote never works for me— climbers differ greatly in strength, flexibility, and height, not to mention skill and confidence, and the holds one person uses could well be irrelevant to another's build and mind; moreover, the topography of a cliff to which you are clinging seems very different from what you saw when standing on the ground. Others climb in sequence as Gordon belays, then my turn comes. I am unpleasantly nervous until I make my first two moves, after which fear falls away, replaced by a deep interest in what I am doing. Holds arise as I need them, almost as if evoked by my need. The thick encrustations of lichen on the rock look like green snow or cucumber soup. Gray liverworts, shingled among the lichens, crunch faintly underfoot like the slender bones of birds. Aside from one tricky place where the holds become what climbers call *thin,* that is, virtually imaginary, I climb quickly and well, I feel. Renee agrees. At the top of the pitch she tells me, "You climbed that like a pro."

As advertised, the rest of the route is an easy scramble and walk. Gaining the summit is almost anticlimactic. I had expected the five of us to be crowded together like angels dancing on a pinhead; instead, the summit is flat, and broad enough for a two-bedroom house. The air is still, the sun almost hot. Renee and Laurie, having located the Tucson

Mountains to the northeast, puzzle over which summit is Safford Peak. I stroll from edge to edge, grinning foolishly. I can't believe that I'm actually here. How can an Impossible Dream yield so readily to a Possible Reality? When I thank Renee for including me in the group, she says simply, "Now that you know the way, you can come back again."

Now I can remove Baboquivari Peak from my mental list of places I yearn to see at least once in my life—West Clear Creek, Aravaipa Canyon, Desolation Canyon, Mount Whitney, Keet Seel, and on and on. The list shows such a strong inclination to grow that I suspect I will never reach the end. Why it exists in the first place is not easy to explain, even to myself: it has something to do with seeing the sights that others guarantee as worthwhile, maybe, or with wanting to discover for myself the lasting appeal of some particular place.

Someone finds the trail register in a jar inside an ammo can under a small cairn. The jar holds a sheaf of paper scraps and several extremely blunt pencils. Laurie writes, "If Georgie Scott had known it would be like this, she would have climbed the peak herself." My mind goes blank, the same as it does when I must inscribe an appropriate sentiment on someone's birthday card at the office. All the time I spent fretting and worrying about the climb I could have more usefully employed in thinking up trenchant reflections for the trail register. I thumb through its pages. Many entries include praise of God and His creation. Some climbers write that they feel closer to God up here. A surprising variety of people have made the ascent: a woman five months pregnant, a group of nuns who thankfully note the assistance of "Señor Julio and his rope," a party who climbed by moonlight, reaching the summit at 2:30 A.M. Suddenly my presence here seems not such a remarkable achievement after all.

Across the Altar Valley, the Tucson and Santa Catalina mountains look like waves on a choppy sea. From past experience, I know that within a week, I will have forgotten how they look today. Within a year, I will have forgotten how it feels to be here looking at them. If I seek out new places only for the sake of accumulating sights and experiences, I might as well stop now. Yet I won't, nor would anyone else with such a list. My persistence, I suspect, has less to do with assembling a collection than it does with attempting a minor miracle: I harbor a noble but futile hope that the next climb or journey will change me for the better, or if not the next, then the one after it.

Psychological case studies demonstrate just how futile my hope is. People clutch their concepts of self as tightly as a starfish clings to a rock. A man who pictures himself as a failure is blind to whatever small successes he does achieve. A woman who has convinced herself that she is unattractive requires more than a look in the mirror to change her mind. Yet, despite our propensity to stick with the familiar, as painful as it may be, moments come when we are capable of assimilating new experience, of adapting our concepts of self to fit experience, rather than the other way around. Could it be that such moments arise most often when we let down our guard? And are we not less guarded than usual when immersed in the sights and sensations of an unfamiliar place?

Even though our favorite places offer a comfort and intimacy not to be found anywhere else, other needs lure us to unknown landscapes. Over time, the details of my climb today might slip away or even become altered in memory, but I dare to hope that being here now—and the courage it took to get here—will forever shape my attitudes and expectations. Whether I find my way back here or not, I hope that Baboquivari Peak will always be part of who I am.

Karen Brennan

INFIDELITY

In the car she notices his beautiful throat against the backdrop of light, the day's rawness folding in on itself, and the heat as visible as dust pulsing against the sides of the vehicle. He turns to look at her, his hand grasps her knee, the gearshift, smiles, then concentrates on the road bending now through high red rock formations and dull green saguaros with jagged holes ripped in their skins. She says, This is infidelity. His mouth curves, on the steering wheel he lifts one large, graceful hand as if to block the sun. She has been seeing him for some weeks. Even so, the beginning is hazy, and because of this she feels there is no chronology in their relationship, no history. Either it seems to her that they have always been together, driving through high red-colored ridges with the heat pulsing against the sides of the car, or that he is no one—a dimensionless figment of her imagination, a stranger. In the motels, already a series of five or six, they had fucked quickly and passionately. Then, because of her husband, she would shower, resolving as the hot water beat upon her neck that it would not happen again. She'd smear her hands on the steam-covered mirror and as if in ambivalent response to her determination to end the affair, her face would seem to shift in the glass, and even to lose its distinction in the moist, blurry heat. They move toward a mountain range, up and up. His foot crashes the accelerator pedal and a smell rises from the wheels, from the shivering clumps of orange wildflowers and cactus. Her throat is dry; she feels a spasm in her groin, not sexual but more violent, as if she'd been shot. At this moment she remembers her husband and is comforted. She envisions him in front of the TV, eating his dinner without her. She feels, as if it were part of her own body, his impatience as he paces from the window to the telephone waiting for her return. They are parked on a crest close to the top of the ridge. The man removes the key from the accelerator and once again she notices a slight convulsive movement in his throat which contrasts sharply with his calm hands. He is younger than she; his face is pure and unlined, his eyes a clear shade of blue. He takes his beauty for granted the way the sky does, fitting between the rivers of ocotillo and the frail limbs of desert palo verde. He touches her face, traces the line from her cheek to her chin, her neck and shoulder. Then he is pinning her down, grinding his body into hers, fiercely parting her thighs. This is the dark night of the soul, is what she thinks, This is what it feels like. The sun has shrunk to a crack, grazing out over the horizon. Dust floats in its last beams, like ashes. When they are done, it is a soft wide blue riding over the desert, sad and unreachable. She takes his hand, kisses the tip of each finger knowing it is the wrong gesture. A bird springs from behind a palo verde and they watch it shriek into the far darkness. He stares out the window and she knows she has no access to him, nor he to her, and their bodies which have so recently been un-done are sealing themselves up again, becoming sleek and impenetra-ble, like the world.

Deidre Elliott

ON SENDING THE RAFT NORTH

"Meg," I said to my youngest daughter, "come get the raft."

"You mean it?"

I heard her turn from the receiver and shout to her boyfriend, "Hey! We're getting the boat!" Even without the long-distance aid of the telephone, I think I'd have been able to hear Hook's return whoop of delight. I imagined Meg and her boyfriend in their tiny kitchen in Bozeman, arms around each other, the two of them jumping up and down as they shouted out the names of the Montana rivers they planned to raft: the Gallatin, the Yellowstone, Madison, Clark's Fork, Bitterroot. But down in Arizona all I felt was sad, as if a part of my life were moving too far away. Maybe forever.

I've rafted for years, ever since my kids were babies and I was a mad housewife and sometime student, desperate to rejoin the world. Each summer I took at least one trip, always in the West, always in a private group among a clan of friends who had hiked, biked, climbed, and rafted together since college. We looked down our noses at commercial outfitters (although secretly some of us would have killed to have a job that involved running rivers every week of every summer) and scorned their clients who slathered themselves with sunscreen and wore color-coordinated safari wear. We sneered as the dudes sat like obedient kindergartners inside the huge womb of motorized pontoon rigs, listening to the drone of the guides' safety lectures.

As for my friends and me, we needed no lectures. We looked out for ourselves and for each other. Together we scouted the rapids, standing in an anxious and almost silent clutch onshore, watching the water

curl and crash and hurl itself against boulders until at last one of us became so uncomfortable that he or she would set out down the channel.
As that first boater reached for the oars, someone would call half-
jokingly, "Remember . . . tighten your tennis shoes and if you fall out,
keep 'em pointed downstream so that you bounce off rocks."

We had our share of screw-ups: a scramble toward the upstream
end of the boat as the waters of the Salmon threatened to sink us; a
wrap around a midstream boulder on the Dolores that required slicing
through two of the raft's four chambers in order to free it; the plucking
of an almost unconscious paddler from beneath one of the Green's hidden underwater ledges. But my friends and I took care of ourselves.
When we messed up, we got out of those messes. We weren't on the
water to have anybody do anything for us. We didn't want to be cod-
dled; we didn't want to be catered to. That way the risks belonged to
each of us. So did the rewards.

And risk and reward were exactly why I began to feel glum when
I sent the raft north. Oh, it made sense to let Meg have the boat. She
had the time and space and aptitude for it. She'd been boating since she
was a kid and didn't mind schlepping two hundred pounds of neoprene,
an unwieldy rowing frame, several bailing buckets, and more than a
dozen paddles around—not to mention the ammo boxes, tarps, first aid
kit, repair kit, on-river and off-river pumps, dry bags and food containers, extra life jackets, a rocket box with accompanying toilet seat, plus a
cooler the size of New Jersey. Meg and Hook were young and adven-
turous, he a summertime fisherman from Alaska and she a student
working toward a degree in wildlife biology. Together they'd have a
blast exploring Montana by water.

Besides, it was time for me to buy my partners out. Elaine, one of
the raft's co-owners, was moving to Chile and looking forward to kay-
aking South America's Bío-Bío. Pam, the other owner, had turned to
even littler craft, one-person inflatables that afforded a fish's-eye view of
the water. I was in graduate school, seldom able to spring myself free
from jobs or homework long enough to sustain an extended river trip.
It made sense to pass the boat on to another generation. I tried to con-
sole myself by claiming that anytime I wanted to, I could simply drive

to Montana, collect the gear, and trundle off downstream. There was
nothing to say I couldn't, right?

My first river trip was a glorious, breathtaking, adrenaline-pumping
shimmy that began at the Green River's Gates of Lodore. Before we
bought our own raft, Elaine, Pam, and I borrowed a friend's aging boat,
labored to patch its many leaks, and finally gave up, deciding instead to
throw in several rolls of duct tape to use in emergencies. We entered the
water, paddles in hand, just as sunlight hit the first waves.

   In the corner where northwestern Colorado and northeastern
Utah meet, the Green River makes a forty-five-mile dash through a
series of canyons, creating one of the premier whitewater runs in the
United States. The Green slices through the scarlet Precambrian cliffs
of the Uinta Mountains, the largest east-west range outside Alaska, in
spectacular fashion. Statistics hardly do the river's awesome, thundering
power justice. The average river gradient through Lodore Canyon is fifteen feet per mile, and six of its thirty-six rapids are major. Lodore
Canyon is followed by Whirlpool Canyon (eleven rapids and a drop of
ten feet per mile) and Split Mountain Canyon (thirteen rapids, a river
gradient of twenty-one feet). In other words, the Green River kicks
butt.

   Major John Wesley Powell described the river in richer terms.
Here, he said, a boat "leaps and plunges along with great velocity." A
one-armed Civil War veteran, Powell led the first U.S. survey expedition through the area in 1869, a trip that also included the first official
traverse of the Grand Canyon. Along one section of the Green he
wrote, "All this volume is set eddying and spinning in whirlpools . . .
the waters waltz through the canyon." But, unable to row and strapped
to a wooden chair on the deck of his boat so that he wouldn't get
bumped out, Major Powell also had a terror-filled view of each and
every rapid. He gave them names like Upper Disaster, Lower Disaster,
Cascade, Triplet, and Hell's Half Mile. The lovely, musical word *Lodore,*
the name affixed to the first and most technically demanding section of
the river, comes from a Robert Southey poem. Powell chose the poem
because it accurately reflected the complex waters of the Green:

Retreating and heating and meeting and sheeting,
Delaying and straying and playing . . .
Recoiling . . . toiling . . . boiling . . .
Gleaming . . . streaming . . . steaming . . .
Flapping . . . rapping . . . slapping . . .
Curling . . . whirling . . .
Thumping . . . plumping . . .
Dashing . . . slashing . . .
Splashing . . . clashing,
And so never ending, but always descending . . .
All at once and o'er with a mighty uproar,—
And this way the water comes down at Lodore.

And sound is exactly what I remember about my first river trip.
Especially the ominous hum of yet unseen rapids. In the last bend or
two before a major obstruction, a river often slows and seems to become positively placid. But this deception is caused by the very downriver constrictions that create rapids in the first place: boulder fields,
chutes, log jams, two rivers conjoining. The calm, silken surface of a
backed-up stream is only an illusion. Yet, almost always, the river fails
to conceal the rapid completely and gives itself away by shouting about
what's up ahead. Words like *bellow, boom, rumble,* and *crash* are simply
not adequate to describe the effect a major rapid has upon a boater's
body. It is as if the boater has yanked the thick tail of a tiger, placed her
head inside the feline's great maw, and is now waiting for the resound-
ing roar to liquefy her bones. She knows she's in a bad place, a very,
very bad place.

My first day on the water we ran all the rapids in the Canyon of Lodore
because Bill, one of our companion boaters piloting his own raft, was
afraid of water. He couldn't sleep well, he claimed, with the clamor of a
nearby rapid in his ears, and so he pushed us to cover twenty river
miles, pushed us almost past good sense.
    All my friends seem to fear something, even though they are
more-than-competent outdoorspeople: world-class climbers whose
names are registered in books of first ascents, boaters who knew Glen

Canyon before the BuRec drowned it, explorers who thrill when a Chiapas native says, "*Sí*, the river flows on, but part of it goes underground." After all our years together, my friends and I are well aware of one another's particular phobias. We take them in stride and think no less of a person when she (usually me) asks for a belay in order to cross a particularly exposed rim of sandstone or when he asks that we exhaust ourselves running the thirty-six rapids of the Lodore in a single day.

On that initial trip down the Green, Elaine had hoped for a shorter first day so that we would have plenty of time to scout even the smallest of rapids. That way she could stand beside me on shore and teach me how to read the river. With time to scout, I'd learn to recognize the many ways a river cuts through the landscape. I'd understand wave patterns, including diagonals, haystacks, and standing waves; sleepers, deceptive pillows of water hiding boulders; holes, a simple name for the huge and treacherous reversals of flow that can easily flip a raft; eddies, low-pressure areas where the current slows or flows upstream; and the tongue, the (mainly) unobstructed V that marks the main current's most prominent—and usually safest—path. With time and practice and the coaching of good friends like Elaine, I'd learn to maneuver a boat myself.

And so, despite a long and frantic first day on the Green, I did learn. On that trip and on others, I learned to read the river at low water and at flood stage. I learned to captain a paddle raft and to row an oar rig. I learned to thread my way through snaggle-toothed side channels and power through giant-sized back curlers. I learned to crisscross the river in order to surf the biggest waves and yet also avoid the biggest holes. I even became proficient enough to take my children on the water and not worry too much about what might happen if I misread the river's cues. Most especially, I learned that time spent on the river in the company of family and friends creates some of life's sweetest moments.

That's why I began to feel sad after I sent the raft to Meg. Running a river is like living Zen. You are riveted in each and every moment, fully alive, intensely aware. You are present. When I sent the raft north, I saw my youth floating away. I thought I'd nevermore experience times as vibrant as these:

• Floating the Yampa, especially the long, meandering section before the horrendous Warm Springs rapid, and lazily bobbing past the
Tiger Wall, a riverside cliff striped with vertical bands of desert varnish
made from dark manganese oxide deposited by ancient seeps onto a
pale sandstone face. Nancy and Steve played their recorders; music
drifted up the cliff face, gliding, floating, hovering in the blue desert air.

• Finding the ruins of a granary with tiny Anasazi corncobs still in-
tact. Puzzling over petroglyphs and pictographs. Were those three
broad-shouldered beings shamans or hunters? There were spears in
their right hands, shields in their left, elaborate curved headdresses
above the trio. A herd of miniature deer surrounded them, each tiny
hoof laboriously picked from the rock's surface, each hoof anatomically
correct.

• Uncovering a dozen *manos* and *metates* on a hillside. Knowing
that people, families and friends not all that different from my own, had
camped in the same sheltering bend of the river. Did they also tell stories under a crescent moon, yawn as bats danced overhead, and fall
asleep in a soft cradle of sand?

• Hiking up a side canyon of the Colorado River for lunch and
happening upon a burial. Hal found a skeleton wedged under a narrow
sandstone overhang. In a space no bigger than a coyote's den, the body
was still folded into the fetal position. We gathered brush and tried to
conceal the remains for another thousand years.

• Finding glowworms one stormy evening, their pink heads curled
downward, phosphorescent bodies glowing yellow-green.

• Watching cliff swallows zoom across the water, every beak cap-
turing an insect, while baby birds poked their heads out of mud daub
homes, searching for Mom, anxious for supper.

• Laughing as Camille, from the banks of the Salmon River, told
us how she'd found these great big leaves to wipe with and then worrying when I asked, "They weren't shiny green, were they?"

• Being surprised by a doe at dusk, both of us seeking the solitude
of the same stand of tamarisk. Me eager to rinse silt from the crevices of
my body, she yearning for a cool drink after a blistering day.

• Savoring curry or chili or gumbo in the evening, schnapps and
evaporated milk in our coffee, all of us trying to outdo each other and

tell the biggest lie. Snatching a few quick mouthfuls of oatmeal for breakfast, gorp and sardines for lunch. Being grateful for fresh water whenever we found it. Being grateful every single time.

· Cutting the front canvas from my tennis shoes because the constant flow of river water and the abrading sand carried within it had rubbed the tops of my feet raw, wounded my heels, and obliterated my toenails.

· Tearing Edward Abbey's *The Monkey Wrench Gang* into seventeen-page sections so that all of us might simultaneously read and chuckle as we floated down the Green through the Gray and Desolation Wilderness.

· Listening to, consoling, cajoling friends through the birth of children, death of parents, breakup of marriages, acquisition of recalcitrant stepchildren.

· And always—always—surrendering to the river, knowing that running a river is equal parts strength, intelligence, and luck. Remembering, too, that sometimes it's only luck.

Before I handed the boat over to my daughter, I took her on one final boat trip, just to make sure she could read the water as well as she claimed. Pam's stepdaughter, Jenny, went along as well. Both girls had plenty of experience in one-person craft, baby boats that ride so low in the waves you're little more than a cork bobbing along the surface. In order to fit into these small boats, you sit and wedge your knees almost up to your chin, then recline against a minuscule stuff sack barely big enough for a sleeping bag and an extra pair of socks, and attempt to operate tiny oars. The most you can do in a little boat is flap against the current, flail furiously in order to avoid rocks and aim yourself toward shore. Tiny boats force you to stay alert. With experience like that, I figured I wouldn't really be teaching Meg and Jenny much of anything. Still, I knew I'd feel better if I could double-check how well they handled a full-sized raft.

My raft is a fourteen-foot, four-chambered craft, a boat designed to carry six paddlers or one oarsman and two or three passengers. It's nowhere near as big as a motorized J-rig or a Grand Canyon pontoon raft. It's nowhere near as small as the rubber ducky my daughter first learned to paddle. A fourteen-footer has three sections: gear is lashed into the stern, passengers ride in the front, and the oarsman operates from a plywood rowing platform in the middle. It's a serviceable type of raft, just large enough to withstand really big water, just small enough to elicit really big thrills.

Two other boats joined us on the Green River trip. In a raft similar to mine was Jean, sixty-eight years old, a longtime boater. Her original World War II surplus craft, complete with patched bullet holes, is the boat I learned to row in. It now resides in the museum in Green River, Utah. In the museum her raft is sandwiched between one of Georgie White's pontoon rigs and a replica of Major Powell's *Emma Dean*. The other boater on our Green River trip, Hal, was a BLM archeologist from Colorado who hoped for a gentle river in order to christen his newest boat, a fancy neon blue cataraft. A cataraft is simply two narrow pontoons with no floor and no cargo area except for an open net lashed behind a delicate-looking rowing frame. The oarsman hovers like a dragonfly just above the water. A cataraft affords incredible mobility, but to ride in a cataraft means that you see water piling up beneath you—and feel it pushing onto you—constantly.

So off we went, once more through Gray's and Desolation Canyons, a supposedly easy jaunt. Probably Jean and Hal and I should have figured things wouldn't be all that easy when the ranger at the Sand Wash check-in station gave us the latest river flow statistics. The Green River carried a higher than usual volume of water the day we put in. Much higher than usual. End of May, end of the spring run-off season. End of an unusually quick spring thaw following a winter of especially high snowfall. In the water before us, logs floated—whole trees, that is. Dead birds too, killed by upstream storms, spun for a moment and then moved on. Their bloated bodies, no matter what color their original plumage, were maytagged by the constantly twisting and turning water. In a matter of days they would be bleached completely white.

Then, too, Jean, Hal, and I should have remembered why Major Powell named this stretch of river Desolation. In 1895, traveling on yet another survey expedition, he wrote, "The canyon is very tortuous, the river very rapid. . . . Piles of broken rock lie against these walls; crags and tower shaped peaks are seen everywhere, and away from them, long lines of broken cliffs. The walls are almost without vegetation; a few dwarf bushes are seen here and there clinging to the rocks, and cedars grow from the crevices—not like the cedars of a land refreshed with rains, great cones bedecked with spray, but ugly clumps, like war clubs beset with spines. We are minded to call this the Canyon of Desolation." Yep. And the *Emma Dean* upset in Steer Ridge rapid as well, just downstream from where he wrote that journal entry. The biggest rapids of either Gray's or Desolation Canyon were still ahead.

Nevertheless, for the first few days of our journey, as long as the oarsman paid attention to the current and as long as someone else watched the river map so that the oarsman *could* pay attention, everything went pretty well. The rapid at Nine Mile Creek, a perennial stream adding strength to the Green, was washed out, creating nothing more than big water and standing waves that called for steady, continuous forward motion. No big deal so long as you didn't reach for a stroke and feel the oar simply suck air. A ways downstream, Rock House Rapid (caused by a moraine of boulders carried into the river opposite the entrance to a lateral canyon) occurs where the canyon is over 5,000 feet deep. In low water the rapid should have been little more than a riffle, similar to Nine Mile. But this wasn't low water. I let Meg row Rock House and saw the muscles in her arms and thighs strain for each stroke.

Six miles downstream we drifted by the cliff wall where Powell's companion, George Bradley, saved his life on July 18, 1869. The pair had climbed the wall in hopes of reaching the top of the plateau and thereby attaining a much-needed long-distance panorama. But climbing in canyon country can be hazardous—especially if you have only one arm. Powell and Bradley reached a point where Powell could go no farther. He describes it this way: "The moment is critical. My muscles tremble. It occurs to Bradley to take off his drawers. I seize the dangling legs, and gain the top." What the journal does not detail is in Bradley's report. In order to grasp the makeshift "rope," Powell had to let go of his single handhold and leap upward several vertical inches. Ai yi yi! When Meg and Jenny ask if we can stop and try a climb, I say no.

For consolation, Jenny rowed the third biggest rapid on this stretch of the Green, McPherson's. McPherson Rapid is just downriver from abandoned McPherson Ranch, once a sometime hideout for Butch Cassidy and the Sundance Kid, today a freshwater stop for boaters who also enjoy picking pears and apples from hundred-year-old trees.

I promised myself I'd stay silent while Jenny rowed, even though her upper arms seemed to lack much strength. Nevertheless, she could read the river well. We shoved off and I fastened my life jacket, nodded to the girls to do the same.

McPherson's Rapid, like the one at Nine Mile Creek, was washed out by high water. If Jenny kept the bow pointed straight into the biggest waves, we'd roll right over any submerged obstructions. No problem.

She powered out into the current, caught the tongue, and began confidently roller-coasting us downriver. Delighted, Meg and I whooped and hollered as water jumped the bow and drenched us. Just to be on the safe side, I reached for a bail bucket. Then I heard Meg say, "Jenny? Jenny."

I glanced up. Somehow the bow of the raft had slipped to the right. If the rest of the boat followed, we'd be crossways in the current and the next big wave would flip us for sure.

I looked back at Jenny. Her lips were pulled into a thin, straight line. The muscles of her narrow arms rippled with effort. She was try-ing with all her strength to right the boat, but the sheer volume of wa-ter beneath her hindered her efforts. Her left arm pulled back on one oar as her right arm pushed forward on the other. Just keep doing what you're doing, kid, I thought, and we'll be O.K.

But when she reached for the next stroke, she missed. The left oar, the one that would have afforded her the most powerful stroke, the most necessary stroke, dipped air. I wanted to shout, "Try again! Pull harder!" but I kept silent. Then as the next standing wave was about to crest, I heard myself or maybe Meg—maybe both of us—yell, "Do it!"

At last the left oar dug beneath the surface of the water. The boat spun forward, straight into the tongue. We rode the wave, the raft tee-tering only momentarily at its crest, and then plunged down the chute, all of us safe, all our adrenaline pumping.

After that, I took over the oars. The girls complained, threw lines at me such as "I thought you said we could row some big ones" and "What about teaching us to read the river?" Still I held firm. Coal

Creek was ahead, the most technically challenging rapid on the river. Jean had made Hal and me promise to stop and scout it. If she hadn't made me promise first, I'd have made her promise.

Unlike most other big rapids, the river before Coal Creek does not slow and become like the smooth surface of a hand mirror. Wire Fence Canyon enters one mile upstream from Coal Creek and creates a rapid that, while not in itself technically difficult, makes pulling in to land and then scouting the next one quite challenging. You're concentrating on negotiating Wire Fence and, in the exuberant success that follows, are likely to miss the landing point for Coal Creek.

That is, until you smell the rapid. If the sound of a rapid is ominous, then consider what smelling one is like. Sulfurous seeps in the banks near Coal Creek impregnate the air with the odors of hell. As we trundled off the rafts and swatted at the spiny, tasseled wands of tamarisk, I felt my stomach clench. Meg was right on my heels when we climbed the rocky path to the overlook. My nostrils constricted with sulfur, my stomach tied in knots, my arms scratched by tamarisks, my daughter pouting behind me . . . I was in great shape to run a rapid.

Hal, Jean, and I stood for a long time studying the water. Meg and Jenny, still miffed at not being allowed to row this one, didn't bother with more than a glance. Jean pointed to first one boulder, then another and another. Coal Creek is the rockiest rapid in either Gray's or Desolation Canyon. What makes it even more difficult is that the current, the tongue, seems to divide. One side tends to suck you into a series of huge holes along the right river wall. Boat-eaters. The other way, the preferred way, requires that you row upstream from the landing point (no easy job at flood stage), avoid a newly created hole at the top of the rapid, thread your way through a series of pillowed sleepers, and hang on while the raft careens up and down a fence line of haystacks. *If* you miss the hole where the tongue is, *if* you keep the bow straight, *if* one of the sleepers next to the far wall isn't more jagged than imagined, then *maybe* you make it through.

Jean went first. Meg, Jenny, Hal, and I stood on shore watching her. Because of the tamarisks, we couldn't see how she pulled away from shore nor how she set up, but whatever she did must have been exactly right because her ride through Coal Creek was perfect. Her run gave the rest of us confidence, and we raced off, back to the boats, ready to make our own perfect runs.

Hal untied the cataraft and leaped for the rowing seat. He waved quickly, then concentrated on stroking upstream in order to gain the far side of the river. Somehow he miscalculated, though, and the cataraft began to slide toward the series of boat-sucking holes near the right shore. He hit the first one dead on, but the cataraft rode it well. Then he powered around the next hole and ping-ponged his way through the rock garden in the center of the channel.

By the time he slipped from sight around a bend of the river, Meg and Jenny were seated in our raft, tennis shoes and life jackets secure, ready to go. But all I wanted to do was unload the boat, portage the gear, and try to line the raft down the rapids. Suddenly all my confidence had evaporated. I smelled sulfur.

"C'mon, Mom," Meg called. "We gonna do this or what?"

I bit my lip and climbed on board. Set a good example, I told myself. Don't let them see that you're afraid. If you're afraid, they'll be afraid. I began to talk to ease my fears.

"Look," I said. "I know you girls didn't scout this rapid much, so just in case I mess up, I'm going to tell you what to look for so that you can help out if you need to." I described the long pull upriver, the confusing tongue, the sleepers, haystacks, and boulder field beyond. "Just in case," I repeated, "you two know what to do, right?"

They nodded.

The hardest part of the whole rapid was rowing upstream to get into position. The waters of both Coal Creek and Wire Fence seemed to have tripled the flow of the Green. Seemed to, but maybe not. All I know is that, not more than ten yards from shore, the current was already so swift that I had to launch myself against the oars in order to make any progress at all. I strained to use every muscle to full advantage and doubted that we'd ever reach the far channel.

"Girls!" I called. "Girls! We're not gonna make it!"

"Mom . . . Mom," Meg said. "Yes, we will. Just keep pulling. You're doing fine."

"You can do it," Jenny said.

"Girls . . ."

"Pull, Mom. Pull."

I forgot about the smell of sulfur, forgot about most everything except the two young women in the bow and the water ahead. Somehow I managed to almost bring the raft into line with the far half of the split tongue. We glazed the edge of the first hole, spun around once on a curler, and ended up pointed downriver again. Then we scraped over a partially exposed sleeper and luckily headed into the series of standing waves, bow first. By then my strength was just about gone, but somehow I kept pulling on the oars, trying to work with the water and not against it. I concentrated on reading the river, not wanting to master it, not wanting to merge with it but simply to understand it.

"Whoo-eee!" Meg yelled as the height of the river's undulations gradually subsided. "You did it, Mom! You did it!" She and Jenny hugged each other. Jean and Hal, floating ahead of us in calm water, waved.

After that, I let Meg row Rattlesnake, the second biggest rapid in Gray's and Deso, the place where Flat Nose Curry, a member of the Wild Bunch, was ambushed and killed during the winter of 1899. But no one died on or off the river the day Meg rowed us through Rattlesnake. She scouted the rapid, accurately predicted trouble spots, handpicked her route, and followed it precisely. She skirted the fallen log on the right shore, wove her way around a rock garden in the middle, and powered through big water at the very end.

She did this confidently and all on her own. Jenny and I just hung on. Well, Jenny did and I bailed because I had to do something. I didn't dare speak. But as I bailed, I smiled. Once I glanced back at Meg. Her jaw was tight and she didn't look at me. She kept her eyes on the water. My kid, my child, my daughter was reading the river.

Suzanne Freeman

THE CROSSING

Swimming unclothed
through our own perihelion, so close,
so close we were,
we gathered the long light
gentled
by the shadows of sycamores.
Our footprints
in the sugary tan of sandbars
chronicled the creekly things,
how we read the waterlines on immaculate boulders
& gave the maidenhair a drink
    (we thirsted not at all).
Big green fish led us down
channeled limestone,
    surprising depths,
then vanished in translucent hours.
A tiny exoskeleton adrift
in a pool of brightness
implied: some other life
as did a silent jet
in the distant dome.
We left
the leathery leaves of old regrets
behind on the bank
for the next flood to take.

GOING TO THE CREEK

Days of increase:
I walk the sundown path through the field,
sleepy as the heavy-headed grass
that droops with the weight
of maturity.
The weedy wayside
dissolves the line between the seasons,
middle & end; a summer will be consumed
by its own momentum.

Buzzards sail & circle
the gradual evening,
they teach me patience.
One has a gap in its wing feathers.

Under willow canopy, I search again
for the frogs & fireflies
(gone now for years),
magic fragments of creek memory.
Dark water glides by and doesn't look back.
Spiders of twilight
cast their webs across a trail
that recedes into the sound of crickets
(may their lacy nettings catch me
as I fall).

YUCCAS AT 70 MPH

Spiked heads crown stout torsos
& shred the air,
an armless army in a permanent lean.
The Interstate splits their midst
near Van Horn
while they go about their ancient business
holding down the desert,
catching the tumbleweed runaways.
They bow to the breath
of the sun,
to what's been given them.

An 18-wheeler blows a hole
in the wind
and I follow it through,
propelled by the fool engine
of a restless heart.

Ray Gonzalez

THE TURTLE

Beauty is nothing but the beginning of terror—RILKE

I found a dead turtle in the dirt lot
across from my house.
It's head had been cut-off,
stiff claws and wrinkled legs sticking
out of its shell like a tiny man
who let the world fall on him.
Someone crushed the turtle into the sand
like the tribe forcing the prisoner to kneel
in the red soil where they abolish his beliefs,
change the colors he paints on his back,
tear the tough skin off his movements.
Someone crushed the turtle, left it
as the glistening coin that marks the path,
believed in its silence,
then tossed it in the weeds.

I stood over it in fear, a twelve-year-old
who had never seen opened life before,
but knew the shell gave strength to those
who wanted to climb inside
a shattered bowl of ugly wisdom,
learn how to hide without losing ground.
I stared at the remains of the turtle,
saw its geometric shape grow into the soil

as if dried blood formed a sign,
or it was going to rise and hiss at me.

I stepped back because I smelled an odor
I didn't recognize, thought I saw movement in the weeds.
Staring at the turtle drew me into an old dream
where I ran after a pack of dogs
who galloped ahead of me, trying to keep up
with an enormous black shape
they chased into the canyons.
I ran after the dogs,
but their barks disappeared
as they were swallowed by what they chased,
the thing that entered the canyons
becoming the turtle lying down,
too slow to know, too old to live
with its impossible head that expands
and contracts for birth, for the impact
that sent us both to the ground,
the weight of what caught us
the hush of beauty and forgiveness.

TWO STRIPED LIZARDS

They look like miniature orange and brown tigers
clinging to the concrete blocks in the back yard,
two lizards looking up at me as I lift the wood
off their hiding place.
They stick to the bricks, flatten themselves
except for their heads and enlarged eyes,
tiny faces looking curious and human,
staring at me when I move,
blinking as if I was about to grab them,
one of them springing out of the brick,
disappearing into the grass to lead me away
from their home.

Two striped lizards is a good omen
from the man who knew the reptiles,
the one who followed them across the desert
because they would lead him to the well.
Two striped lizards are a sign of
abundant thirst and plenty of water,
their rapid movement and suspicions
leaving me with something to grab—
a blade of grass, an abandoned spider web,
a concrete block I won't move
because I learned what the striped lizard means,
was told by the lizard man that

a tiger in the canyon is as good
as the escaped dragon of the heart—
the second striped lizard not moving,
as I leave it alone and close the lid
on the muffled source of the beating heart.

THE HEALING LEAVES

When my legs and arms ached
with growing pains as a boy,
my grandmother pulled out
her bottle of rubbing alcohol,
a muddy-brown oil full of soaking leaves.

Strong smell of a healing aura rose
when she opened the green bottle,
tipped it in her large palms,
rubbed me down with the leaves,
black shreds of wet skin,
shining pieces of strong branches.

Overpowering plants fermented
in a bottle that carried a dark swamp,
a fire that cured me as hot hands traced
the shape of leaves across my trembling arms,
covered my legs like a small animal
wrapping itself around the smoking trees.

When my legs and arms ached,
I went into the cloud of curing,
the fumes of touch transforming my pain
into a hidden bone of passage,
a throat clearing odor that burned me
with a secret I do not speak.

Barbara Kingsolver

FROM *HIGH TIDE IN TUCSON*

Not long ago I went backpacking in the Eagle Tail Mountains. This range is a trackless wilderness in western Arizona that most people would call Godforsaken, taking for granted God's preference for loamy topsoil and regular precipitation. Whoever created the Eagle Tails had dry heat on the agenda, and a thing for volcanic rock. Also cactus, twisted mesquites, and five-alarm sunsets. The hiker's program in a desert like this is dire and blunt: carry in enough water to keep you alive till you can find a water source; then fill your bottles and head for the next one, or straight back out. Experts warn adventurers in this region, without irony, to drink their water while they're still alive, as it won't help later.

Several canyons looked promising for springs on our topographical map, but turned up dry. Finally, at the top of a narrow, overgrown gorge we found a blessed tinaja, a deep, shaded hollow in the rock about the size of four or five claw-foot tubs, holding water. After we drank our fill, my friends struck out again, but I opted to stay and spend the day in the hospitable place that had slaked our thirst. On either side of the natural water tank, two shallow caves in the canyon wall faced each other, only a few dozen steps apart. By crossing from one to the other at noon, a person could spend the whole day here in shady comfort—or in colder weather, follow the winter sun. Anticipating a morning of reading, I pulled *Angle of Repose* out of my pack and looked for a place to settle on the flat, dusty floor of the west-facing shelter. Instead, my eyes were startled by a smooth corn-grinding stone. It sat in the exact center of its rock bowl, as if the Hohokam woman or man who used this mortar and pestle had walked off and left them there an hour ago. The

Hohokam disappeared from the earth in A.D. 1450. It was inconceivable to me that no one had been here since then, but that may have been the case—that is the point of trackless wilderness. I picked up the grinding stone. The size and weight and smooth, balanced perfection of it in my hand filled me at once with a longing to possess it. In its time, this excellent stone was the most treasured thing in a life, a family, maybe the whole neighborhood. To whom it still belonged. I replaced it in the rock depression, which also felt smooth to my touch. Because my eyes now understood how to look at it, the ground under my feet came alive with worked flint chips and pottery shards. I walked across to the other cave and found its floor just as lively with historic debris. Hidden under brittlebush and catclaw I found another grinding stone, this one some distance from the depression in the cave floor that once answered its pressure daily, for the grinding of corn or mesquite beans.

For a whole day I marveled at this place, running my fingers over the knife edges of dark flint chips, trying to fit together thick red pieces of shattered clay jars, biting my lower lip like a child concentrating on a puzzle. I tried to guess the size of whole pots from the curve of the broken pieces: some seemed as small as my two cupped hands, and some maybe as big as a bucket. The sun scorched my neck, reminding me to follow the shade across to the other shelter. Bees hummed at the edge of the water hole, nosing up to the water, their abdomens pulsing like tiny hydraulic pumps; by late afternoon they rimmed the pool completely, a collar of busy lace. Off and on, the lazy hand of a hot breeze shuffled the white leaves of the brittlebush. Once I looked up to see a screaming pair of red-tailed hawks mating in midair, and once a clatter of hooves warned me to hold still. A bighorn ram emerged through the brush, his head bent low under his hefty cornice, and ambled by me with nothing on his mind so much as a cool drink.

How long can a pestle stone lie still in the center of its mortar? That long ago—that recently—people lived here. *Here,* exactly, and not one valley over, or two, or twelve, because this place had all a person needs: shelter, food, and permanent water. They organized their lives around a catchment basin in a granite boulder, conforming their desires to the earth's charities; they never expected the opposite. The stories I grew up with lauded Moses for striking the rock and bringing forth the bubbling stream. But the stories of the Hohokam—oh, how they must have praised that good rock.

At dusk my friends returned with wonderful tales of the ground they had covered. We camped for the night, refilled our canteens, and hiked back to the land of plumbing and a fair guarantee of longevity. But I treasure my memory of the day I lingered near water and covered no ground. I can't think of a day in my life in which I've had such a clear fix on what it means to be human.

Want is a thing that unfurls unbidden like fungus, opening large upon itself, stopless, filling the sky. But *needs,* from one day to the next, are few enough to fit in a bucket, with room enough left to rattle like brittlebush in a dry wind.

Ann Ronald

A NEVADA TREASURE

Sky bridges all Nevada wilderness, including places some of us can't go. The military has preempted huge tracts for national defense purposes. The Nevada Test Site, neighboring Nellis Air Force Range, and land conscripted by the U.S. Naval Air Station in Fallon together total more than four million acres of land withdrawn from public access. In the middle of the state, a guardhouse protects a barred gate cemented in a ten-foot steel fence; beyond, what appear to be offices and barracks stand in governmental lines. Signs told me, "Keep out." Not a single human being brought life to the scene. Way out on the playa, taller structures glistened in the noon sun—a ghost enclave as extensive as downtown Tonopah, locked and apparently deserted. South of this science fiction complex, Groom Lake is a "remote desert test facility" undaunted by the end of the Cold War. No one knows exactly what goes on there, although 737s fly a dozen daily round trips to and from Las Vegas. Citizen watchdog Glenn Campbell imagines they're building a spy plane of some sort, "a U-2 on steroids," he figuratively speculates. Recently the Air Force requested withdrawal of an additional four thousand acres to prevent public observers like Campbell from "spying."

While the complex southeast of Tonopah and the Groom Lake facility remain mysterious, the greater Nevada Test Site has a new 1990s posture. With appropriate credentials, I was permitted inside the gates. There, I perceived a chilling disjunction between wilderness and wildness. Beauty and the beast, I fear. The topography might be anywhere, with names like Silent Canyon, Buckboard Mesa, Banded Mountain, Gold Meadows, and Quartzite Ridge. Red Canyon tumbles magenta rocks down shiny black and amber folds. Conglomerates of black and yellow form brown mudballs in the dry wash. I climbed through red spires, then dropped into white and pink and beige and pale mauve tuff. A landscape befitting a national park, I dreamed, until I stepped over a shovel, a bootprint, foil, a tire track, and a maze of disconnected wires. I also saw where soldiers drove tanks on maneuvers, where scientists perched to watch nuclear explosions. Wide-track swaths cut to a hilltop platform, then smashed straight to the basin below.

While I ate my lunch, I read my maps more carefully, and found sites like Plutonium Valley, Camera Station Butte, Parachute Canyon, News Knob, Groom Lake Road, and Smoky Blast Center. I could see three nuclear-made depressions from where I sat—Buster-Jangle Crater, Teapot Crater, Scooter Crater—and I could see Yucca Flat bomb towers too. I remembered a 1980s tour, when a guide pointed out bleachers where reporters and visiting dignitaries watched 1950s atomic blasts explode before their eyes. They wouldn't have seen the panorama I could see, because mushroom clouds blotted out their distances. Our guide then drove us to the bunkers, the bank vault, the cinder-block motel buffeted by megaton "devices." That was a wet year, when dark-stained mud oozed on the Frenchmen Flat playa. I carefully kept the muck off my shoes.

Twenty miles away, another canyon forks namelessly. I hiked alone past an ironstained cave hidden in puckered red conglomerates. The rest of the wash cut through khaki. Where the dry streambed finally ends at a cliff two hundred feet high, slabbed rock leans heavily on porous stone with hard eroded mud compartments. Seeking isolation, I failed. I heard trucks shifting gears, deep growls of machinery, drifts of a loudspeaker, a siren twice piercing the silence. Someone had flagged the hillside on my left. Backtracking, I followed the right-hand fork. White caves and yellow marked a path between tuff and darker limestone. Soft underfoot, the earth was the color of muslin. I forgot about khaki until I reached the ridgetop, where I looked directly down on a borrow pit, a sewage disposal, adits, a vent, and a radio tower. I also looked down on Camp 12, an outpost once teeming with life where, several years ago, I stood in a long cafeteria line and dodged cars on Mars Street, Neptune Street, and Antler Avenue. Now nearly deserted, Camp 12's parking lots stand empty. Only a handful of men dressed in

white protective suits waited for something I can't define. Above Camp
12, man-made tunnels burrow deep in the mesas. Horizontal ones
housed tactical nuclear weapons tests; perpendicular excavations, underground nuclear bombs. Once I plumbed the depths of what now is a
national showpiece for the Department of Energy. Like any ordinary
mine, Tunnel N has rough walls, a boxcar grinding over rails, darkness
penetrated by fixed lighting, a slightly claustrophobic ambiance. I wonder what the workers thought.

In truth, I find the Nevada Test Site an amazingly beautiful place,
with its own basins and ranges, colors and water and ghosts. The road
to Rainier Mesa, a 7,600-foot-high plateau, circles above tuff ten to fifteen million years old. Like a Utah highway lifting itself through Capi-
tol Reef, it traces puce cliffs, pink horizontal layers and folds, white
perpendicular gargoyles. Not far from Stockade Wash stand cherry-
stone formations, a swirl of desert varnish, a tinaja with rock art. Only
when I looked out the corner of my eye did I focus on a tunnel entrance cloistered in steel and cadaverous towers in the distance.

Rainier Mesa looks the way woodland Nevada once looked everywhere, with juniper, bunchgrass and buckwheat, deep thickets of
pine. When I drove through the fresh green mosaic landscape, winter
snow mounded under the trees. No one maintains the high roads, now
that underground nuclear tests have been discontinued. I dodged snowdrifts and rocks and unattended potholes. Wireless telephone poles, un-
attached sensor wires, and useless copper strands signal the way to an
aging DOE Repeater Site. There, standing by the metal trailer tipped
with fifty-foot antennas and an even taller lightning rod, I again felt the
Jekyll-and-Hyde personality of the Nevada Test Site. A cold wind blew
cloud layers in from the north, past range after range painted in shades
of winter blue. As far as I could see, I traced mountains to climb and
playas to explore, space withdrawn from public access. Overhead skeletal aluminum hummed discordant notes whenever the wind gusted—an
eerie ghost lament for treasures found and lost.

At Tippipah Spring, NTS ghosts converged. Flaked obsidian, obviously worked by prehistoric people, nested alongside a worn-out house
of sod and stone. An Antiquities Act sign cautioned souvenir hunters to
keep their distance. I might be anywhere in the state, but second look

confirmed I wasn't far from Mercury. Hanging between white poles
with red stripes another sign told me, if I understood the code, my exact military location—"16-7-C." A third sign warned of leftover explo-
sives. Barbed wire coiled around posts and lay in disarray, while twisted
sensor wires crisscrossed dirt roads leading to and from the spring.
Black cliffs armored the closest hillside; tawny tuff lightened a far-off
ridge. A low-flying helicopter drowned chukar conversation. Hyde and
Jekyll every time I turned my head.

 More United States citizens view the test site as a potential nuclear
waste repository than imagine the landscape a treasure. A barren anal-
ysis led to the creation of NTS in the first place, and an ongoing misunderstanding of desert beauty suggests potential misuse by future
generations. For me, this place is a microcosm of the way outsiders treat
Nevada—an unfortunate misinterpretation of distance and space and
earthtones and so-called emptiness, a regrettable assessment of what is
valuable and what is not.

Sharman Apt Russell

GILA WILDERNESS

Perched high on their horses, completely unafraid, the children are pre-
tending to be English tourists.

"I say, look at that over there, old boy!"

"Old boy, old boy. Look at that!" Maria repeats gleefully. She is
not quite five and Eric is seven. They have squabbled off and on all
morning over who would ride in front and then who would ride in
back and then who would ride in front again. Eric's mother, Lana, is
leading the horse, in part because I am nervous when we walk downhill
and the big animal crowds behind me. I wonder where these children
have picked up the nuances of satire and funny accents. Videos, I suppose. TV. Their ideas, to be sure, are still vague. When we ask Eric
where England is, he looks shifty and then says with authority, "In
Pennsylvania."

There is plenty of time to talk on this five-mile hike and family
pack train. My son, nearly two, is fulfilling a dream he has held half his
life, for he, too, is high on a horse, his excitement contained by Lana's
ten-year-old daughter, his horse led by Lana's husband. At the back, my
husband leads two more horses packed with camping gear. At the front,
Roberta and her married daughter Carol Greene walk the trail. Carol
has left behind her family in Wisconsin to be with her mother now, and
while I am freshly creating my children's memories, Carol and Roberta
are sorting through their own. A little high in protest, Carol's voice can
be heard as they ascend a hill. Roberta's answer is carried away by the
wind.

Although I have lived here for eight years—although I can see
from the ridge above my home the green edge of the Gila National

Forest—the next four days will be my longest trip into the Gila Wilderness, my fourth trip only, the one in which I will best comprehend wilderness, and the one in which I will start scheming, immediately after, as to how I can return.

It's ironic. Like most people, I associate wilderness with being alone. The 1964 National Wilderness Act, which legislated our country's system of wildernesses, is specific about this and includes "outstanding opportunities for solitude" as part of its definition of what a wilderness is. Historically, bred deep in our cultural bones, we think of the solitary explorer and hunter: men with righteous-sounding names like Daniel Boone or Jedediah Smith. Socially, we believe that the point of wilderness is to get away from people. Spiritually, we want to meet Nature stripped of our accoutrements and modern "superficial" selves. We want to be that vulnerable. We want to be that arrogant—the only human being on earth!

Yet here I am, with four children, five adults, and four horses. My husband and Lana's husband are partners in a new outfitting company, and they have condescended to treat their families to what they provide paying customers. Thus we are well-equipped, with therma-rest pads, big tents, and down sleeping bags. We have disposable diapers and storybooks and sunscreen lotion. We have pork tenderloin for tonight's dinner, fresh asparagus, wine glasses, and a cheesecake. As a mother and wife and friend, I have all my usual concerns. We have, I think, left only the dogs, the cats, and the videos behind.

Our trail runs through dry rolling hills dotted with juniper, scrub oak, and piñon pine. There are three colors: the parched yellow of grama grass, the dark of evergreen trees, the pale blue sky. This is peaceful country, and if its vistas are not grand, they call, nonetheless, to those parts of the body which have always yearned to fly. Sometimes the trail crosses an outcropping of bleak rhyolite or a bed of pink, eroded stone. Sometimes we swing around the side of a hill, and Lana's daughter gets nervous, unsure of her horse's footing on the narrow path.

"Davy, Davy, horsie, Davy," she comforts herself by crooning to my son. Ahead of her, Eric and Maria are much alike; three quarters in an interior world, they squeal so hilariously that Lana, whom I admire for her patience, must tell them to be quiet.

We all stop to watch a red-tailed hawk.

Then we began our descent, down Little Bear Canyon to the Middle Fork of the Gila River.

For my husband, this loss of altitude is a psychic passage. Rather quickly, the canyon begins to narrow and the sky shuts down until it is a swatch of blue in a pattern of pine boughs and fir needles. In a world grown suddenly cool, we are walking on the stream bed with its trickling flow and ledges of rock that rise above us. A grassy bench shelters a stand of yellow columbine; we stop again while the girls exclaim and wax sentimental. All around us, in contrast to the hills above, the murmuring life has been nurtured by water. Insects hatch and burrow in the mud. Emerald green algae swirls in a puddle. The canyon deepens and the rock rises above us, so close we could almost extend our arms and touch each wall. Now there is only rock and water and we are moving darkly to the center of the earth.

Then, like the odd turn in a dream, the stream bed expands to the size of a living room. Above is a small cave which my husband announces as a prehistoric shrine. The children are lifted down from their horses; the older ones scramble up the rock face. My husband tells us that not long ago you could still find prayer sticks and arrowheads here, scattered on the ground. These artifacts were from the Mogollon Culture: weavers, potters, basket makers, and farmers who by A.D. 900 had upgraded their pithouses into multi-room villages of stone and mud. Slighter and shorter than we are today, the Mogollons had a life expectancy of forty-five years and babies who died rather frequently. At this site, they have left a few faded pictographs—a squiggle I might generously call a lizard, a red hand that is oddly evocative. Carefully, Lana's daughter puts her own hand over the ancient print, covering it completely.

We emerge from Little Bear Canyon, as my husband said we would, into the light. Streaming down from the center of the sky, reflected in the water and trembling cottonwood leaves, bouncing up from banks of white sand, the sun seems to explode around us. It is a

drought year, and the Middle Fork of the Gila is not as large as usual.
Still, it looks grandly like a river, with riffles and pools and a fiery gleam
that disappears around corners left and right. High over the water, red
cliffs form the towers of an abandoned city, with tapered ends eroded
into strange balancing acts. Here the riparian ecology includes walnut,
sycamore, cottonwood, willow, wild grape, and Virginia creeper.
Herons and kingfishers hunt the shallows. Trout rise for bugs. These
sudden shifts in environment, accomplished in a few hours of walking,
are not unusual in the Gila Wilderness. On some day trips, a hiker can
move from the Chihuahua desert to a Subalpine forest. Diversity is the
rule, with five life zones and a thousand microclimates, all determined
by water or its lack.

Water is our goal as well, and the mothers take the children to the
river, letting the men deal with horses and lunch. Maria joins Lana's
daughter, who is busy making dams and catching tadpoles. Eric attempts to disappear forever, but Lana knows him well and is prepared
for this. She hauls him from the underbrush and informs him firmly: he
is only seven, he cannot leave her yet. My own son picks up a stick and
begins to splash me. Then, who knows why, he is suddenly anxious and
wants only to nurse.

A half mile from our planned campsite, we eat in a small grove of
ponderosa pine. When it is time to pack up, Maria wants to sit in front
on the horse again. It's not your turn, we tell her, it's Eric's turn. Maria
has a tantrum. Six parents stand around, cajoling a little, making deals.
She can ride in front later; we'll tell her a story. She accepts the good
part—she'd love a story—but rejects the bad. Finally, my husband takes
a stand. Maria cannot ride unless she rides in back.

So I am left amid the ponderosa pine with my screaming child.
Ponderosa are beautiful trees. Unlike other local conifers, their long
needles extend out and away, giving this pine an oriental delicacy. In
many parts of the Gila, ponderosa form vast, parklike forests where the
trees rise a hundred feet, the crowns do not touch, and the accumulated
needles make a deep carpet free of undergrowth. These are, as well,
trees with a secret: breathe deep into their reddish bark and you are suf-
fused with the faint scent of vanilla.

I try to show this to Maria as she cries fiercely, piercingly. I hug her, in a physical effort to contain an emotion of which she has clearly become the victim. Following one school of thought, for a while I simply let her express the emotion. I wait and admire the beautiful trees. My patience for waiting is not long, but in that time I am surprisingly content. This is my job, I think. Socialization. Taking turns. I am grateful for where I am. In a public place, or even a friend's home, I could not endure this blast of feeling.

"Maria," I say, like a fisherman baiting a hook, knowing well she will succumb, "I'll tell you a story while we walk."

The storm subsides slowly; Maria is beached on shore, looking bewildered. Where has she been? We hold hands and follow the trail along the riverbank, through shady groves and then out, once more, into the sun. I tell her about Hansel and Gretel, and when we reach the campsite, everyone is happy to see us. The camp itself is full of miraculous signs. In a pool, deep enough for bathing, a group of fish sway in the shadows. Nearby, three baby birds with wide mouths complain from their nest. A swallowtail butterfly circles the stalk of a purple bull thistle. Two trees for a hammock stand perfectly apart.

As we go about the business of setting up camp, our son opens and empties a bottle of brandy on our clothes. In the rustles inside newly erected tents, I know that other family dramas are going on, and I am beginning to see that older children bring a whole new set of interesting problems. Roberta is hurt by something Carol has said. Lana's daughter is unhappy about the dinner arrangements. Lana is trying to keep Eric from under the horses' feet.

The horses themselves are engaged in complex social arrangements. I had never known that they could be so human, so insistent in their desires. One horse doesn't like the other and won't be picketed beside her. Two of the horses are set free to graze because my husband knows they are too loyal to leave while their partners are tied up. Much later, in the middle of the night, the mare begins to scream with jealousy and rage: another horse has broken loose and is eating grass. This she cannot abide.

The afternoon slips away with the sounds of children playing in the river. Around the evening campfire I shelter my son just as these green cottonwoods shelter us. Lana's husband also holds his ten-year-old daughter, the girl's long legs crowding her father's lap. Roberta and Carol are thoughtfully quiet while Maria and Eric can be heard from a tent, whispering secrets.

We are not the first family group to laze under these trees and count our riches and our sorrows. In a wilderness, relatively few humans have come before and it is permissible, I think, to imagine an intersection. I imagine an Indian family, descendants of Asians who crossed the Bering Strait and came to this area after the Mogollons and before the Spanish. The Zunis christened these nomads Apache—the word for enemy. I imagine wicki-ups instead of tents, pine boughs for softness, hides for warmth, *metates, manos,* beads from Mexico.

"In that country which lies around the headwaters of the Gila I was reared," dictated Geronimo when he was old, exiled, and still homesick. "This range was our fatherland; among these mountains our wigwams were hidden; the scattered valleys contained our fields; the boundless prairies, stretching away on every side, were our pastures; the rocky caverns were our burying places. I was fourth in a family of eight children—four boys and four girls. . . . I rolled on the dirt floor of my father's teepee, hung in my cradle at my mother's back, or slept suspended from the bough of a tree. I was warmed by the sun, rocked by the winds, and sheltered as other Indian babes."

As a boy growing up in these forests and mountains, Geronimo's life would have been greatly envied by Lana's son. In the Apache's words, he "played at hide and seek among the rocks and pines" or "loitered in the shade of the cottonwood trees" or worked with his parents in the cornfields. Sometimes, to avoid the latter, he and his friends would sneak out of camp and hide all day in some secret dappled meadow or sunny canyon. If caught, they were subject to ridicule. If not, they could expect to return at twilight, victorious and unpunished. Geronimo's father died when he was small and at seventeen years of age—1846, the year the United States declared war on Mexico—the teenager was admitted into the tribe's council of warriors. Soon after, the young man married his version of a high school sweetheart and together they had three children. This first wife, Alope, was artistic. To beautify their home amid the vanilla-scented pine, she made decorations of beads and drew pictures on buckskin.

Later, as Geronimo tells it, he and his tribe went to Mexico to trade. There Mexican troops attacked the camp while the men were in town. Geronimo's mother, wife, and three children were killed. Stunned, the warrior vowed vengeance and went on to fight both Mexicans and Americans in a guerrilla warfare that was mean and dirty by all accounts and on all sides. "Even babies were killed," one Apache warrior regretted later. "And I love babies!"

Here in the Gila headwaters, local chiefs had long fought the parade of settlers and prospectors. The end was inevitable. In 1886, Geronimo, the last holdout, surrendered and was shipped to Florida along with every other Indian who had ever made the Gila a home. Even the Apache scouts who had helped bring Geronimo in were loaded onto the boxcars. In the 1890s a newspaper reported with nostalgia and some compassion that a "wild and half-starved" Apache family had been seen foraging in the rugged Mogollon Mountains. Desperate and surely lonely, they died or left by the end of the century.

In the morning, my husband gets up early and walks with David and Maria to the nearby hot springs. I follow later and for half an hour, I am, in fact, solitary in the wilderness.

Self-consciously, I look about the scene of a fast-flowing river, lined with leafy trees, against a background of rock. It is conventionally pretty. It is also hard edged and muscular, Southwestern tough. I have the strong feeling that I am not the dominant species here.

This, too, is an echo of the 1964 Wilderness Act, which declares that "a wilderness, in contrast with those areas where man and his own works dominate the landscape, is hereby recognized as a place where the earth and its community of life are untrammeled by man, where man is a visitor who does not remain."

Frankly, I like this lack of power and control. I like being a visitor. Here in the wilderness I can put aside my grievances against humanity. I can exchange, at the very least, one set of complexities for another: the dappled slant of a bank, rustling leaves, straight white trunks, crumbling cliff faces, gravel slopes, turbulent water—all glowing with sunlight, intertwined, patterned; rich with diatoms, moss, algae, caddisflies, dragonflies, damselflies, stoneflies, trout, suckers, bass, minnows,

chubs; pinchers, mouthparts, claws, teeth; photosynthesis, decomposi-
tion, carbonization. None of it is my doing. I am just a large mammal
walking the riverbank. Ahead is my mate.

When I was fifteen, I lied to my mother and hitchhiked from my home
in Phoenix to camp out in a sycamore-lined canyon above the desert.
The point was to do this alone. The point was to be alone and serene
and in touch with beauty. The trip, unsurprisingly for a girl raised in
the suburbs, was a disaster, and I ended up leaving a day early. On the
way home, the old man who gave me a ride tried once to put his hand
on my thigh. The image lingered with me for many years. The stubby
white fingers. My revulsion. My ignorance.

When I was eighteen, a girlfriend and I planned a summer-long
backpack trip that would take us four hundred miles up the Pacific
Crest Trail. The girlfriend dropped out at the last minute, and I went
on by myself, determined this time to live alone in the woods. Outside
Ashland, Oregon, I watched the dawn beneath layers of a plastic tarp
against which mosquitoes hammered and whined for my blood. At that
time I was still concerned about my alienation from nature, and I perceived a sheet of glass, a terrible wall, between me and life, me and experience. For days, I hiked through a pine forest that never seemed to
vary or end, until my thoughts too began to hammer and whine at the
bone of my skull. One evening I cried after swimming in a lake and
finding my body, my legs and crotch, covered with small red worms. A
week later I met a boy my age who was also alone, and we traveled together the rest of the summer, hitchhiking north to mountains that began where timberline ended. We never grew to like each other. We
never had the slightest physical contact. Yet we hung on, gamely,
blindly, to the comfort and distraction of another human being.

When I was twenty, I set out again, this time bicycling with a college classmate up the East Coast. She ended her tour in Maine, and the
next day I started for Nova Scotia. By now I knew what it meant to
travel alone as a female: I knew about circumspection, reserve, hiding.
In Canada, the ocean exploded against a lushness of farmland, and for
me this was exotic, stupendous surrealism. I tried my best to internalize
the scenery. But it seemed that I could only turn wheels, pushing my

limit, sixty miles up and down the green hills, a hundred miles on the flat inland highway between the tips of the island. By now I knew as well when to recognize misery, and in Halifax I prepared to pack up and head back to school. Instead—a postscript—I met another bicyclist, fell in love with him, and stayed on through a long winter.

Somewhere in all that, I gave up on my ability to conquer solitude. I had tried to be my version of Daniel Boone, brave and self-sufficient, to seek distance and the lonely sound of foreign names. My model could have come straight from the Gila Wilderness. I had tried to be—not Geronimo, who was too much the warrior—but such a man as James Ohio Pattie, a twenty-year-old who trapped beaver on the Gila River five years before Geronimo was ever born. By his own account, Pattie left Missouri in 1824, traveled to Santa Fe where he rescued the governor's daughter from Comanches, managed the copper mines in Santa Rita, escaped massacre by Pimas in Arizona, floated the Colorado River to its salty mouth, starved in a Spanish jail, and crossed Mexico to sell his memoirs to a publisher in St. Louis.

In this case, as I walk beside the Middle Fork, it is not fanciful to imagine that I am following Pattie's footsteps. In his narrative of the 1824 trip, he clearly reaches the hot springs where we will picnic this afternoon. Typically, his description is more dramatic than seems reasonable. He writes of catching a fish and throwing it in the spring's boiling waters where "in six minutes it would be thoroughly cooked." Other tales are equally elongated, and it has become a historian's game to match up Pattie's journey with the rest of history. His account of daily dangers are the most credible: the terror of meeting a grizzly bear or the hunger that forced him and his partners to shoot their dogs. On one sad day, Pattie wrote piteously, "We killed a raven, which we cooked for seven men." By the end of his adventures, he had probably become what he most admired—the quintessential mountain man. Still, it is a lesson to me that James Ohio Pattie, living out the romance, felt so strongly the need to romanticize. For at that time the governor had no daughter, it was another trapper who fought the Pimas, and another man who killed the grizzly.

In 1924, a hundred years after Pattie explored the Middle Fork, three-quarter million acres of the Gila National Forest were designated by the Forest Service as "an area big enough to absorb a two weeks' pack trip and kept devoid of roads, artificial trails, cottages, or other works of man." This was the first official wilderness in the United States, the beginning of our national wilderness system, and the brain-child of a thirty-seven-year-old forester named Aldo Leopold. In my own history, upon returning from Nova Scotia and my first, unsuccess-ful love affair—upon giving up the idea of becoming a mountain man—I settled instead on becoming Aldo Leopold. I read his famous work *Sand County Almanac* and I changed my college major from drama to natural resources. I took courses in wildlife management, the field that Leopold pioneered, and wrote papers on deer herd reduction. I even took a course from Leopold's son, Starker Leopold, whom I glamorized on the slightest of proofs. My hero became not the man who lives wil-derness, but the one who manages it.

Years later, when I came to live near the Gila Wilderness, my at-tachment to Leopold increased for an odd reason. I learned more about his mistakes. They were not small. After a boyhood beside the Missis-sippi River, Aldo Leopold went East to the Yale Forestry School and then Southwest as a greenhorn foreman of a timber crew. At first, this sportsman thought mainly in terms of hunting and fishing. He had no problems with grazing either and eventually had friends and relatives at both of the big ranches in the Gila Forest. With these connections, and in his later role as a game and fish manager, Leopold pushed hard for predator control and vowed to extinguish every killer of deer and cow, "down to the last wolf and lion."

In the Gila area, he hired hunter extraordinaire Ben Lilly, who by 1921 had a lifetime lion kill of five hundred. Today there is a Ben Lilly Monument in the Gila National Forest with a plaque dedicated to the memory of a man who shot more wildlife in the Southwest than any-one else would ever want to. With all his outdoor expertise, Ben Lilly is not a man I would want my children to emulate. Violence was his tie to nature. And when his dogs "betrayed their species" by being poor hunters, he beat them to death.

In the late 1920s an irruption of deer in the Gila and nearby Black Range caused Aldo Leopold to rethink his ideas on predator control. Twenty years after the fact he describes shooting at a wolf and her half-grown cubs from a high rimrock. In seconds, the mother and children were dead or scattered. Leopold rushed down in time to catch a "fierce green fire" dying in the old wolf's eyes.

"I thought that because fewer wolves meant more deer, no wolves would mean a hunter's paradise," the conservationist wrote in his essay "Thinking Like a Mountain." "But after seeing the green fire die, I sensed that neither the wolf nor the mountain agreed with such a view. Since then I have lived to see state after state extirpate its wolves. I have watched the face of many a newly wolfless mountain, and seen the south-facing slopes wrinkle with a maze of new deer trails. I have seen every edible bush and seedling browsed, first to anaemic desuetude, and then to death . . . In the end the starved bones of the hoped-for deer herd, dead of its own too much, bleach with the bones of the dead sage, or molder under the high-lined junipers. I now suspect that just as a deer herd lives in mortal fear of its wolves, so does a mountain live in mortal fear of its deer."

By the time Leopold himself died, in 1949, he saw wilderness in a much richer light than the one that prompted him, in 1924, to push for a "national hunting ground" in the Gila Forest. Wilderness areas were still important as sanctuaries for the primitive arts of canoeing, packing, and hunting. But they were also necessary as part of a larger land ethic and as a laboratory for the study of land health. Culturally, wilderness was a place where Americans could rediscover their history and "organize yet another search for a durable scale of values." Wilderness even had something that Leopold could not name. "The physics of beauty," he noted, "is one department of natural science still in the Dark Ages."

It is, perhaps, not surprising that as the country's first wilderness, the Gila may also be the most mismanaged. In part due to its bloated deer herds, in the late 1920s a road was opened through the heart of the wilderness to allow access to hunters. Another road to the Gila Cliff Dwellings National Monument would later be paved. In 1964, historic grazing leases were granted "in perpetuity," and along certain streams cattle have clearly become the dominant species. The imperfections of the Gila carry their own lessons. To become a visitor, to relinquish control, is not easy.

When I reach the hot springs, I have reached a place like my husband's passage through Little Bear Canyon, a place that conforms to a place inside. Surrounded by ferns and vegetation, the two pools are sheltered against a massive rock upon which the hot water trickles down in a cascade over slick moss and lime green algae. A hand-built dam of loose stone creates a four-foot-deep swimming hole in which the older children play and splash. The water temperature is about a hundred degrees. My husband stretches full length and lets his nose touch the tiny yellow wildflowers that bloom at the pool's edge.

I carry my son David against my chest. He is developing his sense of humor and, to amuse him, I simulate disgust when he sticks out his tongue so that it fills his little mouth. "Oooooh!" I make a face. He laughs with power and sticks out his tongue again. "Ooooh!" I say. He grins and sticks out his tongue at everyone. All the girls, excepting his sister, want to hold him in their arms and glide away with him in the warm water. He skims over the surface of the pool and then cries out so beseechingly that they float him back to me. Clinging, he rides my hip like a cowboy in the saddle. We go through cycles with our children, as they do with us, and for now my son, who is twenty-two months, and I, who am thirty-five years, are besotted with each other. I adore his skin and his smell and every stray expression that informs his face with intelligence and personality. This is mutual, unconditional love—an exotic interlude. This has been going on in these hot springs since the first Mogollon mother, since Alope and her children.

The rest of the trip passes in this way. We take turns riding the horses farther up the Middle Fork: here the rock walls loom a thousand feet above a canyon floor that narrows dramatically to the width of its river. Another few miles and the trail runs downhill, faster and faster, as the horses hurry to a grassy bottom land known as The Meadows. The scenery is breathtaking and we claim it as our own. No one has ever seen it, just this way, before. In the cooling twilights, we swim in the water hole. During an afternoon rain, we lie in our tents. We cook. We talk. We clean. Roberta and Carol take long walks together. Spouses, as usual, spar a little, and the children bicker. On our therma-rest pads, we all sleep well.

Later, driving home, I have to wonder why these four days have been such a success. Who was it—my husband, my children, my friends—who helped me to see, just a little more clearly, that I do not need to become more than I am to have a place in the wilderness? I do not need to love solitude more than the company of my own species. I do not need to become a man. Or a manager. The shrine is here already. The graves. The bowls and the baskets and the way we touch a baby or tell stories to children. I need only walk in.

Leslie Ryan

THE MOUNTAIN

It was too late to have left for the mountain. She wore her grandmother's
lavender dress. It was a summer dress from 1926, in four sheer layers of
silk. Her grandmother had dropped the waist and omitted the sleeves,
following the flapper style. Below the waist her grandmother had sewn
three yards of fabric for each layer, so the dress draped and touched itself
in many places. Her grandmother had rolled each hem to weight it
slightly, and in each rolled hem could be seen the fine, even stitches of
her grandmother's lavender silk thread.

Across her shoulders she pulled a sheer cotton scarf printed with
birds, to cover her breasts if necessary, as they could almost be seen
through the dress. The things she should have taken up the mountain
she left in camp. The knife she left in camp. The hat she left in camp.
The raingear, compass, snacks, and lamp—all these she left in camp. She
hadn't meant to leave them all, but neither did she care to gather and
carry them. It was late, and by the time she returned from the mountain, it would be night.

People didn't care to visit the country nearby the mountain. The
stream was not picturesque. It flowed sometimes milk-white and sometimes red, like old blood. It wasn't glacial silt or iron deposits. It wasn't
sulfur or erosion. The water just came up out of the earth that way periodically, and it hadn't been explained. No one cared to explain it.

The land had little to boast of. Many hours on washboard were required to reach the head of the trail. Its wilderness was a long thin strip
attached to a steep swath of crumbly rock, not good for climbing.
There wasn't a panorama until just below the mountain. The long trek
up, several days in length, had to be made in plain woods and meadows.

The mountain was unremarkable, one among many, not the highest in the region nor the most dangerous. Even the animals were plain ones like elk that had not been made dear by peril. The whole place was a gangly flower growing on the wall of crumbly rock, and it was regularly passed up in favor of the more comely wildernesses to the south, whose spectacular needlelike mountains spiked fourteen thousand feet into thin air.

The earth pounded like a wooden bridge as she walked. Her workboots drummed on the path. Silk brushed her bare shins. When the wind blew, a pointillism of light flashed in the aspen leaves. Scars that appeared to be lidded eyes stood out on the aspen trunks where the trees had pruned themselves of branches. She followed elk tracks between the white trunks. There were deer tracks too. All had been casually walking, browsing on forbs and bunchgrasses.

At the trailhead five days ago, she had stood at the trail register. Spiders had spun the box shut. She could have pulled up on the lid and torn the netting in half. She could have scraped off the webs with a stick. She had wanted to write her name in the box. But her mother had said silkwork was a long strand of hours threaded through a tissue of invisible labor. In the end she had not sundered the mesh, and her name had never been written.

Since then they had walked a good distance. They had come up four thousand feet. During that time they had seen their own sign, but none of other humans. There was only one trail, this one, which died in the sheer crumbly wall of the mountain.

Green plants—false hellebore and larkspur—touched her thighs through the lavender dress. Elk urine had left runnels in the mud. Her shins had been injured, so she had to step carefully onto stones. She turned and looked behind her often to see the backside of the trail. She had hiked for many months of many years, and she did not have to think what to do.

Her lover was sick at camp. Against her nature, she had left him alone. He was lying in the tent. He was having trouble breathing. It wasn't too bad. It wasn't high-altitude pulmonary edema. He had said, "Go on up the mountain."

Back in camp her letter was lying on a rock. It was wrapped in a bag in case rain came. The bag was weighted down with another rock, and a goldeneye flower she had knocked down while gathering water. The letter wasn't done yet. In it she was considering something she had lost. It had slipped out of her when she was a girl. It had slipped out of her, like a lozenge. It could not be described correctly. But previously it had communicated with her like a compass. It had glowed a ruby red color when she turned in the right direction. It had paled to gray when she turned the wrong way. When she was a girl approaching woman-hood, she had lost it, two thousand miles from the mountain. By the time she had noticed it was gone, it was too late.

The trail left the aspen and ascended through spruce. It side-hilled north through subalpine meadows and then became thready in nature. Past this point the trail was used very infrequently.

The trail veered to the east. Where subalpine fir first appeared with the spruce, the path began to unravel. The route was poorly main-tained, and some of the game trails looked better. Fallen trees blocked the way. To step through the branches, she lifted the edge of the skirt, twisted it as if to wring, and cinched the rolled cloth at the hip. At times there was no trail at all, only wide circles of dry spruce needles. She chose a path where the most branches had been broken. At one time someone had cut blazes into the trees, but now the bark had healed back into thin, lumpy seams.

She became aware of water moving a little to the south. Its sound was the drone of silent places, which could always be heard, even in the desert, if one cupped the hands and bent the ears forward. It was a con-stant aaaah, like a washer filling with rinse water, or an iron steaming, or a sewing machine being treadled in a distant room.

The firs closed in and the trail entered a cleft that cut east to west. A flock of pine siskins spun into the trees and hung on the low dead twigs. "Friends, hello!" she said. All around, in the branches and trunks, delicate squeaks sounded.

The silk bounced on her shins. Some few hundred yards into the cleft, she crossed the stream on stones. It was running clear. She crouched to fill the flask she had lashed to her waist. She touched the surface of the water with her palms. It pressed up into the lifelines. She could smell the sap from the forests. She could smell the must of grasses from the meadows. When she removed an iodine tablet from the small pouch tied to the flask and dropped it in, she could smell that too.

The trail switchbacked up through spruce forests on the north-facing side of the cleft. She was partways up before she remembered to shake the threads on the flask. She stopped, opened the lid two turns, and tilted the flask back and forth at arm's length to keep iodine off the dress. Then she continued walking.

To the east more trees were down. Instead of stepping through the trees, she wove around the root clumps of dirt that stood up sideways. The trail grew slighter and slighter. She scouted for blazes. The thin seams visible lower down had disappeared. The old maps would have called such a path a "man-way" rather than a trail. The man-way grew more and more subtle, until it became a pleat of space that had to be intuited between the trees. Still, the man-way was not difficult to find, and, except for the steepness, she passed along it with ease.

As the man-way curved north again, the incline grew less steep, and the trees more stunted. Tundralike meadow spread between dwarf atolls. Near treeline it was evident that the wind beat the firs like rugs, knocking the cones and needles from them and bending them to its positions. Finally the man-way passed beyond the trees entirely and crested out into a rolling meadow. She preferred to step from stone to stone when there was no trail. She watched the brown leather of her boot. She watched the light-colored stitches welting the vamp to the sole. She watched the soil, rocks, and plants the boot passed over. When the boot came down on a rosette of oval leaves, she said, "Sorry, friend, I'm sorry, I did not mean to crush."

In the meadow the path reappeared periodically as patches of gravel among small plants. She oriented from patch to patch, but the way grew more faint, until the pattern of depressed clearings in the short vegetation appeared to extend in all directions equally, like the twill on damask. There she lost the path entirely. It died out into the scarlet gilia. But all around, in its place, rose the view.

A thousand feet of brown rock loaded the edge of the meadow on three sides. Chunks and jumbles of it hung against blue sky. The wall hooked around the meadow at some distance, perhaps three miles away at points. It caught the gray-green hillock of the meadow in its crook. At the wall's northernmost curve, directly where a hook would catch an eye, stood the mountain.

The mountain bulged out from the crumbling wall into the far end of the meadow. Though its flanks ascended to a definite peak, the mountain itself was clearly as rotten as the walls around it, looking more like a pile of old brick or broken-up houses than a solid, individual, proper mountain. It appeared as a bulbous aberration in the wall, a conglomerate of avalanche chutes and scree slopes, as frayed around the edges as a bent-up wirebrush, entirely lacking individual integrity and isolation, leaning too unassertively against the wall to command much attention.

Down from the peak, ridges scalloped into two high saddles, one to the east and one to the west, and from them the two arms of the brown hook extended. The one arm bordered the meadow to the east, then crumbled and grew slender as a wrist, and finally gave out after several miles, as if its hand were hanging off the far contours of the meadow in sleep, permitting a view into the spires of the other, more famous ranges to the southeast.

The other, western arm of the hook dwarfed all features in the landscape. Looking back along the way she had come, as far as she could make out, squinting, the massive escarpment blocked the view to the west. Never growing weaker, never submitting to drainages, never losing altitude, the brown arm stretched thirty miles south, flexing against the wilderness, a wall without apparent terminus, protecting the wilderness from whatever terrors lay on the other side of it, yet at the same time seeming to crowd and shunt the trees and meadows off the eastern edge of the divide, as a cleaver shunts food off a cutting board. She had walked many miles in the wall's shadow without fully understanding its magnitude.

To the south the meadow rolled downward. The sun lit its southernmost edge, so it hung clear as the curve of a ball against the far dark foothills below. Then the meadow plunged out of sight into the cleft. Beyond the foothills she could see the flat ranchlands of the valley. They were sixty miles away.

Rufous hummingbirds zoomed through the meadow. They visited the gilia. They chitted broad-tails off their nectar. She cast around for the trail. There were many cushion plants about. That was when she found it. It was there, between a harebell flower and a yarrow. It caught the late afternoon sun. She knelt down beside it. She examined it closely. How it glistened! There was no dirt on it. There was no dust on it. It was small and red, like a garnet. It was just as she'd remembered it. There was a heart of fire in it. It glowed.

She knelt there beside it. She breathed in and out. The small plants around it trembled in the wind.

She didn't dare to touch it. She was afraid it was still wet. Because it was not the ruby that had slipped out of her. It was a piece of candy from someone's mouth, recently spit into the meadow.

She stood up. She softened her eyes to detect motion on the distant periphery. Nothing moved but flowerheads in the wind near her feet, and the lavender hem of her dress. She scanned the side of the mountain and believed she saw a broken zig of switchbacks ascending it. She should have shielded her breasts with the scarf, since someone was decidedly near, but she did not. She did not wish to restrain the sensuous fabric the wind had been touching her with.

She knelt again and checked the moist cushion plants for crushed stems and leaves. She looked for the damp or dusty undersides of overturned pebbles. She searched for rips in the knitted vasculature of the tundra. She found no sign that anyone other than she had passed through the meadow since snowmelt.

After that she stood again. The scarf covered her shoulders and trailed down her arms. She held one corner in each hand. She left it that way. She walked on. Lavender birds and peach-colored fruits billowed out behind her.

She picked up the trail again by a mat of alpine forget-me-nots. At the next crossing she stopped and filled the flask for the second time. She looked back and checked again to see where she had come up from the cleft; the knotty atoll with three dead-white leaders marked the distant southeast corner of the meadow. The wind carried the cold smell of damp rock. She stepped out easily across the clean, open meadow, watching the tiny oval leaves of plants. Her hair hung along her spine, pressing like the hand of someone behind her.

The meadow began to climb steeply. Long ribs of brown scree had slid into it. The trail was a subtle line of flattened rock traversing the scree of the mountain. Volcanic boulders had rolled down the slope. A halo of coolness surrounded each one. The trail passed among the boulders. She observed the chartreuse lichens growing on their surfaces. She observed her steps on the broken stones. She tamped the talus first when it looked too loose. Even the secure talus clattered and scraped underfoot.

Ahead a massive boulder had cleaved from the mountain and split in half. One half stood on either side of the trail. A thin stretch of scree passed between them. It was dark in shadow.

As she approached the portal, a slight rustle sounded behind one of the rocks. She stopped.

She stepped forward, to be sure she had heard it correctly. It sounded again, this time more clearly.

"Shhh," from behind the rock. She froze. It was a man.

The blood rushed down to her feet and hands. She felt the empty place between her breasts where her knife should have hung. Without moving her head, she looked to the side for a stick. Immediately she was sickened by the vulnerability of her skin under thin silk. The leather flask hung against her abdomen like a liver.

She could not turn her back. Out of fear, she took a step forward. "Shhh."

He was shushing another man. He could see her. He whispered just as she moved. He stopped just as she stopped.

The hair on her forearms rose. She could almost touch the portal rocks. A coldness crept into her wrists. It was not the chill of the air. It was a sinister intention, emanating from behind the rock. The dress skimmed the length of her body, suicidally feminine.

Because her lover was sick many miles down the trail and she was standing between two men in a wind-scoured wilderness in a diaphanous dress without even a stick or a knife to protect herself and there was nothing else to do, she took a step forward.

Exactly as she stepped, she heard the man's voice again, this time coming up from between her legs. It was her own legs, brushing against one another.

She continued up the mountain, walking on her toes to avoid hurting her shins. Hard breathing drove the thoughts from her mind. Knots formed just below her calves. Cramps pinched her quadriceps. Lungs bellowed air in and out. Without stopping, she sashed the scarf to her waist so her hands would be free. She lifted the hems of the skirt. As she ascended, she tucked them under the waist scarf at four points. They draped like petal hems. This left her legs free for climbing. The shadow of the wall crawled up the mountain as the sun set. She used hands for balance as she worked her way into it.

Cairns on big stones must have once marked the trail. Occasionally a single flat stone lay conspicuously atop another, and she followed these. At times the trail was a compressed ledge in loose scree. At times it was a disconnected series of sturdy stones in a chute of loose ones. Above, at the ridge, the wind was blowing hard. It could be heard buffeting the ridgeline. She was protected from it by the mountain.

Sunset projected a yellow wedge onto the mountain. Near a whiplash saxifrage she regained the sun. She leaned down and put her hands on the two rocks by the yellow flower. "Friend, you are beautiful here."

This man-way would end in a summit. Along the way there would be flowers. The last man-way she had climbed, in midsummer, had ended in a hanging alpine lake. The desolation, the absolute uninhabitability of that place, was its triumph. In three directions around the lake, ratty ice fields plunged a thousand feet down into the lakebed. They curved out onto the surface of the lake, so three shores were floating ice floes. Permanent high winds scoured the lake's one remaining shore. That shore was a jagged tumble of boulder cubes. Waves smacked their flat sides. Small white ice islands with blue bottoms floated in the water.

There was no place to lay a bivy sack and hardly a place to sit in the tilted rubble on the one shore of the lake. Even soil could not find a niche. No vegetation could survive there. Only black lichens stained the granite tops of the rock. She had scrambled out to the edge of the lake, climbed a boulder, crouched down, and placed her palms on the rock's cold surface. Then she had leaned out and looked down through the clear waves into the lake. Twenty feet underwater, the squared-off faces of boulders with all their fissures and cuts sat crisp as ice.

As she had scrambled back, hopping off a stout rock, her boot had hit near something strange. She had jerked the foot back. There it was, tucked alongside the hunkering boulders and bludgeoned by geologic starkness: a patch of vascular green. A little crowd of five-petaled flowers smiled up from the mat. Alpine phlox, the most open-faced and cheery of blossoms. At the heart of adversity, this is who resides: smiley little flowers, as neat as the print on calico kitchen curtains.

Before she reached the ridge, she untied the scarf from her waist. She bent forward and threw her hair over. She knotted it up in the scarf. She twisted the ends of the scarf. She twined them around like rope, binding her hair to her head. Now her arms were bare.

When she stepped out onto the ridge, the wind blasted her back. She lunged forward into it. It hit from all sides alternately and sometimes from two sides at once. She planted her feet in the rock.

The ridge was six or seven feet wide. At times it narrowed to four. It was composed of rocks the size of tea saucers, some loose and some packed down hard. Shadows outlined their edges. Occasionally the larger stones beneath were revealed by clear spots in the shards. Eight hundred feet of exposure slipped away on either side. She could die, she would most likely die, if she fell here. But this could also be true of a bathtub.

Blood pooled down in her hands. She did not look down the sides of the mountain. She focused on the thin strip of stone. She had to keep steady in the wind. The dress whipped wildly around her. She balled up the silk in her fists and held it in tight to her thighs.

She dug each boot into the saucers of rock until she had a firm foot. She let the bigness of her calves and thighs keep her steady on the ridge. She watched her boots stomp, seat, and lift in the shadowed clutter of stones. She looked straight along the blade of rock in the sky.

At a stable spot she stopped and looked back to the east. On the eastern horizon, sunset appeared as a thin rim of vermilion. In the four directions, the sky was clear and blue.

At the summit of the mountain, land fell away on all sides. The rest of the mountain seemed to have slid into a hole in the earth, down at the bottom where the earth sounded hollow. Only one point had stayed up in the sky, and the sun was setting below it.

She stood clutching the dress to her hips, staring into the sky. A coldness outlined her knees. The turban protected her ears from the wind, but the wind was prying it loose from her head. One strand of the scarf hit her lips. She bit it and held it between her teeth to keep the turban from unraveling. A pressure built on the south side of the turban: a bubble was being lifted in it. Twists of hair loosened underneath. Moving air tugged at the roots.

She opened her fists and let go of the dress. At once the wind flattened the twelve yards of silk against her northern leg and whipped them out to the south. It blew the fabric out over the edge of the ridge. The rolled hems lashed at her legs and then sailed away from them.

She flipped her head over and bowed to retuck the scarf. The skirts filled with air and bulged into her face like laundered sheets being clothespinned upwind. Even in the fresh, basaltic wind, she smelled the delicate soap she had swirled the silk in and, beneath that, the faintest trace of the attic.

When she lifted her body again, she did not attempt to grab the lavender fabric. In the absence of clouds, sunset had leapt into the dress.

The wind hurled and split the four layers apart. It flew them out in different directions. Saffron from the west flapped against blue south. Northern purple slipped under the east. The wind beat blue shadows into and out of the folds. Amethyst, saffron, and azure flashed in the surround—molten, quixotic, as when she had swum in an ocean at sunset, and the waves had folded around her. Light clasped and released her limbs. Dark forearms broke through amber. Trails of gold slid down her wrists. The wind beat a wild topography into the skirts, obscuring and revealing the landscape beneath. Forest and meadow thrashed in the lavender gauze. Cliffs whipped west and east. Lightning-struck snags appeared small as thorns at the meadow's edge, then disappeared behind patches of light. Stones undulated opaquely, like dancers hidden by scrim.

For instants at a time, she could see all the way back to where she had come from. She could see the dark thread, sometimes white, of the stream running into the cleft. She could see the dark sides of the mountain shooting down into the scree. She could see other mountain ranges cuffing the one she was on. She could see the far side of the west wall, its warp and weft of hillocks extending down into the flats. And somewhere out of sight, down in a hollow deep in the earth, she could see a brown wooden box into which her name had not yet been signed.

All the known and unknown friends, all the land she had traveled and all she had not, vanished and emerged in the wild, flapping fabric, whose sound was the beating of wings.

On the way down, off the ridge, she unknotted her hair from the scarf. Still above treeline, she passed a branch that looked to be bone. And later, farther down, an orange flicker feather rimmed in black. She had to step lightly on her toes, as elk do. The earth crackled and drummed beneath her.

It was the time of evening when lavender looks most beautiful. Just before dark. She had far to go on the switchbacks, and soon it would be night.

The dress glowed against the brown trail as it was kicked by her shins. Light was removing itself from the paintbrush and from the little purple gentian. The meadow had turned bluish gray. Only the bottle-brush flowers and the lavender dress, and sometimes the edge of a pearly everlasting leaf, could be seen well in the dusk.

She lost the trail again in the same place where the candy had been spit. She didn't see it again. The man-way resumed near the three dead leaders in the southeast. Wherever the view was not obscured by trees, she was looking south, into the shadowed foothills and the unlit valley.

Six hundred feet above the water, she curved to the west. On the north-facing side of the cleft, the air darkened. She perceived a different kind of silence. It occurred as a pressure from above the trees. Not even the sounds of squirrels or birds were present in it. She side-hilled through the silence, hearing the drum of her toes on the earth. She felt uncertain about the man-way going west. The fall-line of the cleft kept pulling her down too soon. She had to keep to a certain contour and hit the stream at a certain point, or she would get cliffed out and have to reascend in the dark.

She stopped and stared around. It was getting dark. The trees stood dry and uncrowded, and the silence opened around them eerily, like a doorsill expecting to be crossed. Witches' hair lichen hung in the trees. Spruce budworm bolls stood out against boulders. She looked down the length of the dress. A faint glow of reflected light was evident in its southernmost folds, a differential illusion caused by the darker ground of the uphill behind it. When she turned downhill to the north, the background of needles and stones seemed brighter, and the glow in the skirt dulled. She walked on, ducking around limbs and keeping the light in the dress.

Indentations in the surface of the earth were no longer visible, though protruding white rocks could still be seen. In very steep spots she pushed on the needles first with the side of her foot to see if loose plates of dried duff would slide out. She tried to keep contouring high. She traveled west among spruce and fir.

The static sound of water occurred occasionally, brought up the hill like a chill creeping up from a cold sink. It must have been lifted from the depths of the cleft by the wind, but the wind did not rustle the branches. She kept walking on her toes as elk do.

Suddenly, from the bottom of the cleft, a woman with a strange, low voice said, "Oh!" The voice was serious and surprised.

She stopped in the trail and listened for more.

There was only the distant sound of rocks being clunked by the water.

She continued to walk. The pressure of silence from above began to give way, and from the cleft she could hear murmured conversation. At times one of the people was singing.

She pulled the scarf shut over her breasts. She knotted it at her sternum. She prepared to give way to the others, who were drawing nearer. It was not right for them to be walking so late without a trail. She hoped they were not drunk. She hoped they had not hurt the woman. She felt the fine hairs on the sides of her face rise up, to check for their location. But then their conversation began to fade, and it seemed to be receding, until finally it was engulfed completely by the sound of the water.

She met the stream not far east of the crossing. She picked a way down on stones. At the crossing she balanced on two white stones to fill the flask again. She leaned out and placed her palms on the cold, relaxed surface of the water.

When she reached the clearing at the other side of the crossing, she knelt down and felt the mud. She searched for the people's footprints. She could see dim shapes in the soil. With the tips of her fingers she explored the pitch and the roll of one shape. It was the mark of her own workboot. She touched the cliff edge inside another track. It was the hoofprint of an elk that had stopped to drink. There were no prints of other humans. She crouched again and rinsed her hands in the water. In her ears there was the sound of water rushing, and somewhere upstream in the water, the hollow knock of one stone against another.

On the south-facing slope of the cleft, where there were fewer trees, the whole dress grew slightly brighter again, and she walked more quickly. Goldeneye leaned dimly into the path. The pilled mounds of soil belonging to pocket gophers made darker humps among the darkened meadow flowers.

Her workboots drummed on the earth. The dress had turned a dark blue-gray. The last of the light gave out. She heard the sound of the aspens before she could see them. They made the sound of exhalation. By the time she reached them, the undergrowth of hellebore and larkspur was black. The trail made a gray line through it like a pencil mark on black paper. Only the lighter vertical lines of standing aspen trunks, and fallen humps of trunk on the forest floor, broke the darkness.

She felt her way with her feet. When the trail became steep, she either leaned uphill into it, feeling the stretch of a decreasing angle between shin and top of foot, or tap-stepped down it, testing the earth with the toe of her boot before committing to a step. When a strong branch took up the skirts, she halted, stooped, and disentangled them by touch, sliding fingers between budscale and gather.

To the south the night sky appeared at times as a dark blue glow through the black leaves of aspen. She did not bother looking down.

Everything, even white stone, had turned black. She walked with chin lifted high. Her lips felt the air for approaching limbs. The skin on the sides of her hands, between thumb and forefinger, also became attentive. Soil pressed information into the soles of her feet. When the trail was not too steep, she flapped her feet out flat on the earth, kicking them out from the knee with the ankles loose. Channels in the earth grasped each foot and led it, turning her body from side to side. Divots in the earth swirled her partways around and released her. When a twig tugged the dress, and it was clearly not a strong branch, she bent in a curtsy without losing stride, flicked the skirts up, and curled away.

As she tap-stepped on the trail, she considered this walk to the mountain. Humans and human drama had been anticipated at every turn, and yet, in reality, none had been there. No human had talked in the canyon. No human had spit a red lozenge. It had been a regular day in the wilderness. A rock had said "oh!" to the water. One thigh had shushed another. Wings had dusted pollen off petals. Sun had scrubbed shadows from portals. Wind had swept junkos off meadows. Jewels had been mistaken for candy.

When the wind came, the aspens breathed in and out. Occasional creaks sounded from the forest, which could have been two trees squeaking against each other in the wind or the call of the long-eared owl. The scarf of birds fluttered against her elbows. Her skin had grown cold and alert. A sensuous, beloved feeling arose in her shins where the hems touched them again and again. In the darkness she knew the eyes of the aspen stared out at different levels, like figures on a totem pole. Some of their gazes hit into her. Most of them, though, spread out on higher or lower planes, looking into each others' branches or into the stars off the downhill side of the mountain.

When the light of her lover's small fire became visible through the trees, she thought of her mother. Her mother would be glad she had made it back to the fire. She considered telling her mother, in the letter, about this walk to the mountain. She considered telling her mother about the fabric of her life—the one in which nothing, really, happens.

Reg Saner

CHACO NIGHT

Years ago during a June night in Chaco Canyon I truly believed I had lost any need for the future tense. There, then. My panic, replayed, now seems exaggerated as great dismay in a silent movie, but it hasn't dwindled to merely that. And though it was a night I'd never choose to relive, its effects—perhaps predictably—have become the healthy reverse of morbid.

Therefore the point isn't adventure. In physical terms, the incident was prosaic: I'd been messing around alone in New Mexican desert where nobody was, and got hurt. Nor is the point fear. Yes, I was scared plenty, though "scared" may trivialize what happened inside me. Whatever it was, hours of fear went into it, whereas split-second terror—on highways, for example—is over so fast it hasn't time to dismantle what we prefer to be made of.

It had been a blazing New Mexican afternoon. He was sweating, I was sweating. Backlit by adobe wall, he had stood framed at my car window, politely listening. "I seem to be turned around here. For Chaco Canyon, which road do I want out of Santa Ana?" Given the surroundings, I had supposed his dark skin and black hair were Hispanic; but his accent wasn't. Navajo maybe. Or Pueblo? After all, we were on the Jemez Indian Reservation. My memory of it now is of red dust, red roadcuts—shallow ones—through low rolling hills splotched with desert green; and of the blue cloud shadows moving over them. Beyond simply his badge and neat creases in the beige twill of his shirt, two things have stuck with me ever since: first, that I had liked him on sight; second, that, as he spoke, a subtle amusement in his brown eyes seemed to be answering something in my own look—as if we were sharing the same smile, but differently.

Motor running, my sweaty face looking into his, he answered simply, briefly, politely, said nothing unusual. I listened, thanked him, drove on. We do it all the time.

I fell toward evening. A flake of sandstone came away from cliff that a moment before had been solid rock, and my handhold. When it happened, I had climbed only a little way above the broad shelf that broke my fall. Because I had fallen feet-first, and not far—barely more than twice the height of a man—I needn't have been hurt at all. As it was, I got knocked out, though for how long I'll never know. One moment the sky had been the shady blue/orange of sundown already verging on dusk; then a white flash like round lightning, and the sky I lay looking up at was night.

The reassembly of one's first person singular would be interesting to witness, except that no one who has been hit *hard* awakes with mind enough to preside over such a putting-back-together. As cartoon characters come to, they ask, "What happened?" or "Where am I?" Wordlessly someone not quite "I" groped toward those very things. All I knew was that I was lying twisted, looking up at dark rock I'd never seen before, and a night of stars that wouldn't resolve to a focus. My head ached so tremendously it wasn't a headache but something else. My left side, my left shoulder, my arm, my left hand: hurt. "I fell." Yet it was only some fragmentary "I" who knew that. This partial self also knew the wetness was blood.

The inventory began. Despite hurting, I could untwist, move my body parts. "Nothing broken?" Apparently not, nothing major anyhow, not a hip, not a leg. Then, as I tried to get up, the starry sky and cliff began to veer. The rock was moving, accelerating. I eased back down, the nausea ebbed like a tide going out. So I just lay there, looking up with double vision at stars twinned, yet paying less attention to that aberration than to my own panic. Hair on the left side of my head was sopped with blood. "Jesus!"

I was well off any beaten path or trail. Nobody knew I was even in New Mexico, much less this remote Chaco area. My small pack's one-quart canteen was already half empty. All the first aid stuff which for years I've toted unused—including codeine and other pain pills—was back with my big pack four miles away in my car. Because when simply strolling around I don't carry so much as an aspirin tablet, my resources amounted to that pint of water, some repellent, a much-crumpled bandanna, and—ironically—a small cassette player I'd forgotten to remove from the daypack and leave in the car. Again I tried to rise, again waves of nausea rose with that effort. I lay back down, more frightened than ever. Apparently the exertion produced more bleeding—not profuse, but wet blood added to the panic.

Though my kind of safe adventure can hardly be called "mountaineering," even tromping up and down mountains entails risks clear as arithmetic. Chances of injury may be slim; still, the more time you spend around rock, the likelier. Any rock, big or small, has moved often in its long past and will move again. You want not to be in its way when it does. Perhaps canyons are safer. I don't know. I had slept in Tsegi Canyon one night where another sleeper—who had unrolled his sleeping bag too near the cliff—was drilled through the head by a down-streaking fragment of sandstone. Hardly more than a pebble. From several hundred feet it had reached speed enough that he surely never knew he had died. As an overnight guest I had, in Grand Junction, been offered the bed of a man whose mountain hikes, like mine, had always gone off almost routinely. Then a boulder got him.

That's why, in addition to an assortment of Band-Aids and gauze pads getting more crumpled by the year, with no occasion to use any of them, my homely little kit included pain tablets: for the day I hoped wouldn't happen. Yet I had imagined it, had imagined myself pinned. In some of those fantasies a friend went for help while I swallowed codeine pills and hung on, waiting. In others, there was no friend. I never cross slopes of big talus without imagining how easily, and with how sickening a bone-severing grind, one of those ten-ton slabs could amputate a leg or arm if it suddenly shifted. Unhealthy as that may sound, it had seemed merely a way of remaining alert to possibilities my alertness meant to keep remote.

Toward evening, I had been wandering up by-branches of Chaco, miles from its central complex of restored Anasazi ruins, keeping an eye out for petroglyphs among the many rough ledges of sandstone, with their rust reds and animal forms. Outside its canyons, that part of New Mexico is completely accessible to eyesight. Nothing withheld. Everywhere, an opulence of aridity, tawny sand; a world of solitudes, and their secrecies. The canyon that Chaco Wash has carved there—to fill it again with alluvium—varies from a half mile wide to three-quarters. Compared to Utah's deeper, far narrower canyons which the sun can look into only obliquely, Chaco is both quite shallow and broad. That and its alluvial soil had lent its twenty-mile length to dense settlement by the Anasazi—whose ruined villages are now the sole reason people go there, a past presence making actual cliffs half mythical.

Where runoff from many thousands of years of desert rain has streamed *off* those cliffs my gaze had poured with them, following their bone-dry streakings, their rain sashes of black. But no petroglyphs.

Instead, I paused to watch hundreds of cliff swallows sip at a water catchment which Anasazi hands had chipped troughlike out of a sandstone bench. Late evening sun coming through their wings had produced a translucence making the swallows even less substantial, more weightless than their own feathers. With a steadily nervous fluttering each bird kept its wings erect, extended upward. Quivering and all but airborne while sipping at that puddle, they danced nervously on tiptoe, never settling entirely. It was as if those trembling, backlit lives were afraid of forgetting their avian natures. At least a hundred swallows sipped there, yet not one had entirely left the sky. And each, after drinking, had blurted up toward clusters of mud nests stuck to the nearby cliff wall; to lumpy, bottle-shaped nests with entry holes just wide enough to slip through. One by one each swallow had alighted almost upside down on the lower lip of its nest, then at a wink disappeared inside.

At several ancient Indian cliffsites in the Southwest I'd seen other, much smaller catchments where, in the black rain-path marked by streakings, prehistoric inhabitants had hollowed small basins in stone shelves. Up cliff walls I'd also seen vertical dimplings where villagers long ago carved footholds for ascending to squash and corn and bean plots above their settlements. The holds had always looked precariously feasible, provided you took your time and used both hands, though

Anasazi farmers and their women must've often ascended while en-
cumbered with baskets of corn, water pots, firewood, dead game such
as jackrabbits or quail.

In Chaco I had more than once taken long, speculative looks at
the "escalade" now called "the Pintada stair"—and let it go at that. In
fact, a day or two before my fall, I had stopped at the campsite of a
French couple at the mouth of Canyon de Chelly. They were doing a
rock climbing tour of the Southwest. Having just come from Joshua
Tree National Monument, they would visit buttes at the Arizona/Utah
border before going further north for some slickrock climbs outside of
Moab. "We tried those stairs at Chaco," the woman told me, "but they
were not easy."

Her muscular thighs and calves, and her experience as a technical
climber, had made "not easy" hard to believe. On reflection, however, I
realized that such steps as we see today must have become—in the nine
or more centuries between us and their daily use—eroded enough to
make ascent trickier than when Anasazi farmers had first hacked them
out. Up Butler Wash, for example, west of Monticello, Utah, when
sunlight rakes the sandstone walls at just the right angle, you can spot
more than one set of Anasazi footholds—though what they lead to
nowadays are further plateaus of sandstone scraggled hither and yon
with piñon pine, thorny shocks of blackbrush, yucca clumps, cliff rose;
plus the inevitable, ubiquitous juniper. A lot of nothing? Maybe so,
from our point of view; but food, firewood, roof traves, hoe handles,
digging sticks, baskets, sandals, rope, and twine to the Anasazi, for
whom those clifftop plateaus of hardpan were—incredible as it now
seems—part of the Fourth World, the land long promised.

My impulse to ascend, to put a hand where so many Anasazi hands
had once rested, put my own foot exactly where their sandaled feet by
the thousands once poised, had never quite overcome the timidity calling itself "good judgment." Then in Chaco it did.

Chaco sandstone spalls away in natural cleavages that lend themselves to masonry. Five-story chunks can and do break from its cliffs.
Though their sheared faces look clean as yesterday, archeologists have
proven that—to cite merely an instance—one such monolith at the edge
of the spectacular ruin called Pueblo Bonito had separated from its par-

ent rock close to ten centuries ago, but hadn't toppled. Already in pre-historic times its free-standing form had threatened parts of that pueblo, so Anasazi builders tried to check erosion at its base. As metaphysical reinforcement, prayer sticks had been buried there to induce Anasazi spirits to stave off that monolith's grand collapse—which they did, till it finally let go in 1941.

What's more, the foot of every such cliff in the Southwest is littered with reminders that stone can flake away. And if shearing and flaking over time spans geological isn't the same as every ten minutes, those clues should nonetheless have kept my timidity at full strength.

Not so. Having come upon quite a feasible set of Anasazi hand-holds and footholds that had been there since the end of Europe's Dark Ages, I actually tried them. And had fallen. But that memory is half recollection, half supposition. It's what "must have happened"—because parts of "after" are still lost to me, as well as phases of "before." The gaps are less like page-leaps in a mismade book than a quirkily spliced film. Your blink says, "They must've cut something there," but you've no idea what it was, except for theme: life as it almost wasn't.

Even unhurt, climbing back down to Chaco Canyon's floor in pitch darkness wasn't anything I'd have cared to attempt; dizziness made it impossible. There I was, eighty miles from a doctor, and the first thirty, dirt road. Time to time, I watched the twink of a jet's wing lights drawing its whisper across the night sky. If I lasted till morning and still couldn't move about, dehydration would finish me off in two days, three at the most. You can't simply will to do without water.

The fact is, however, it didn't seem I'd live long enough to dehydrate. The next dawn would happen without me.

Wavelike episodes of numbness and tingling were pervading my upper body as far as the lips. Frightened, I had kept clenching and un-clenching both hands, testing my ability to move feet and toes. The left leg and side, especially the buttock muscles and thigh, had begun to spasm. My heart—whose resting pulse earlier that summer had been as low as forty-one—was now beating arrhythmically and very hard, al-most like blows with a fist. "You're panicked," I had told myself, "calm down, breathe deeply." I inhaled deliberately slowly, exhaled slowly. I tried not to think beyond "air in, air out." It actually helped. But the leg spasms continued, at intervals of maybe twenty minutes. The way my pounding heart kept shaking my body terrified me. When one of my hands chanced to pause on my chest or abdomen, or even my groin, the jarring felt so alarmingly ominous I at once moved the hand. The heart no longer beat: it simply whammed. And kept whamming. As if a large animal were throwing itself again and again at a door.

Out of an almost nil understanding of the neural system, my guess was "head injury." Brain signals were misfiring. Otherwise, why would my left side be spasming like a dead frog given galvanic shocks in the lab? And how long could *such* a heart rate stay well over a hundred beats a minute? After a certain time wouldn't it just quit? A cracked skull had thus seemed all the likelier.

Intervals of twenty minutes or so would elapse between episodes. During the lull, hope crept back. Then the next onset would rape me with fresh panic. And since nausea attacked every time I tried lifting my head, I felt real despair. So I just lay helpless. "Maybe I'll feel better after a while." But the realist in me said, "This is the place you've wondered about, wondering where you'd be. The road ends here. Now you know what it looks like."

So I lay that way, looking up at a night sky of stars whose double- ness, over hours, closed by degrees to a blur. Thinking, trying not to think thoughts in which life and death trade places, I'd ask myself "How much of this do I belong to?" and I'd realize, "All of it." The spasms would lessen their intensity, take longer to recur, and I'd say, "I'm better, maybe it's passing." The tingling and numbness would wane. Then my left leg and thigh would start thrashing about, muscles of the left buttock would spasm with them, till my whole body throbbed violently, as if I were being driven fast over rough road. That happened many times. In the longer interims I'd think, "It's better now," while aware how wishful that was. Then the next onslaught. Each new wave of spasming laid morale even lower. Finally I had to face what seemed inevitable: "I'm not going to get out of this. I'm going to die."

Hair on my head's left side was messed with blood half-congealed, the left shoulder and back of my chambray shirt felt sticky, but the bleeding had apparently all but stopped. Yet for a long while I was afraid to let my fingers explore. If . . . but no, the idea sickened me. I wouldn't let my hand touch there; wanted to know, but—especially because I was alone—couldn't bear to know, not yet.

Deep fear carries its adrenaline charge only so long. Then something else sets in—not so much "resignation" as realizing, "No use kidding yourself." My left side felt bunged up, not broken; but my heart kept whamming away. My head hurt more than I had believed anything could. As my mind returned to something like itself, somehow it was aware that it was still more than half stunned. Meanwhile, "I didn't know" recurred, moaning, like a grievance. "I didn't know anybody could be hit that hard." "I didn't know anything could hurt so much. Why doesn't a head spatter open?" My dismay stuck at that same level of unbelief: "I didn't know you could be hit so hard and not be killed." "I didn't know I could hurt this much." Again and again.

For how long? An hour? Two hours? My medical expertise was close to a minus sum. I remembered only that nausea can go with skull fractures, and that people are kept "for observation" because the worst effects may take a while to set in. Finally, despite the headache, I had tried a few tongue twisters aloud. "Peter Piper picked a peck of pickled peppers" should've made me laugh. It did no such thing. The ludicrousness was purely sardonic, and those words simply a tool about which only one thing mattered: could I say them? Was there brain damage? The jaw ached too much to say anything fluently. Mouthing words aloud felt like chewing harness leather. Not only that; I discovered my tongue had been cut, and that I'd chipped a couple of teeth in the left jaw. I tried remembering the English words to one or two short poems by Japanese poets, and found I could mentally say them. I tried remembering each room of the big house I grew up in. I tried naming as many of the NFL's back-up quarterbacks as I could: Kubiak, Tomzchek, Young, Hilger, Kramer, DeBerg, Herrmann, and so forth. That too, OK. Then lost sight of myself.

That's how the night had gone. I'd be staring up at stars, shivering, then nothing. After which, even to close my eyes seemed dangerous. With what felt like physical effort I fought off unconsciousness: to keep the universe *there*. At one point it was as if a spider's filament had been spun from each star to a tumpline round my head, its thinness unbreakably strong. Each star was tied by such a filament to a thousand stars unknown, in cosmic space beyond it, and each of those tied to other thousands, and so on, indefinitely outward. Despite my repeated lapses, the illusion persisted. By willed effort I *had to pull* back, continuously, against every star's inclination to drift away into some high, distant, and final dispersion.

When I came to, the stars would have moved, but not much, so intervals of sleep or unconsciousness must've been short. And the sleep of nervous exhaustion was indeed a possibility, because in the previous several days I had spent a ton of physical energy. From my pack I managed after much grunting and tugging to pull out a Gortex parka, which helped surprisingly to cut down the chill. However, that cost me. Getting it on produced appalling dizziness. At times when my vision seemed to be closing from its periphery inward, my heart rate surged. Runaway cowardice? I didn't care. Even if the cardiac muscles didn't self-destruct, even if their seizures and pounding lasted till morning, lack of water would guarantee the final result. Vertigo would make climbing down to the canyon floor or up to the rim out of the question. Under New Mexican summer sun, the last rain-filled hollow would dry up. The shelf that had saved me would become a rock oven. The feel was something like, "Well, this time you've done it. You won't get out of this one."

It had seemed that where I lay, right there, was indeed the spot vaguely named even as we shrug it off in the phrase "sooner or later." Yet most lifetimes do learn what it looks like. Billions of persons have learned it—the ground their steps had all that time been leading them toward. Now I had.

And now, with my life about to end, I could see it wasn't complete at all. It would just stop. More happenstantial than intended, patternless, no real structure, it had filled itself with its own randomness. Its two or three biggest decisions hadn't been rationally made; they had been emotions, impulses. Given a second chance, I'd have done so much differently!—yet with similar results. All the words I had ever spoken now streamed past my inner ear like one long word made of run-together nonsense syllables. Nor was that a judgment, an evaluation. It had seemed a physical fact, as certain as when the fingers let go, a held pebble drops. Not a word I had ever said mattered, *only what I might have said*. Retrospectively, my effort at what I'd thought was a life seemed just oddments that added up to . . . nothing much. Not bad, not good, just me.

The sandstone stratum that had broken my fall had, itself, been laid down countless millions of years ago. Even while its stone warmed my back and the backs of my calves with night radiations giving up the day's heat, the life I contained felt less substantial than smoke. But I had felt substantial, like everyone, having turned away from the dumb truth of stone, the fathomless annals *any* stone implies. From all that time alive in dead matter, I had turned, as one must, in order to live at all. Straight overhead the ghostly, galactic glow of the Milky Way told the same story: "You weren't. Are. Won't be." And that would hold true for longer than even its fires could reach. Cassiopeia's "W," below and to the right of Polaris. The barely visible Pleiades at the sky's zenith. Orion to the south, halfway up the same sky . . . and a hundred hundred thousand others. Their great swarms. Bonfires, fuel dumps. Those nearest and brightest, most personal. Others, fainting at their own distance.

Under their gaze, Chaco's ruined dunes had roved for millions of windblown years, had hardened to stone, been buried, had been thrust again into starlight by crustal collisions; had again been eaten to rejected cathedrals.

That starlight was just now my summer sky, with an immense fragrance of lives not ours, out there beyond the limits of visibility. I thought, "If anyone ever returned from oblivion this would be his first memory." But isn't, because nobody does.

Knowing "each life must die" had brought not the slightest consolation. On the contrary, that was nearly worst of all. Death made of our planet only a holding tank from which, one by one, everyone is effaced. Nor did it bother me that my friends' features would, next morning, be alive when my own had congealed. I wanted everybody alive to go on living. That is, wanted it as much as I could want. My altruism gland had numbed. For family and relatives, for my wife and sons I *should* have wished much that I was empty of. I simply thought, "Well, the world will go on being the world, they'll just have to cope. And they will. People do." My sons would, in part, become me just as I had become my own father, for better and worse, dearer and more recognizably so the longer gone. It had taken twenty years of his death for me to turn and finally see who he was. It didn't matter; nor matter that my sons would need years to see me. I didn't care. Didn't care what they might see or fail to see, good or bad. It had indeed felt strange to realize that both my sons would perhaps live to a great age, and go through this, and die. Surely that had mattered? Here, today, I can't be sure it had.

Instead I suspect it had felt like simply the way things are. With our whole species swept over an edge denying even brief continuity, geological and human history had seemed a pathetic flicker compared with the furiously burning stars whose light kept arriving at my up-turned face. Though they too were mortal, in the face of their stellar immensities mere planets lacked duration enough to matter. All of it over the edge. It would fall forever.

At the same time, and to my considerable surprise, I saw that despite its fits and seasons of self-contrived turmoil, my life had been blessed. Extraordinarily so. From Chaco's night-long revelations, that had been perhaps the strangest of all. Facing its death, a lifetime had thrown aside its posturing and now stood revealed as what it added up to: fortunate, happy.

But of course, "The Tao you can Tao is not the Tao. The name you can name is not the name." So too the death we can talk about has nothing to do with the death anyone really dies. What I felt myself being drained away into that night bears no relation to anything I'd ever read or heard or thought of. It was neither logical nor self-consistent. Dark, vaporous, without edges. Death was nothing whatever—whose enormousness terrified me.

I saw that poets and novelists maundering or intoning about "death" haven't a clue. Nobody on this side of it has, nor do I; not now. I just know how that one night felt, alone, with *hours* to look straight at the real. I remember enough to know that "death" in literature may be literature, or it may be a writer's cheapest trick, but it isn't remotely like what I saw—which cannot be talked about. Literary death gets talked of on paper, which will put up with anything. Inertness of the body is nothing. That's easily and often eerily described; and is trivial. On the other hand, to feel everything past and to come, the pattern everything makes, the power and delicacy of creation simply vanish as if none of it ever had been—that hit my dumbstruck awareness like a dark comet.

Even so, my feelings had been at odds with themselves, and with logic. In one moment I had felt that "the world would go on being the world"; in another moment I knew it would not be "as if" the universe died when I did. In all its tangibility it would empty, be sucked from time, forward and backwards. Utterly. That filled me with an anger giving way to deep grief at the canceling of all creation retroactively. I had never dreamed anything so hideous could happen. Our cells, senses, suppositions had lied to us. There would be no world to "leave behind." Remembering it now as delusion doesn't produce in me the slightest reaction. Back there it felt real, thus sickening.

At a certain point, during that long night, often as my mind formed the words, "I'll . . ." an irony mocked the futurity in "will." Feeling I had lost any use for the future tense wasn't, as it is now, a point in grammar. Through losing my use for the habitual "I'll," my face got shoved into life's very essence, taken from me. I had discovered how continuously each human moment leans toward the next, preferring to travel rather than arrive. Whenever I doubt my own fear that night at Chaco, I have only to recall how hair stood up on my skin as a thought begun with "I will . . ." or "I'll . . ." whimpered to silence. I lay at the end of possibility. Thus "I will" had left me, and left in its place an awareness: every thought we have implies a presumption we can't do without, the one called "tomorrow." We eat, drink, and clothe ourselves in it. How conceptual it sounds, "losing the future tense." To feel I *had* lost it—that was far and away the very worst single moment I have ever known.

If my heart's serial explosions, I had told myself, were mainly panic or some peculiar sort of anxiety seizure, music might help. Might at least alter the aloneness. I fumbled the tape player and earphones from my pack, pressed the play button, heard Sonny Stitt's alto sax continue, midnote, on "Spanish Harlem." It was welcome yet bizarre, unsettling. I was listening to a roomful of 1975, a reed player, his guitarist, drummer, bassist, his two trumpets, all back there in some New York recording studio, a few years before Stitt himself had died of a heart attack. "The Way We Were," "Funky Interlude," "Never Can Say Goodbye." I tried believing it was music, but in my state it wasn't, just human sounds, recorded ones, barely better than nothing. Also, a shade worse than nothing. Still, I listened. "Too bad Sonny Stitt isn't around any more. Too bad we all . . ."

Too bad? In the context of New Mexico's tremendous space, of the solitude of that canyon, under a sky whose depths sparkled with stars, nobody's living or dying—compared with even silicon grains in the very sandstone I lay on—lasts long enough to have lasted at all, much less "too bad." I heard fellow animals doing peppery Afro-Cuban things with time. It felt weird, dissonant, wasn't really the company I wanted to feel it was.

Maybe the cassette's other side would feel better, a Charlie Byrd album titled *Top Hat*. Battery-fade began distorting Byrd's acoustic guitar to a bass viol. Not good. If the music stopped, that would be the worst sort of omen. In my pack were extra batteries. When they too began to lose energy, I put the tape player aside. Better not to listen than to hear the notes slowly stall, come to a standstill.

Another awareness then stunned me: the JVC player, a favorite possession, wasn't really mine any more. By morning neither it nor my pack, nor my watch, nor my wallet. Nor my boots, nor even my bloody shirt. The body inside them wouldn't be mine.

In imagination he stood over my face. The enormous change in me was invisible to him; he hadn't the slightest recollection of our eyes ever having looked into each other. By the light of midmorning he and his patrolman sidekick were discussing what must've happened. The buddy, an Anglo, pulled my wallet out from under me and was giving it a fast, professional rundown. He slid forth the Colorado driver's license, pinned it under the clip on his board, jotted down its relevant data. He then opened the wallet wide to show its folding money to his dark-haired partner: two twenties, a ten, a few ones. Each drew out a twenty, leaving the rest.

When the dark-haired officer, his chin and jaw freshly shaven, his tan shirt still morning-fresh, bent to pick up the tape player, I could hear his leather gear creak. Hefting the mechanism, he turned it over in his hands, appraising.

His pal's shrug said, "You want it, it's yours."

The other nodded, stuffing the player in his pocket, the earphones inside his shirt. "Yeah," he said, "it's a good one. You can tell just by the feel."

That theft infuriated me. Yet I still liked him. He might as well take it.

My fantasy made no sense. And there he was, the New Mexican cop who'd given me directions way back on the Jemez Reservation. He had tested my right thigh with the toe of his shoe, while the other presided over my face, his own features blocked from view by the clipboard. He was filling in blanks on his report: where found, when found, how found. What found with. But of course state troopers aren't rangers. They never get more than a hundred yards from their patrol cars. My Navajo/Pueblo cop wouldn't be out footing it along trails. That didn't stop me imagining his shoe nudging my body.

My terminal mirage also included ants, desert ravens. Liking an Indian cop hadn't altered my preference: I'd rather be nibbled away by more straightforward animals than my own kind, however small and swarming. Even turkey vultures would be some consolation.

It was then I had decided that if I were going to die I'd at least die looking up at those stars. Clear night, the galaxy in full bloom, no town glow to kill it. And the stars, as usual, "unreal"; yet familiar and fresh, the undiminished constellations of once-upon-a-time. Out of their fire-wealth I made one star mine, no idea of its name, just a bright one; not Altair certainly, not Vega, just one more incandescence among our galaxy's 200 billion suns, among the estimated 100 billion *major* galaxies. All that out there; me, here. Except, where's "here"? Lifelong, it had been the single thing I most wanted to know.

Maybe the thing I'd been truest to was that curiosity. From early boyhood, stars had fascinated me. The telescope I had pieced together of magnifying glass, eyeglass lens, cardboard tubing and black friction tape hadn't been the success of boy geniuses in movies. It had taught me, by way of rainbowing the moon, only that chromatic aberration— avoidable with better lenses—has a beauty of its own. Summer stars had been my furthest-out boyhood adventure. Even hurt and shivering, therefore, I had been able to realize my good luck: What better place than here in Chaco Canyon, among so many thousand Anasazi? The nearness of their own various deaths seemed company worth having. Though I knew they were fossil dust, I felt myself inside what was left of their passage. And what better way to go than looking at stars I had wondered at and loved all my life? "No better way, no better time, no better place. So be it." And that had been my breakthrough.

I no longer felt sorry for myself. I was alone, yes; but that's how dying gets done. I had stopped wallowing in self-pity. This thing would have to be gone through sooner or later. Conditions *then*—would they be more to my liking? Surely not. To die alone, surrounded by South-western space, under stars . . . no, what lay down the road wasn't likely to improve on that. I was glad I had collected all those sunrises. Each had been a sort of unrepeatable virtue no life could embody or imitate, beyond watching it happen.

Having learned I could face my extinction without freaking out, I had relaxed my deepest conviction enough to utter a sort of testimony: "Lord of the center and the edge, of the magpie, the springtail, the neu-ron, the spruce cone, I'm grateful for my life. I'm glad I had it. I was a lucky man."

Had I felt I owed creation some final assent? Obviously, the cosmos doesn't give a damn. But I must've felt, "We're humans, we ought to say something." It had seemed fitting. Life and consciousness being so exceedingly rare in this cosmos, the least I could do was to ac-knowledge having been lent them. I knew there was nobody not equally mortal out there. I spoke to it anyway.

But "Lord" had felt vaguely disloyal, sinful. "Lord" isn't a person. Creation doesn't "see," doesn't "hear," doesn't "know." Radiant, inex-haustible, it makes and unmakes; raises up, crushes flat. Woos into exis-tence, then splats. Endless smithereens. Doesn't "care," doesn't "love." Is. Should I therefore have said simply, "Dear Is"? No, not "dear." Is.

If at the time I had felt deeply moved, it was not because I verged on "meeting my maker." I verged on a black vacuum. So were my words a small ceremony for my own disappearance? No, they really had been for whatever underlies the design that the whole shebang makes and floats on, or within. Because English lacks a pronoun for which no antecedent is conceivable, "Lord" was the name I had found myself saying. That archaic choice notwithstanding, I had said what I meant.

No longer panicked, I began to feel hope enough to be superstitious about losing the particular star I had made "mine." As Earth turned me toward morning, the cliff overhead had been about to occlude it. I couldn't let it happen. My solution: give that star leave to go, as if its disappearance had my permission; then quickly choose another till it too neared the cliff rim—whereupon I had given it leave, had again chosen, and so forth. Any straw seemed worth grasping toward. As for life, I hadn't known I loved it so hugely, frantically.

Despite desert chill and shivering uncontrollably for long periods, despite headache, bashed up left side, clotted scalp, bitten tongue, I began to take heart a little. Without my noticing, blurred stars had resolved themselves from so many twins to sharp points. Similarly, my heart rate had slowed, the spasms had lessened so gradually I can't say when the last one occurred. I do remember, however, that when it seemed dawn might happen again, my mind had already grown suspicious of its own fears. How could a dying man think so busily about so many sorts of things? I had simply fallen and lacerated my scalp, not broken my skull. Dizziness and nausea were the effects of severe concussion.

As for the muscle spasms, my chronic back trouble might've been thrown into fast forward by the jolting impact of the fall. Any number of lower-spine, pinched-nerve possibilities could have triggered them.

Dawn was too much consolation to entertain more than skeptically—like hardly daring to believe bad weather is finally beginning to lift. When light seemed less than an hour away, I had sat up every now and again without feeling woozy, except for my imagination vaguely mimicking the nausea I was afraid of. Come sunrise, downclimbing might not be so impossible. For the first time I stopped fighting to stay conscious. Till then I seem to have thought death might come if I weren't looking. I fell asleep, neither well nor deeply, and, a half-hour before dawn woke to the barking of coyotes. And to cries of piñon jays. Exhausted, I welcomed daybreak but without joy. Instead I felt dirtied, humiliated by my fear, glad only to be rid of it; like a dog soldier hearing his relief approach after a miserable stint of guard duty.

Retrospect suggests that at Chaco my personal being must have actually touched something like the nothingness we have a word for, but no meaning. Though I don't understand it now, I *thought* I did then. My fear at touching it wasn't physical. Somehow it was worse, far worse than anything that can happen to one's body, which, paradoxically, is our sole receptor for that sort of intuition.

Receptor? No, more. One's body is it. At Chaco I had seen that my own should have been better cherished, not treated like a draft animal. So my body/mind had resolved I should take better care of it, out of gratitude for years of good service.

Within three days, however, after minor stitchwork in the emergency room at Farmington, New Mexico, that night's immediacy had already begun to wane. Old turns of mind soon crawled out from their hiding places. Another resolve had been, if I survived, to behave wisely. Having seen what I had seen, henceforth I could not help living with the clarity of a sage, ever after. But that too gradually hazed over. Like hundred-mile-distant ridgelines, my intended reforms grew to be only occasionally visible, and then only if I shaded my eyes and squinted far into my past—as if trying to actually live by what I had seen might not be wise, or for me anyhow, even possible.

At the time, there had been something about both Sonny Stitt's tenor sax and the Charlie Byrd pieces which had felt dangerous, eerie. It puzzles me therefore that to this day I can bear listening to that same cassette almost indifferently. Why haven't I chucked it? Because its music retains a doubleness I want never to lose? Just as the scar from a considerable gash in my scalp isn't visible, just as hair shaved away the better to suture the wound has now regrown, so too has the living tissue of my human complacency regenerated. Once more I'm encoded to fear dying and to sense I never will.

Yet an otherwise banal moment may all at once suffuse me with strangeness when I realize: "This is a day I didn't think I'd have." All the days since have been those. At any odd moment, a room's most prosaic object—a terra-cotta pot, for example—may say: "This light from red clay is light you might not have been around for."

If Chaco gave me that, it also gave me the dark twin to go with it: "nothing matters." In a healthy sense, the latter realization doesn't cancel its sibling. Their two ways of looking differently at the same thing may amount to no more than seeing the evanescence of what's cherishable—except that to leave one's own body out of what went into its deepest knowledge yields a wisdom thin as paper. It takes the actual, that full flood of bodily terror, long continued, to widen the pupil of one's inner eye. Once it has, we forget—though never completely, and rarely for long. Out of the trivial chaos of an afternoon, rain on a manhole cover may suddenly give back the sweetness of existing.

The glossy black tip on a magpie's wingfeather can do it. Checking the body for deer ticks can suddenly bathe one's calves and thighs with gratitude. Iridescence in sun-stricken paint on old cars. Sweetness of the plainest, most everyday faces. Richness of one's boredoms, their motions and textures. Of a bank teller's eyes that, for a half-second, look into mine with normal and therefore intricate brilliance.

Stephen Trimble

ON THE BACK OF THE DRAGON

The crack of thunder snapped me awake. I reached for my bathrobe and scuffed into slippers and walked outside to look up at the red cliff that soared away into the darkness. No rain yet.

The weather had been strange last night, cloudy and heavy, more like Massachusetts than Utah. I didn't like weather like this, and I didn't like rain.

More heat lightning crackled far up the canyon, dendritic sparks traced against the clouds. Then a big bolt again struck the rim. The afterimage floated inside my eyes. The musky tang of ozone filled my mouth and nose. I recoiled into the doorway and whooped nervously in chorus with the roll of thunder. All the while, I kept my eyes as wide open as possible. I felt like a camera shutter locked open for a long time exposure, waiting for the next high-voltage zigzag to flash onto the emulsion.

Footfalls came from the sandy track that led up to the house from the road. Lillian. As I sensed her lean shape dark against the white of the drive, she spoke.

"I knew you'd be out here, Doc. I was on the terrace at the lodge, but this is too good to watch alone. Besides, you have the best spot for rimfalls in the whole canyon."

"God, woman. Come over here."

I wrapped my arm around her shoulders and held on, anchoring myself to her warmth. Thank heavens she came. I looked up again at the sky, and felt the curve of her upper arm, the span of her back through her canvas coat. Lillian leaned into me. She put her arm around my waist. But she kept her eyes up, searching the rims, placing a gentle boundary on our intimacy.

This was as close as we had been since I moved to Blossom. One month, and we were standing in the dark together waiting for lightning, hoping for rimfalls. What will come next?

The rain came next. The first drops splattered into the dust of the drive, loosening the aroma of the canyon the way a few drops of water release the bouquet of scotch. The air smelled like weeks and months and years of dust and ground rock. The storm set free the smell of dryness.

The pace quickened, the raindrops fused into sheets, and water superseded air as the medium filling the canyon. A hint of detail appeared as dawn light diffused into the gorge—enough to show us the rimfalls. My terrors receded as the blackness faded.

"There!" Lillian spotted the first feathery plunge in the neighboring alcove downcanyon.

"Over there, too—across the canyon." I nodded toward the opposite rim where three separate falls lipped over three low points, spilling toward the river. All the water that fell from the sky poured down off the slickrock, a trickle in every crack, falling free from the rim in cataracts the rich colors of the layered formations, brick-red Wingate, purple Chinle, tawny orange Entrada.

Ever since graduate school thirty years ago, when I first read John Wesley Powell's descriptions of flash floods and rimfalls, "rivers of bright red mud, leaping over the walls," I had yearned to see these dreamlike torrents. I had been out to visit Lillian and her family before the war, but the storms always struck in the dark or when I was off in the mountains or out on the range. I had never been here in the canyon at exactly the right time.

I started sifting my memories, looking for a particular image, a distinction the Navajos made between male and female rain. After years of teaching, I pictured my brain like a row of poorly organized and overflowing filing cabinets. A lot of information lay buried in there, but it was sometimes hard to retrieve.

A crash of thunder rattled me back to the canyon. The rain took me away again, to Katharine and Wesley, to the night at the pond, rain streaming off me, desperate to find a flicker of movement in their still faces.

In dreams I see them, trapped in the car. Sobbing, I scream at

Katharine, "You killed my son!" I run to her. "I've lost you." And then, "Why you? Why Wesley? Why not me?" I still ask. Every time. In dreams.

I slumped a little against Lillian in the doorway. I shivered.

She turned to me. "Are you all right?"

I nodded. "You know what I'm thinking," I said.

She tightened her grip around me.

The rain misted us, but the porch roof blocked the full force of the downpour. Two streams ran around the little bluff where the cabin perched, seething through the rabbitbrush and willows, running down into the river.

Jacob's River rose quickly, brimful in no more than fifteen minutes. Lillian's family called it The Jake—a perfect sample of the Burns family's take on this place they had made their home, a quicker, wittier vocabulary than the one used by the Mormons who stolidly planted themselves here in the rocks of southern Utah a few decades before them. The Burns's lodge made an ideal touchstone in the wilderness. They had helped me buy my little cabin. They were becoming my family now. All of this made Blossom a comfortable place to ease into, to come back from the darkness. It was as far from rain as I could go, and yet here was the rain again, still terrifying.

"Doc." Lillian's voice brought me back. She spoke sharply to be heard over the storm. "Let's walk down to Jennie Thunder's. We'll be able to look for more rimfalls. I doubt she needs any rescuing, but she'll surely have something interesting to say about this storm."

Downcanyon, the old Paiute healer's cabin was on a rise, a small one. I looked toward the river, now up and over the road. But the trail along the cliff should still be passable.

"I'll get dressed," I said. Lillian followed me into the kitchen.

She sat and fidgeted with my insect-collecting gear on the table, pins and paraffin and small boxes pleasing to handle. I went back into the bedroom, toweled off the film of warm rain with my robe, and began to pull on my clothes. A wool coat and straw hat would have to do. My Massachusetts rain gear still lay buried somewhere in a storage box.

The rain drummed on the roof. I sat on the bed and worked on my boot laces with stiff fingers. Male rain. That's the image. The Navajos understand the connection between rain and fertility, rain and sex.

The flickers of the buildup are like foreplay. Lightning bolts begin the thrust toward climax. And the driving rain is surely orgasm, or, at least, male orgasm.

The smell of the rain, the wetness. Katharine and I often made love on rainy afternoons, when neither of us had to teach, when Wesley was in school. She lay on our bed against the white sheets. Outside, female rain fell on New England, gentle, prolonged. You could see the grass green, the flowers shoot up. Afterward came the deep peace, the sleep that follows lovemaking.

In these canyons, though, climax is sustained. Rimfalls come nosing over the cliffs. Flash floods build and roar down washes. This is a raucous and heady coming, a screamer. The release is physical, connected with the relaxation of the electric air. And psychological, after the keyed-up interval of the storm.

I finished my second boot. I reached out onto the sheets for Katharine.

"Move it, Doc," Lillian said. She was peering out the south window. "The river is still rising." And then, "How are you doing with all this water?"

"I'm okay" was all I could muster.

The red roil of the Utah stormwaters did feel different. Full of the threatening energy of the storm but not the sucking evil that took my family. New England water is bottomless. Here the floodwaters swirl over sand and rock. The warmth and solidity of the earth underneath promise an end to it all.

Together, Lillian and I entered the storm. It was full light now. We dashed for the shelter of the cliff like infantry troops moving on an enemy trench. I had the same tense cramps an infantryman would have.

Jennie Thunder's alcove was a third of a mile downcanyon—the last irrigable land at the end of the road, a pause before the gorge of Jacob's River narrowed to plunge into the heart of the Black Dragon Cliffs.

Jennie had moved here from her hermitage high in the Henry Mountains when her arthritis began to make winters difficult. With the help of the Burnses, she built her cabin below the Black Dragon itself, the painted beast that gave the cliffs their name. I always thought of Jennie Thunder as the guardian spirit of the canyon.

The path close along the cliff was virtually dry. We moved down-canyon, walking purposefully. Lillian led.

I watched her weave between boulders and duck under overhangs and low cottonwood branches. She moved along the trail with the methodical and efficient care of a craftsperson, like the skilled pilot that she was. As she passed each panel of petroglyphs, the bug-eyed and head-dressed creatures carved by long-ago shamans, she touched the rock near them softly.

Lillian's beauty was unceremonious and robust. She kept her jaw forward, giving the clean lines of her nose, her cleft chin, and the strength of her cheekbones and brows a surprising elegance. She often broke this smoothness by throwing back her head of auburn hair and turning loose a deep-throated laugh full of joy, irony, and intelligence.

As she had aged, she'd stayed lean. I liked the fact that she looked older. Grayer. A little more weathered.

Lillian had come to Powell College as a student in 1926, a slim young woman who knew more about the world than she should for someone from such a backwater. The Burns family had given her a ceaseless curiosity and a power to observe that complemented her rural physical ease and forthrightness. Her strength drew me. Even at the beginning, long before Katharine, it was hard to maintain my professorial distance.

I stopped for a moment to reach up and rub my neck. I was suddenly aware of my skin, the warmth of it, the soft hollows between tense muscles. I remembered the touch of a woman's hand. I realized I was imagining Lillian's touch, not remembering Katharine's. It made me both exhilarated and uncomfortable.

Overhangs protected us until we reached Buffaloberry Canyon. The normally dry tributary was surging over the trail, cutting through sandy banks usually barely noticeable. As wild as it seemed, Lillian was already on the other side. She turned and yelled at me, "Come on. Jump onto that rock and you won't even get your boots wet!"

I jumped. The stone was farther than I thought. But I landed solidly, pushed off with the right bounce, and reached Lillian without a dunking. Not bad for a short, increasingly creaky, sixty-two-year-old retired professor.

"You make a good adventurer, Doc," she said. "Sam Singermann: the John Wesley Powell of 1950." We touched each other lightly on the forearms, a gesture that surprised me with its tenderness.

"Let's go," I said. "Rain never bothered Major Powell. It shouldn't bother Professor Singermann, either."

Around a last buttress, we came into Jennie Thunder's alcove to see a red pouroff cascading over the curve of cliff that backed her bend of the river. It looked like the classic images of Vernal Falls at Yosemite, broader than most western waterfalls, but the wrong color, like a startling scene crayoned by a toddler, brown sky, black shrubs, water the color of smoked salmon.

I looked past Lillian to Jennie Thunder's house on a ledgy rise above the branching arroyo channels leading outward from the cliffs. A melange of rockwork, logs, adobe chinking, with a tarpaper-covered plywood roof, it looked like a cliff dwelling, updated.

Jennie Thunder stood on the lip of her hill, the rain drenching her. A large fire, now smoldering, lay at her feet. As always, she wore a gingham dress, an apron, and a sweater. Her heavy braid of gray-white hair looked like a basketmaking material she had gathered in the marshes— substantial and alive. Rain streamed over her quiet face. A broad nose, deeply hooded eyes, wide mouth, deep lines framing all these. Her body was made for the long haul, like a weathered boulder. She was smiling, in a kind of rapture, into the downpour, up into the alcove, toward the Black Dragon.

A woman of the desert, reveling in rain. One look at her solidness, her face, her home, her clear connection with ancestral voices, and I understood the certainty of her self-sufficiency. We were invading her privacy.

Her alcove itself was exceptional, an arc of sandstone as graceful and sheltering as the inside curve of an egg. My eye went first to the rim, then downward over the fractures and streaks and stains to the base of the cliff.

There, back behind a huge boulder, a protected slab of sandstone had served as a gritty canvas for the ancient artists.

I thought of the line of broad-shouldered beings dancing across the wall up there as Jennie Thunder's kin, celebrating the rain along with her. They were painted the colors of dried blood: vermilion, purple, brown, cinnamon. One, twice life-size, held a big-handed arm upward, balancing a delicately drawn spray of Indian ricegrass on its middle finger. Small bighorn sheep walked along the arm raised to the sky.

Down the row, an earringed female silhouette stood between a frame of ricegrass bouquets and flying birds. The birds were stylized, but with their motionless hovering, I always thought of them as hummingbirds.

To the right of the medicine people, a dragon flew across the cliff. Dragon was the only word for the creature. Lanky legs, long upright neck, horns, a serpent's tail, and two billowing bat-wings. All drawn in black, with a red eye.

I pictured the beast. I saw my wife and son in its talons, its wings undulating, the limp bodies of Katharine and Wesley rising and falling with the rhythm of its flight. The Dragon felt implacable, silent, and strong, inexhaustibly strong. The other painted figures felt as kind as Jennie Thunder, and together the rock beings and the Indian woman eased the threat.

We watched Jennie Thunder raise her hands to the sky, a bundle of small bags in her left hand. I imagined the bags as buckskin, but they looked more like brown paper from the five-and-dime. She reached into one, held up benedictory fingers while she spoke something we could not hear, and then cast whatever was in her hand into the small flood below. It was still floating on the surface as it raced by us, and I recognized a yellow dusting of cornmeal before it swept away, catching on the flotsam washing along, juniper twigs, piñon needles and cones, a drowned woodrat, pieces of a raven.

We picked our way over to her, jumping the small channels of muddy water threading through the peach orchard that filled her alcove. These peaches had a unique syrupy intensity from ripening on the rim of wildness. Or maybe from having Jennie Thunder and the Black Dragon hovering over their growing. The Burnses, and everyone else in Blossom, called them Jennie Thunder peaches.

Jennie Thunder looked up to the sky and back to us. "Come here," she said.

We stepped closer. She reached in the smallest of her bags and retrieved a bit of yellow pollen. I knew it was supposed to be cattail pollen, but couldn't tell if Jennie Thunder still followed that old Paiute law or had used whatever plant was available. She touched her heart and then lifted her hand into the rain, chanting in Paiute.

Waagotsi.	*Ungwangumpaniakwa.*
Moopitsi.	*Pa'a tinkamai.*
Piyini.	*Ninia pavitsingi.*
Nangkatsaka'a.	*Ninia patsitsingi.*
Unuayikwa.	*Moopitsi uvitui.*

The sound of the words soothed me.

She spoke again. "You don't talk right at the lightning, you know. You talk around its edges. This blessing will keep the lightning away from you."

With her thumb, with the protectiveness of a grandmother and the boldness of a medicine woman, she smudged pollen on Lillian's forehead, then mine. I was acutely aware of that yellow mark on my skin. It radiated calm.

"What did you say in your prayer?" Lillian asked her.

"No," I said. "Don't answer." The two women looked at me.

"I need my own meaning, and I have it already."

Katharine's drowned face came floating down the arroyo toward me, peering up from the red current like the full moon in a black sky. Wesley came behind her, his brown hair floating above his round boy-face. Their eyes were lifeless, but for the first time in my visions, there were signs of peace in their faces. I saw them clearly, and then they disappeared, perhaps tugged back under by the Paiute water babies, the spirits of the river that divulge such things.

We turned back into the pelt of the rain and watched the falls stream over the sandstone. The three of us had our own rimfalls running off our noses and fingertips. I sipped the salty mix of rainwater and sweat dripping from my moustache and pulled handfuls of water from my beard. Lillian shook spray from her hair. We were drenched but not cold. The canyon country summer heat hadn't abandoned us completely.

Jennie Thunder started talking. Her voice dropped a note in pitch. This was her storytelling voice, her voice for orations. There was still a gravelly undertone in there, left over from her alcoholic years.

"A day like today is the Black Dragon's day. The Dragon is a water serpent. When lightning strikes, he is flicking his tongue. Flash floods travel on the back of the Dragon, his wings flapping in the current, his tail slithering over the rocks in rimfalls. In between storms, he flies back to the mountaintops."

Lillian was watching me while she listened to Jennie Thunder. She turned and reached down to the shrubs and pinched off a sprig of sagebrush. In the rain-soaked canyon, the earthy spice of the bush lay heavy in the air. She rolled the leaves between her fingers, smelled deeply, then let the sage drift into the remains of Jennie Thunder's fire.

I did the same. I turned and hugged Lillian, holding her tight to my chest, without words.

It was midmorning. The deluge was winding down, the driving male rain softening to female rain. After a long wordless time together watching the canyon, Jennie Thunder spoke first.

She turned to Lillian, with the wry spark that lived in her eyes glittering in the soft light. "In your airplane, you might be able to catch the Dragon on his way to the mountains. You two need to go fly after him. Remember what you told me about flying over the cliffs after a storm, Lillian? You need to show the professor what you saw."

Lillian lit up. "Of course. And I have another idea—somewhere I want to fly you, Doc. We'll need to camp. We can come back tomorrow."

"Do I have a choice?"

"You could say no. But you'd be crazy to." She smiled and squeezed my arm.

I wondered if I was ready to face the Dragon. I wondered if I was ready for Lillian. But I heard myself say, "Okay."

"You watch out for those water babies as you walk back up the canyon, Lillian," Jennie Thunder said, nodding us on our way. "They can make you pregnant if you aren't careful."

Lillian groaned and smiled. "I'm too old to want babies, and besides, I have Doc to protect me."

I had a strong sense of Katharine watching us. Neither approving nor disapproving, just there. I hadn't bantered with a woman in a long time. I plunged ahead, feeling awkward. "Hey, Lillian—you're only forty-two. A young woman. You can take care of yourself, I'll wager, but I'll do my best to fight off your attackers."

"I'm older than I used to be, but not yet as old as dirt," said Lillian matter-of-factly.

As we walked back along the cliff trail, the opalescent gray of the sky became more transparent, thinning, beginning to reveal an underlying blue wash. The rims continued to run with their red and umber floodwaters, but I knew the waterfalls soon would cease. We would be left with full potholes, rearranged boulders and logs in the arroyo channels, new mud banks. The sun would return to bake the land, and by evening the storm would be a dream.

The Jake was dropping, leaving a fresh line of flood debris high in the willows and tamarisk, a wrack of soggy cottonwood leaves, with chocolatey mud glistening below. We came to one little streambed that required three or four quick hops from log to stone to bank to cross the water.

Lillian turned to me. "After you."

"No, after you."

"No, no—after *you*."

Finally she said, "Oh, all right," and with a daredevil grin, she stepped lightly over the rushing creek. I followed. It wasn't bad at all.

We walked along the trail between the highwater mark and the cliff. I brushed the ricegrass clumps with my fingertips. By the time we reached my cabin, the sun was out, and our clothing steamed. The air actually felt humid, an unlikely adjective for the canyon. Maybe, maybe, those flapping black dragon wings have flown on past.

I kept repeating one of Jennie Thunder's phrases, "on the back of the Dragon." I knew it from somewhere, but for now it stayed lost in the recesses of my brain, in one of those filing cabinets spilling with memories.

In the stillness of midafternoon, we lifted off from the dirt airstrip above Blossom. The rumble of the little Cessna made talking difficult. When the thermals dropped us two hundred feet in sudden jolts, my heart dropped with the plane, but I trusted Lillian. The turbulence pressed us together, thigh to thigh.

Lillian was virtually the only woman prospecting for the big payoff in the uranium boom, and her exploits with her airplane had already made her famous in the ore-crazed plateau country. Some of the stories were true, if exaggerated: men telling of being buzzed so low they had to duck, seeing her fly so close to cliffs with her wingtip Geiger counter that she could snag samples by hand with a special hook. The men envied her, and fantasized about her, and tried to talk her into partnerships.

Lillian flew along the line of the Black Dragon Cliffs, about a thousand feet above the slickrock. She pointed down toward the benches.

"This is what Jennie Thunder wanted you to see."

I looked at the sweep of creamy sandstone ledges. Every depression was filled with runoff. Potholes, tanks, pools, tinajas. The little reflective ponds beamed back the golden afternoon light, flashing with watery vitality against the stony desert surrounding them. They looked like the multifaceted eyes of an insect or a sea creature—the eyes of the earth—blinking on and off as we changed our angle. They brought the mesalands to life.

"This happens not much more often than the rimfalls," Lillian shouted. "And you can only see it from the air."

We threaded between the peaks of the Henry Mountains, then dropped down toward the Colorado River, following the deepening canyons that fed into the master stream with the inexorability of capillary leading to vein leading to heart. We swung out over the Colorado itself and began to fly down Glen Canyon. Everywhere on the rims the potholes winked their brilliant reflections at us.

Great blue herons flew up from sandbars below. Agitated beavers swam away into the eddies. We circled Anasazi forts perched on lookout buttes. I thought about where the Colorado came from, tumbling down from the north, joining the Green, then roaring through the grand rubble of Cataract Canyon into the fine-grained Navajo Sandstone, working through this sculptor's medium for 170 miles, clean out of Utah and into Arizona—all the way to where Marble Canyon began the descent into the Grand Canyon itself.

I bellowed over the engine roar, "Jennie Thunder used one phrase that keeps coming back to me. 'On the back of the Dragon.' I've been trying to remember where I've heard it before. I finally have it. Fred Dellenbaugh kept a journal when he floated the Colorado with Powell in 1871. When he rowed from the Green River onto the main stem of the Colorado at the confluence, he wrote of feeling 'at last on the back of the Dragon' itself. I always loved that image."

"It's perfect," Lillian said. "For Cataract Canyon, anyhow. Down here, the Dragon is resting."

I knew what she meant. Glen Canyon of the Colorado was the idyll of the river, a slickrock eden of tapestried walls, side-canyon grottoes, mounds and humpbacks of orange and gold stone, a rock desert imagined by a visionary artist.

I imagined the Black Dragon flying toward his mountaintop. I leaned closer to Lillian and said, "I hope he stays at rest."

Lillian banked the plane away from the river, out over the benchlands, and took aim at a high island mesa rising from the ocean of sandstone. The summit covered perhaps two square miles. It looked enchanted. I spotted a little landing strip in a swale of alluvium. It hadn't been bladed, since there was no way up here for a dozer. The first landing must have been wild. I looked at Lillian, and she nodded.

"That's it."

She came around, straightened out, picked a line, and dipped lower and lower. My heart raced.

Lillian looked from the mesa to her instruments, holding the wheel handles delicately, assuredly, fiercely.

We floated over the mesa rim and dropped to the earth. The bumpy runway slammed me first against the door and then against the taut curve of her shoulder. We rolled to a stop.

"Come on, Doc." Lillian led me away from the plane and out along the cliff edge. Beyond the patch of red dirt, the clean white sandstone resumed, running as smooth as a sidewalk through the sculpture garden of bonsai junipers. The view astonished me, a labyrinth of canyons cut back from the river into the sandstone mesas, toward the high bordering plateaus that flickered like smoke and the tantalizing forested dome of Navajo Mountain. Holy places, say the Navajo and Hopi and Paiute. Their word seemed completely justified.

We wound across the ledges capping the mesa. Near the southern brink, Lillian angled off behind a boulder. When I caught up, she was looking down on a perfect pothole, huge, thirty feet across.

"Someday it will be an arch," she said. "But for us, it's still the world's best swimming hole."

The bowl of stone was countersunk into the edge of the mesa. Its far rim was the rim of the world. The surface of the water that filled it sparkled with riffles in the breeze. I could see the red silt bottom angling up at one end through the metallic clarity left by the settling of the new runoff.

Lillian looked down at this pilgrimage spot, then glanced at me with an expression that balanced peace with exhilaration, anticipation with contentment. I knew this was her place and no one else's.

She bounced down the rock stairsteps, sat on a bench-like ledge next to the pool, and began to strip off her clothes. Boots and socks. Khakis. Work shirt. Underpants. Camisole. Completely at ease with her nakedness, she grinned at me, stepped up to the rim, curled her toes against the grit of the sandstone, and dove into the deep end.

She seemed to hang above the pool for a long time while I looked at every part of her slender body. Then she disappeared into the water.

She came up for air, gasping with the shock of the coolness. "Come in, you wonderful old man," she cried.

I saw Katharine and looked closely at her face, hoping for a sign. When she smiled, I didn't know if this was her decision or mine.

Either way, I knew she would have loved this place.

I stepped down to the pool and peeled off my clothes. The breeze riffed through the hairs on my back and arms, cooled my chest and crotch as it evaporated the trickles of sweat. Lillian drifted to the shallow end, throwing back her arms to rest her palms on the rock. It was her turn to look at me. I felt surprisingly safe, remarkably unexposed. I tugged on my beard, marshaled my adrenaline, and jumped.

Stroking toward her, darkness below me, stunning light above, cutting through the ripples that shimmered between us, I saw Lillian ahead through the glitter of water droplets.

PART III

Living Close to the Land

Rick Bass

THE FARM

It was still the end of winter at our home in northern Montana, but down in south Texas in April, at my father's farm, it was full-bore spring. It was a joy for me to realize that Lowry, just turned three, would now have the colors and sights of this place lodged in at least her subconscious, and that Mary Katherine, just turned six, was old enough to begin doing some serious remembering.

Some children, of course, hold on to odd-shaped bits and pieces of memory from a much earlier age, but around the age of six and seven, nearly everything can be retained—or at least that was how it worked for me when I was a child.

It was like a kind of freedom—a kind of second welcoming her into the world. Now when I am an old man I will be able to say to her, "Remember when . . ." and she will remember.

We had flown to Austin, rented a car, visited my brother, and then driven down into the brush country and toward the live oaks and dunes that lie in braided twists some fifty miles inland: to the farm. As we drove, Elizabeth and I talked and watched the late-day sunlight stretch across the green fields; the girls slept, tired from their travels, in the back seat. Angels. So much joy do they bring me that sometimes I wonder if, since my mother is not here to love and know them, I'll carry also her share of that joy, having inherited it prematurely. For a fact, this joy seems too large. I think that maybe that is what is happening some-times, at certain moments. I glance at them and love them fully and deeply, but then a second wave or wash comes in over that one, as if she is watching them over my shoulder, and I feel it again.

It used to give me a bittersweet feeling, but now I'm not sure what the word for it is. Gratitude, sometimes: to the girls, of course, but also to my mother.

They woke when we stopped to open the gate. We drove through and closed the gate behind us, and because we could not wait, we parked the car there and decided to walk instead of drive the rest of the way to the farmhouse. We walked in the late-day light, the last light, down the winding white sandy road, beneath the moss-hung limbs of the enormous live oaks—trees that were five and six hundred years old. It's so strange, the way there will be certain stretches of time, certain moments, when for a little while it will feel exactly as if I am walking in her every footstep, as if I am her in that moment, set back in time—and enjoying that moment as I know she must have enjoyed it, or one like it, thirty or forty years ago. And I wonder, is it just this way for me, or do others experience such feelings, such moments?

Buttercups, winecups, and black-eyed Susans—before we had taken ten steps, Lowry and Mary Katherine both had picked double-fistful bouquets and had braided flowers in their hair. Another ten steps took us across the culvert that ran beneath the road. There was water standing in the culvert and in receding little oxbows on either side of the road, and as we approached, ten thousand little frogs went splashing into that muddy water. "Frog alert, frog alert!" we cried, and ran down to mud's edge to try to catch one, but there were too many, springing zigzag in too many directions; you couldn't focus, and couldn't chase just one, because their paths were crisscrossing so. There were so many frogs in the air at any one time that occasionally they would have midair collisions; they were ricocheting off each other. The mud around the shoreline of their fast-disappearing pond glistened, so fast was the water evaporating, and the mud was heiroglyphed with the handprints of what might have been armies of raccoons, though also it could have been the maddened pacings of one very unsuccessful raccoon.

We finally caught one of the little frogs, and examined it: the gray-brown back that was so much the color of the mud, and the pearl-white underbelly. I wondered why, when frogs sunned themselves, they didn't stretch out and lie on their backs, the way humans do at the beach. I guess they would get eaten. I guess if a frog had a mud-brown belly it could lie on its back, camouflaged to the birds above, and still be able to listen for the approach of terrestrial predators, but I guess also there's no real evolutionary advantage to a frog being able to warm its belly in the sun. Though for that matter, the same could be said of us.

Into the farmhouse she loved so much—she had lived in it, and loved it, for only a few years before she fell ill, but had loved it so fully in that time that I still cannot step into it without feeling that remnant love-of-place. And it is thin substitute for her absence, but with the exception of my own blood in my veins, and memories, it is all there is, and I am grateful for it, place.

Elizabeth wanted to go for a run in the last wedge of light—after the long Montana winter we were nearly delirious with the gift of these longer days—and so she laced up her running shoes and went on back up the road at a trot. Mary Katherine wanted to go fishing in the stock tank, so we rigged up a line and went off toward the pond, following the winding sand road and walking beneath those old trees.

We stood on the levee and cast out at the ring of flat water. Turtle heads appeared in the center of the lake, tipped like little sticks, to observe us. In the clear water of the shallows we could see the giant Chinese grass carp, thirty pounds each and seemingly as large as horses striding just beneath the surface, cruising; my parents had put them there when they first built the pond as a means of keeping algae from overtaking the pond. The carp are hybrids, so they can't reproduce, though it's rumored they can live to be a hundred years old—and because the carp are strictly vegetarians, there was no chance of them striking at our spinnerbait. It was strange, though, watching the giant fish circle the pond so slowly, their dorsal fins sometimes cresting the surface like sharks, and knowing that we were fishing for something else, something deeper in the pond—fishing for fish-beneath-fish.

On the far side of the pond, a big fish leapt—not a carp, but a bass. We cast to it for a while in the gathering dusk, but I was hoping that we wouldn't catch it. It's good for the girls to learn that you don't get something every time you go out, or right away.

A water moccasin swam past, its beautifully ugly wedge of head so alarming to our instincts that it seemed almost to cause a mild form of hypnosis—as did the eerie, elegant S-wake of its thick body moving across the surface. Floating on the pond were four-leaf clovers that my parents had planted—a special variety in which every one of them had four leaves—and we stopped fishing for a moment and picked some for friends.

Across the field, across the rise, we could see the cattle trotting in front of the blood-red sun, running from something, and in that wavering red light, and across the copper-fading visage of the pasture, it looked like some scene from Africa, some vast herd of wildebeests. The cattle passed from view, and then a few moments later we saw the silhouette of Elizabeth jogging along the crest of the rise—she was what had spooked the cattle—and across the distance we watched her run in that Mars-red light, the sun behind her, as seven years ago I had sat by this same pond with my mother and watched Elizabeth and my father ride horses across the face of that sun.

We resumed casting. A mockingbird flew up and landed in the little weesatche tree next to us, not five hundred yards away, and as the sun's fireball sank (as if into an ocean), the mockingbird began singing the most beautiful song: some intricate melody that, in the blueing of dusk and then the true darkness, was one of the most beautiful songs—a serenade—I'd ever heard.

"Sing back to him," I told Lowry, and so she did; she sang her alphabet song there in the darkness, her "A-B-C's—next time you can sing with me," etc.

Finally it was true dark—the mockingbird was still singing—and we headed back toward the house. We saw a shuffling little object, a humped little creature, shambling down the sand road in front of us, and I cried, "Armadillo! Chase him!"

We set out after him in full sprint, and were almost even with him—he was running in zags and weaves through the trees—when I noticed the white stripe running down his back and was able barely in time to shout, "Skunk! Get back!"

Perhaps it was the four-leaf clovers. The skunk went his way, and we went ours. I had the strangest thought, in my relief, however. I found myself wondering how—had we been sprayed—the girls would have thought of me afterward, growing up. What if they grew up to be storytellers? What kind of mirth would they have with that—

recounting, for the rest of their adult days, the time their father told them to chase and catch a skunk?

How lucky they were, by fluke chance, to remain in normalcy and to escape unsprayed, untraumatized; and how lucky I was, by the matter of a few feet, to not have such identity fastened to me by my children with the permanence of myth.

I remembered the time when I was about Mary Katherine's age, when my cousin Randy was sprayed by a skunk. It was right around Christmas. We were all gathered up at Grandma and Granddaddy Bass's in Fort Worth—my parents, brothers, and myself; Aunt Lee, Uncle Jimmy, and my cousins Rick, Randy, and Russell. I had already gone to bed—I think it was Christmas Eve—but Randy, being a few years older, was allowed to go down to the creek to check his troutlines and his Hav-a-Hart trap one more time.

I had just nodded off to sleep when I awoke to the impression that all the doors in the house had been blown wide open by some awful force. All of the adults had just let out a collective roar—a primal group groan—and then there were gasps and more groans and my uncle's voice, angry and above all others, "Randy, get out of the house!"

Then the smell hit me. Even in the back room, it was stout. I hadn't known that an odor could be that powerful. It seemed that it could levitate the house. It certainly levitated the people in the house.

When I went out to ask what all was going on, I seem to recall a furious, sputtering inarticulation on the part of the grown-ups, until finally—or this is how I remember it—they shouted, in unison and choreographed with much arm waving, "Randy!"—as if that said it all.

Thirty-plus years later the girls and I let the skunk travel on his way, and we went ours, still sweet-smelling. We could see the glow of the farmhouse through the woods and were striking toward it, holding hands and walking carefully in the darkness to avoid stepping on any skunks, when I saw a firefly blink once, then twice, in the distance, and I shouted with happiness.

The girls had never seen fireflies before. I am not sure they had even known such creatures existed.

For the next hour we chased them through the meadow, trying to catch just one. It seemed a harder task than I remembered from my own childhood—I remembered filling entire lantern-bottles with them—and I figured that it might be because it was still early in the spring and they were not yet blinking with full authority or intensity. We'd see only an individual blinking, and always at some great distance. We'd break into a run, hoping to arrive there before the blink faded, but they were always a little too far away, and their luminescence lasted only a few seconds. We would leap at that last instant, toward the always-ascending (they heard us coming) fading glow of gold—leaping with cupped hands and blind faith toward some imagined, calculated place ahead of us where we believed their flight path would take them—and opening our hands cautiously then, in the silver moonlight, to see if, like a miracle—like plucking a star from the sky—we had succeeded in blind-snaring one.

As beautiful as the on-again, off-again drifting missives of the fireflies was the seamlessness with which Mary Katherine accepted unquestioningly the marvel of such an existence, such a phenomenon. As if secure almost to the point of nonchalance, or at least pure or unexamined wonder, that yes, of course, this was the way all silver-moon nights were meant to be passed, running and laughing and leaping with great earnestness for drifting, blinking low-stars against a background of fixed, higher stars.

Eventually we caught one. And one was enough. We went through the time-honored ritual of putting it in a glass jar and punching air holes in the top. We took it inside the house: turned off all the lights. That simple, phenomenal, marvelous miracle—so easy to behold—as old familiar things left us, replaced by a newness in the world. The heck with electricity, or flashlights. Yes. This is the world my daughters deserve. This is the right world for them.

Later that night, after a supper cooked out on the grill, and after the girls were asleep (dreaming, I hope, of leaping), Elizabeth and I went for a long walk in the moonlight. The brightest, most severe platinum light I have ever seen. Revealing more, in the glare of that intense silver-blue light—highlighting certain things—than would the normal broad light of day.

It didn't feel as if we'd been together nearly twenty years. Or rather, part of it did: the good part.

Such strange brilliance.

The next day we all went fishing. It was windy, and Elizabeth's straw sunhat blew off and landed right side up on the pond. We watched it sail quickly, without sinking, all the way across the little lake. Mary Katherine ran around to the other side of the lake and was there to fish it out with a stick when it arrived. She ran it back to Elizabeth, who put it back on and tied it tighter this time.

The joy of children catching fish: there's nothing like it. Most of the few fish we were catching were too little, and we kept throwing them back. Low's pink skin, her bright blonde hair, in that beautiful spring sun. A hundred feet of snow, it seemed, back home, where we live now, though this was once my home, south Texas, and it's a wonderful feeling to be able to come back to a place that you have left and to feel that place welcome you back and to feel your affection for it undiminished across time.

Mary Katherine kept wanting to keep some fish for dinner that night. We finally caught one that was eating size, and as I put the fish on the stringer, I said, "It's your unlucky day, my little friend." And for the rest of the day, whenever we'd catch one, Mary Katherine (while hopping up and down and clapping her hands if I'd caught it, or simply hopping up and down if she'd caught it) would say, "Oh, please let it be his unlucky day, oh please!"

That night, after our fish fry, I took her into town for an ice cream cone; Lowry had already fallen asleep. I get so used to doing things with them together, the two girls, that I have to remember this: to always be there to spend some time alone with each of them. The special quality or nature of that as unique, as sacred, as the unique quality of sunlight early in the spring, seen dappled through a new-green canopy of emerging leaves, or in the late fall, when the light lies down soft and long again after the harsh bright summer.

It was dusk again, and nighthawks were huddled along the edges of the white sand roads as we drove slowly, twisting and turning, beneath

the arched limbs of more old live oaks. Fireflies were out in the meadows again and we rode with the windows down to feel the cool night
air. The radio was playing very quietly—a jazz special, with the music of
Sonny Rollins and Louie Armstrong—and I knew by the way Mary
Katherine rode silently, happily, that she had never heard such music
before.

We got into the little town of Yorktown a few minutes before
closing time. We went into the coolness of the air-conditioned Dairy
Queen and I waited while Mary Katherine pondered her selection, deciding finally on a chocolate dip cone.

She ate on it the whole way home—back through the starry night,
back through the fireflies, back to the rest of our waiting, sleeping
family—just riding and listening, all the while, to that strange, happy,
lulling music from so long ago.

I have never felt more like a father: never more in love with the
world.

Gloria Bird

RAIN

It is the house that does not accommodate us three, my sons
and me. It is a solid, low fortress against intrusion, swirling
wrought iron grates over the doors and windows. I lay awake
this early morning watching the green flash of the digital alarm
fill the dark room in time with rain ticking on the window
glass, aware that the needed rain will save me from watering
un-native trees I have no feelings for. My first thoughts of how
power outage where we live is as common as flooding arroyos
during rain storms, and how the furnace has a short to be fixed,
a reminder of the storm's potential danger. Yesterday, my son
tells me, a fat mouse attempted to move into our bedroom, to
build its nest in the papier-mâchéd balloon made in school
that abandoned to the floor made a green and red finger-
painted cave. What was it I said, speaking in unfinished
thoughts and sentences, mutest meaning trailing off and left
for him to make sense of never quite on the same channel
when we speak? And today, what I mean to say is that much of
what is written is accepted by that force called "Native Issue,"
an *en vogue* mouthpiece for multiculturalism that merely
capitalizes upon ethnicity, and though the liberal logic is to
give us natives exposure, at the same time, this act of
separation reinforces our 'difference' and 'otherness.' This
morning, I am pulled from the warm bed to write while my
children sleep, by thoughts of the *Arroyo Seco,* the name of this
place where we live, where today flooding will erase the sand
floor of dirt bike tracks, human and animal footprints. We

could watch the tumult safely away from the crumbling edges
while sitting in our heated car dumbly staring at the channeled
waste floating by in the muddy water: piñon limbs, empty
boxes *de cerveza,* a flowered polystyrene cross. From the
porch, the field is burnt brown sticker bushes and chamisa
gone to seed. Blanketed by clouds are the stoic mountains,
which does not *mean* that they are resigned. The single mesa
jutting from behind the nearest house has turned red in the
rain. A comforting thought, that: from the carpet beneath
my feet, my freezing fingertips and the distant jagged hills, all
the earth today is as red as stone polished Santa Clara
pottery.

ARROYO SECO, NM
1993

THE HEART'S RESILIENCE

Morning sun skims through the cool, dry air
sears the sleepy eyes torn from the rim of dream
as spiders build their webs across our doorways, crickets
come in through the cracks of windowsill, and mice dance boldly
in the hallway predicting the coming of an early winter.
A field of chamisal in the foreground tempers
the impoverished memory of the desert's withholding hand
feeds my hungry spirit. The arroyo empty of rainwater wakes
alive with good luck lizards leaving their imprint in swirled
sand. Cactus plants guard the parameters of our existence, run
the fence line. The pinnacles of earth formations rise eye level
in the distance, shift our senses.

I am returned here twenty years later with two young sons
not yet a part of the memory of my daughter's birth in this land,
whose presence we feel still as native wildflowers bloom freely
occupying each field of vision in variegated yellows
against the sienna earth, the color of their skins.
In the early morning, we sit on our verandah on freezing benches
facing a rising sun, the powdered air rough with pollens. At our backs
the western slope is streaked by dark rains and slow cloud shadows.
Somewhere on the edge of hearing a lonely puppy yaps to be let in.
Whiffs of burning trash trail in on the living wind.
I plant myself, a toughened yucca to this miraculous land.

My sons, like shoots, lean into the morning sun to grow, blessed
with youth enough to take the path of the heart's resilience.

ARROYO SECO, NM
1992

Steve Bodio

BIRDS, ICE, FIRE

Nick met his new best friend on a blue New Mexico fall morning, after
the flowers had died but while the aspens still made gold impressionist
slashes against the blue of the mountains. He had hoped that his
dreamed-for life of action would just naturally evolve from being in
such a fine place. First, he had reactivated his old falconry permit and
bought a huge, restless gyrfalcon from a breeder in Sheridan. Then he'd
found some work painting birds for a neotropical specialist at the university, rented a four-room house that had once belonged to a ranch
foreman, and painted the inside a stark white, deciding to wait until
meaningful possessions suggested themselves.

They didn't. Life soon came to consist of drinking Black Jack and
beer in and out of the Stockman's Saddle Saloon. His substitute for action became falconry. Every day he flew his silver gyrfalcon, Cara, on
the Plains of St. Augustine, where there was no game, only the ravens
that were both illegal and, in Nick's mind, immoral to kill.

He had had a hangover that day but thought that breathing cold
air and seeing horizons might go a ways toward curing it. He climbed a
rise west of dirt road 70 until he could see the Datils rising twenty miles
away across the old dry lake bed, a Tibetan flat seven thousand feet
above sea level. A line of chalk-white radiotelescopes in the distance
were the only man-made features in the landscape; the bartender at the
Saddle called them "Golftees of the Gods."

He unhooded the hawk and stood with his head bowed until she
ruffled her feathers, filled her wings, and floated her three and a half
pounds off his fist as lightly as though she were a dandelion seed. She
turned downwind, then began to beat her wings, rowing for the

horizon like a slow-motion movie suddenly snapping into real time. Although she looked as though she were running away, he knew better. Soon the hawk was a swallow-sized silhouette two thousand feet above, beating forward into the wind, sliding back down it, beating forward again.

She knew as well as he that there was no game. This was basically jogging on a track. He had a wicker crate of pigeons in the truck. Real athletic training for falcons demanded real pigeons, Belgian racing homers so fast that even a jet-propelled arctic gyr felt challenged, missed, climbed higher, and tried harder. Nick had not been able to summon up the concentration needed to build a sky racer's stable; the basket contained mere fodder, fat grain-fed commons from a farm in the Bosque. Releasing them under Cara was like feeding lab rats to a python. But she had to be served. He groped blindly in the basket, pulled one out, looked it over one last time for signs of disease, then bowled it aloft, yelling, "HAAAH!"

Cara dropped instantly, as though she had been shot, then began to beat her wings as she flew headfirst toward the ground, corkscrewing, accelerating past gravity. Just behind the pigeon, only a hundred feet above the ground, she turned her suicidal plunge at right angles and hit the bird like a baseball bat. Feathers trailed out over fifty feet of air as the pigeon crashed to earth with all the grace of a ruptured pillow. But instead of claiming her kill, Cara was heading up in a curve, out toward the Datils, where a pair of ravens was climbing toward a mutual battlefront above the plain, croaking and circling.

Shit. Not only did he not want to kill a raven—he considered them as intelligent as he was, and believed in spite of himself that to kill one could bring on some obscure doom—but they were good enough fliers to take her the sixty-mile length of the plain before she won or gave up. They could pull her into the mountains and make him chase electronic blips from her leg-mounted miniature transmitter for a week. They could even make him lose her forever. But not this time. In a moment one raven seemed to slide off even as the other rose. The falcon in turn abandoned her climb to peel off after the first. They dipped and flared and menaced, black and white shadows mirroring each other's every move, then fell out of the sky together like stones, into a little grove of junipers back near the road. When they didn't rise, he hopped into the truck and gunned it over the washboard to the grove, vibrating to the edge on every curve. He skidded to a stop as his dust caught up to him, and saw a black Suburban with mirrored windows parked between two of the neatly spaced trees. As he climbed out, the occupant rolled down the window and raised a hand. "They're right in front of you. God *damn*. I've wanted to see that all my life. Can I buy you a drink?"

Caught between relief, disgust at the unwanted kill, and an almost sexual embarrassment at being caught at the death, Nick was never sure if he answered. He raised one finger in acknowledgment and stepped forward. The raven lay on its back, its black wings spasmed into a stiff upward curve four feet across. The gyr stood solidly on its breast, one fluffy black feather grasped firmly in her bill. She looked up at him, shook away the feather, said "kack" clearly and with consonants, and stepped to his glove, her stout little hands shifting and gripping. He murmured meaningless endearments, fished around in his hawking bag for a hunk of pigeon, and handed it to her. Only then did he turn to the intruder.

"Thank you for not walking in."

"I know better than that. I've read the book and seen the movie."

"The movie?"

"Whatever." An impatient wave. "That's a gyrfalcon, right?" He pronounced it as two words: "gyre-falcon."

"Right."

"In that case I have to buy you a drink." The face was long and pale and narrow under a dusty black cowboy hat. A rooster tail of straight black hairs fell over the collar of an ancient brown canvas jacket as the driver withdrew into the wagon's tinted-glass gloom. In a moment it returned over an outstretched hand, holding a shot glass full of golden liquid. "Unless you have some kind of principle against it."

"Not at all, no." Suddenly it seemed the best of all possible resolutions. Holding the heavy bird high with his left hand, he reached out with his right and tossed back the shot. The smell and taste of the tequila burned through his awkwardness. "How the hell does anybody out here know what a gyrfalcon is?"

"Don't be a Yankee asshole. Get that bird fed up and I'll tell you all about it." He paused and extended his hand, adding, "Johnny Aragon."

Their immediate friendship was based on mutual admiration, mutual cultural incomprehension, and mutual excess. It consisted of widely separated marathons of drinking, eating, talking, chasing animals, and general helling around. Nick and Juan Aragon found they shared a fondness for tequila and brown liquor, not to mention the outspoken conviction that they were smarter than everybody else except for a few tough, articulate women who enjoyed the same, especially Juan's difficult sister, Cecilia.

The Aragons were local kids, born ten miles south of the pavement in Leon County. They were the product of an unlikely liaison between a land-grant scion from northern New Mexico's insulated society and a Welsh-Jewish heiress from California. It had apparently been a Romeo and Juliet affair, and their residence in far southwestern Leon County was considered by more conventional ranchers to a be a kind of exile. Ostracism never bothered the elder Aragons. With her familial connections and his savvy, they had made a modest fortune in oil and real estate, with which they built an empire in the mountains. They had died together in the crash of their Cessna, probably drunk, when Juan was seventeen. Drink was a family trait, its excessive indulgence as inevitable an Aragon character as hawk noses, blue eyes, good manners, and horsemanship.

Aragon once described Cecilia, to Nick's secret dismay, as a "bug-zapper—you know, one of those blue-light boxes that buzzes and burns off everything it touches." She was a vegetarian and style queen, an even narrower and more elegant version of her brother, with premature silvery black hair and New York clothes and the kind of deliberately frenetic wit that Nick found almost heartbreaking.

The three of them ran through the year as passionate and furious and thoughtless as children. They slept in the woods, drove all day to rodeos, talked and drank all night in motels, and never got hangovers. They saddled up and rode to the top of ten-thousand-foot Escondida Peak in April, wallowing through belly-deep snowdrifts to celebrate what Juan called Aldo Leopold Day with tequila and champagne. The Aragons showed Nick his first mountain lion that afternoon, hurrying nervously through the melting drifts, shaking drops off a forepaw, looking over his shoulder, leaving tracks the size of coffee can lids.

And, of course, they chased things. Cecy would cast a number-22 dry fly, an artificial dust mote almost invisible from ten feet away, on the nose of a rising trout that she would then release. She led Nick to the tiny headwater streams where the nearly extinct Gila golden trout still spawned, protected by walls of willow, beaver dams, and the indifference of jaded sportspersons. Juan scorned such effete sport. He taught Nick to fish for catfish in the tamarisk bayous along the Rio Grande. They'd go at night, with lanterns and cigars and plenty of mosquito repellent. The surroundings were eerie, the sounds extraterrestrial, the bait scary. Juan disdained the stinking lumps of chicken guts, or "buzzard bait," that worked for channel cats. He was after bigger game: carnivorous "flatheads" that weighed from twenty pounds up past one hundred, monsters that resembled whiskered tadpoles the size of dogs, above all, hunters that only ate things that moved. To attract them, Juan favored neotenic tiger salamanders: axolotls. They were a foot long, cold and mottled and vibrating, with staring eyes and bushy gills and hands like a tiny human's. Nick thought they looked like embryos and didn't like even catching them in cattle tanks, never mind sticking hooks in them. Juan laughed and cast them into the black water, where they swam in tethered circles. Cecy would watch and shake her head, but she, too, would stay all night.

Later in the bird season Juan and Cecy took him to a vast flatland ranch in the prairie south of Portales, where the only things that broke the oceanic horizon were windmills. The owner was an eccentric red-headed millionaire from the Midwest who now devoted his time to bird banding, ballistics research, raising emus, and hunting Cape buffalo. They entered through a mile-long dirt drive with the emus racing along beside the fence like reanimated dinosaurs. Jim's ranch house was full of nineteenth-century English weaponry, dogs—field-trial pointers, Russian wolfhounds, Jack Russell terriers, heelers—and what seemed to be a complete collection of original Audubon lithographs.

He managed the place for cattle and deer but above all for prairie chickens, which he preferred to call "pinnated grouse." Rare and local, they were legendary in bird-hunting history, high-flying flock birds with headdresses that danced like Plains Indians in the spring. Like the Indians, they had followed the buffalo; like them, they were broken and scattered.

But not on Emu Ranch. Nick and the others walked into the gray afternoon skies with the falcon bent like a bow against the wind five hundred feet above their heads. They were an incongruous hunting party. Nick looked appropriate with his moth-eaten gray fedora in an antique Stetson pattern and a game vest over his denim coat. Jim resembled a farmer, with bib overalls and lace-up boots, his chin unshaven and his head bare. By contrast, the Aragons were their usual elegant twin selves: black jeans, black packer boots meant more for riding than for walking, silver-belly hats, silver at their wrists and buckles. Juan also wore his ancient brown canvas barn coat and somehow seemed more in place for that. After a few hundred yards Jim sent his little black-and-white female pointer out to race back and forth in front of them in the precise arcs of a windshield wiper. As she bounded across their bows, arcing and disappearing in the shin-oaks like a spotted porpoise, Nick felt exultant, all his cares flowing out and behind him downwind, to be replaced by clean prairie air.

Just as he tugged his hat more firmly onto his head, the pointer slammed to a point as abruptly as if she had run head-on into an invisible wall. They trotted up to the dog, a sudden statue, only a vibrating tail to show she was alive. She rolled her eyes back to watch her human companions. Juan whooped, sprinted past the dog, and sailed his hat forward into the wind with a cowboy YEEE-HAH! Nick had been expecting a covey flush, a burst of four or five birds. Instead, an acre of dark grouse bigger than pigeons erupted from the stubble, first ten, then fifty, more and more, and finally stragglers in twos and threes. Distracted by the thunder of the wings and the plaintive calls, Nick momentarily lost sight of the falcon. He caught her as she slashed across a grouse with a burst of feathers. It staggered, recovered, and headed for the horizon with the falcon in hot pursuit. In a moment they had vanished over the hillocks on the fence line.

"What do we do now?" asked Jim.

"Follow that bird!" whooped Juan. They raced to the truck. Nick turned on the radio receiver, then paused.

"How far do those things fly?"

Jim squeezed his chin. "They *can* fly forever. But they usually head for trees or structure. There's an abandoned homestead just past the section line . . . right over that little ridge."

The sun was below the horizon, and the colors were draining fast as they bumped along the rectangular grid of section roads. Jim turned on the headlights as Nick, holding the receiver's earphones with both hands, tried to balance and interpret the beep at the same time: "louder . . . even louder . . . WAIT!"

They stopped where two straight dirt tracks intersected at right angles. Nick hopped out, waved the hand antenna up, down, left, and right. "North!"

"That's where the homestead is," Jim said, smiling. Nick climbed in. In a moment the truck's headlights illuminated a ghost building, gray and shivering, with black holes like eyes in a skull, a tattered elm shading the walk. The beeper was so loud it hurt. Nick stepped from the truck to see the silver hawk glowing incandescent in the beams, bent in a curve over a gray-barred bird with splayed black head plumes. She reached down for a mouthful of feathers as he watched, shook her head irritably in the wind to clear her beak, bent again. She continued to ignore him as he picked her up with her quarry, pulled the grouse through his glove, and hid it behind his back. She was calm, almost in a trance, after the flight's storm. After a moment she seemed to come to. She rearranged her feet, stood erect, polished her bill on the glove, and shook down her feathers. Nick looked back and his friends burst into applause. Cecy, the vegetarian, was clapping too, face solemn, eyes as black and enigmatic as the falcon's.

That night, when Jim took two more grouse from his freezer, Cecy reached in for another. "There's still meat I'll eat. I want Cara's, though," she added, looking at Nick, who nodded his assent, as solemn as she.

Later Nick was to assign that evening any number of meanings, ones that shifted and would not come into the same focus twice. That night seemed to be more fun than he had ever had . . . the friends, the food, electricity, the aftermath of action, even the fact that Cecilia had chosen the bird. He was high before he ever touched his wine. The wines were magical old Bordeaux from Jim's amazing cellar. The table was lit by candles that illuminated his companions' faces from below, so that they seemed to glow softly in the dark. The conversation bounced like a ball tossed higher and higher. One moment they would be laughing madly at the sound of a word—"javelina" nearly reduced them to hysterics, as though they were stoned teenagers—the next moment they would sit and shiver as Juan told of a beloved horse he had shot when he thought it would never regain its feet, who had returned to stand blood-drenched in the moonlight in front of his door after he'd had to drink himself to sleep, forcing him to, as he put it, "kill him again." Jim described his ninja-style dispatch of a persistent poacher: he had ambushed and beaten him while wearing a black hood over his head, then dumped him hog-tied at his favorite bar after pissing all over him.

Juan raised his glass in a toast. "To the old ways! Prairie chickens forever . . . and Comanches and cowboys. . . ."

"Grizzly bears and wolves!" Jim countered.

"Lions and tigers and bears." This from Cecilia. "Well, our own *tigre* anyway." She stared darkly at Nick, who felt compelled to raise the ante.

"Imperial mammoths and dire wolves!"

"Thunderbirds and moonhorn buffalo!" Juan again.

"Revive the Pleistocene!" hollered Nick, remembering a poem. They all raised their glasses to that one, yelling and hooting as the prairie wind rattled the windows.

When he made his way to the guest house under the cold moon, he felt as though heat were being sucked out of him by the black void above him, as if the world were falling under his feet. The air was unbearably sweet and cold, breath boiled out of him like smoke, and the hair stood up on the back of his head. He walked toward the wind again, knowing he couldn't sleep yet. When he turned back toward the little adobe hut, he saw Cecilia standing by the door like a ghost. As he approached, she put her hand over his mouth, then turned and led him to the narrow bed. When he opened his mouth, she touched her finger to it again, not smiling. "No." She pushed him down backward onto the bed, stood, and began to remove her shirt, never taking her eyes from his. After a moment he sat up and unbuttoned his.

II

They made love strenuously, almost painfully. Every time he began to speak, she put her hand or her mouth over his, harder each time. She gritted her teeth and bit her lip and his and refused to scream when she squeezed her hips against him so hard that it hurt, though at the end he had no such inhibitions.

A few minutes later he jerked, jumped awake from his postcoital daze to see her gathering her clothes in the cold gray light. "Quiet, don't worry," she whispered, and was gone. In spite of the cold and his puzzlement, he was asleep again in an instant.

In the morning only her smell remained to tell him her presence had not been one of those half-waking dreams that plagued him when he was drinking too much and sleeping too little. At breakfast he and John and Jim ate venison sausage, tortillas, eggs, and chiles while she carefully dismembered a tangerine, washing it down with several cups of black coffee. She did not seek or avoid his eyes and seemed, if anything, more hyper and sardonic than ever, making quicksilver references to Nick's "attack fowl," Jim's feudal empire, and her brother's love life. When Nick tried to speak to her in the hall, she gave him a long and enigmatically sad look, saying only, "Later, maybe."

When they returned to Leon County, Nick found himself unable to call her, whether out of fear or puzzlement being a question he would not ask himself. Juan invited him for dinner the next week, where he was introduced for the first time to Marguerite Rossi and her brother, Tom. Marguerite was a childhood friend of both Aragons who had been working as a farrier on a Wyoming ranch, a big, vivid, hawk-nosed woman of thirty-nine whose Swiss-Italian family had lived in one place for a hundred years, twenty miles north of the pavement, thirty miles east of the Aragons, and two miles north of a jagged wall of cliffs that often cut the Rossis off from the towns for a week in winter's snows or summer's rains. Her father, now dead, had been a famous hunter of cats and bears; her mother was a former nurse and teacher who was also a serious reader, a trait she had passed on to her daughter.

Marguerite had long, perfect legs, a mane of red-gold hair, and she loved horses and books. Cecy told Nick that she was the best shot in their wild childhood group and that she loved every living thing on the old ranch, from cows to bobcats. She startled Nick with her familiarity with what he still thought would be pretty esoteric writers for a cowgirl—the great African adventurers Karen Blixen and Beryl Markham, and Sybille Bedford, whom Nick had just discovered. She whooped with delight at his ill-concealed astonishment.

She also informed him she was not a "cowgirl" but a woman who was a cowboy. Like Juan, she wore her worn silvery Blanchard spurs everywhere. Nick knew enough to realize that these were working traditionalists' dream tools, like his shotguns; more dollar-oriented cowpokes sold them or hung them on the wall. She seemed at least as close to Juan as Cecilia, treating him a bit like a younger brother but with more tenderness.

Young Tom, only twenty-three, lived for the hunt. He was heavy but not fat, innocent and very western. Nick found them both attractive and a little intimidating, she despite or perhaps because of her kindness and a quick intelligence, and he because Nick suspected that Tom's easy competence did not conceal a little contempt or at least condescension for effete Easterners, though he never showed it.

Overnight, Marguerite became the fourth of their group, going everywhere with the Aragons and accepting Nick as a new member of their family. Nick was fascinated with her. He thought her air of undefined melancholy when she was not outdoors or telling stories, her mix of country and bookish interest, evinced a certain restlessness. Although she was as sane a person as he had ever known, she seemed haunted by several different pasts.

They continued to run together through the early part of February, hunting quail behind a new dog that the Aragons had acquired from Jim, drinking in the Saddle at night, crashing at each other's houses, riding horses over the plains. Nick did not again attempt to raise the issue of the night he had spent with Cecilia, although he knew it was not to his credit. He put some energy into getting to know Marguerite. She was another instant easy friend, but her eyes always seemed to be on Juan. One evening when he and Cecilia had preceded the others to the bar, she told him that Juan and Marguerite had been sleeping together since Juan was thirteen and Marguerite sixteen.

He was mildly flabbergasted. "Why are you telling me this? Are they still . . . ?"

She grimaced. "What do you think?"

"You're—unhappy about it. Jealous of big brother's time?"

"You really *can* be an idiot. I think he's a complete fool for not marrying her. But she can't have babies. . . ." She stopped as they entered, and Nick again decided against raising the issue.

On February fifteenth, the last day of the quail season, they went to a place that the New Mexicans called "Uncle Tony's." Tony Arzeni, who had homesteaded there, was an ancestor of the Rossis. His father had come into the country in the nineties with the rest of the historically unnoticed influx of Basque and Swiss-Italian families that became the founders of more than half of the so-called "Anglo" ranch dynasties of the region. Like his compadres—Arrietas, Croces, Gineras, Echeverrias—he had run sheep and goats and cattle in the kind of high dry pastures that reminded the immigrants of their gorgeous, impoverished, hardrock former homes, finally building a walled retreat thirty miles from the railroad and later the road that connected Socorro to the cattle-shipping terminal at Raton Quemado. At that time the foreign speakers had been considered a sort of new breed of Mexican, but the ambitions that had driven them across the ocean had allowed them to succeed in places that both the older Spanish settlers, mostly townsmen and farmers, and the post–Civil War Texans who preferred to stake out their cattle empires in the lusher fields of the high mountains to the west never even considered.

The site had permanent water and a defensive security that must have mattered in the bloody old days, but it looked at first glance like a place in Afghanistan or on the moon. Although the walls did not close in until you descended another half mile, they still rose in steep waves from the dry river bottom until they crested hundreds of feet above the house, lion colored and treeless and austere. The only greenery visible in the dry months was around the spring and beside the house, the feathery green of the black walnuts that gave the canyon its name. The arroyo's channel ran uphill in sweeping curves until it entered another canyon, a notch like a rifle's open sights centered on the remote blue ridges, ten thousand feet and more above sea level, where three-foot winter snows and midsummer thunderstorms drove the waters that scoured the sandy bottom.

But the Aragons and Marguerite, and doubtless old Tony, loved the homestead exactly for its bleak charm. They took Nick up onto the old porch and sat on the edge overlooking the spring. Juan built a fire on the bare rock. They toasted it with enough shots of tequila that Nick's recollection of the conversations that evening were blurred. Was it Juan or Marguerite who called young cowboys known as the Wild Bunch "the last romantics"? Probably it was Marguerite, for he could remember that it was said without an edge.

But it was Juan who began to talk about the old days with rising heat. He spoke of the last recorded jaguar in Leon County, a wandering male that had taken to killing calves in the deep snows of February. He had been poisoned by a ranch wife, who dumped the strychnine that everyone kept then to kill wolves into a bucket of milk and left it in the corral. "That was nineteen-oh-two," he told them. "The end of the beginning. We thought we were doing good, but we were just killing the old country. That's when the Salado dried up, south of Thieves' Mountain. We didn't know enough then. Now we do." His identification with the old-timers was so intense that his friends nodded solemnly and raised their glasses.

But he wasn't done yet. "I had this old karate instructor in Albuquerque. He was a mean old Korean, about sixty-five, head like a bowling ball. . . . Anyway, one day I showed him some pictures of up here. He looks at the mountains and says, 'Are tigers here?'

" 'No sir,' I said. 'We got deer and elk and black bear and mountain lion. Used to have wolves and jaguar, and bigger bears. No tigers.'

"He looks at me like I was a little slow. 'Looks like tiger country to me.' "

The next day Cecilia was gone, with the dog and a suitcase, on an early flight to New York. Although she had an apartment and friends there, the suddenness seemed more than odd. Juan seemed as surprised as Nick, though only Marguerite expressed any worry.

Ten days later Nick received a postcard. On its face was a black-and-orange beaded lizard, on the back the word "Nick?" and Cecilia's address on 22nd Street. He didn't do anything. That evening Marguerite's pickup pulled into his drive as he was about to turn in, sleepy from four strong drinks. She pushed in past him and said, without any preliminary, "Cecilia's dead."

He stared at her, knowing that somehow he already knew, knowing that his unease with Cecilia had real roots, knowing he did not know a fucking thing. "How?"

She paced, arms wrapped around her as though she were cold. "You know Cecy—no halfway measures. She seems to have took about fifty pills and slit her wrists. And given her dog some kind of injection so she's dead beside the bathtub."

"Did she say. . . . ?"

"Not so's you know anything. A note: 'Why not? Sorry and love to all.' "

"Jesus."

"I know, this is too much. You gonna be okay? I've got to get back to Juan. You want to come over?"

"I'd feel intrusive. Could I come over later? When's the. . . ."

"They're doing an autopsy tomorrow. And shipping her home. No date for the funeral yet. . . . Call us or come over. Later, 'bye." And she vanished into the dark.

He built himself another whiskey, and then another, staring into the fire with a feeling of dread he had never experienced before, even with Carole. He woke up in the morning in the same chair, stiff and headachy, with a foul mouth. After a shower, a handful of vitamins, and three pills, he knew he had to see Juan. A whiskey to strengthen his resolution calmed his shaking. When he arrived at the house, he saw Aragon on the porch, waiting. As he opened the door, Juan stooped and picked up a whiskey bottle and staggered off the porch. He took aim and flung it at the corral, hollering, "THIS DOES NOT HAPPEN TO RANCH FAMILIES!"

He didn't go to the funeral or go to see Juan for several weeks. He went out hawking every day, letting the gyr roam, daring her to be lost as she tail–chased ravens over the horizon. On a day of almost Mongolian cold, twenty-two below in the monochrome dawn, they went out into a brown plain laced with crusts of old snow, under a sky of no color at all. The air was so still that he could hear the swish of her pinions and the sound of her breath as she mounted in circles around him. Fifteen minutes later she chased a shrieking raven to cover in the corrals sur-rounding an iron cattle tank, diving at it repeatedly as it cowered under the lowest rail. As Nick jogged up, she flew vertically to the top of the windmill and lit, only to explode into a hissing sparkler that burned for a moment before she fell like lead to the ground below, feathers burnt to ash, blackened feet curled in rigor, clutched to her breast. Nick stood in sudden tears, wondering why those left alive so unfairly felt like victims.

Pat Mora

EL RÍO GRANDE

Maybe La Llorona is el Río Grande
    who carries voices wherever she flows,
the voices of women who speak only Spanish,
    who hold their breath, fluttering
like a new bird, cupped in their own hands high
    above their heads.

Maybe La Llorona is el Río Grande
    who rolls over on her back some afternoons
and gazes straight into the sun,
    her hair streaming brown into fields of onion
and chile, gathering voices of women who laugh
    with their own fear.

Maybe La Llorona is el Río Grande
    who penetrates even granite, gathers the stars
and moon and tells her cuentos all night long,
    of women who scoop her to them in the heat,
lick her on their lips, their voices rising
    like the morning star.

A RIVER OF WOMEN

A river of women
  softened this valley,
    hummed through the heart
    of night lulling
      babies and abuelas
        into petals of sleep.

El río de mujeres
  gathered the peach light
    of dawn for warmth like a shawl,
    slid the glow
      into the desert's roots,
        eased its greyest thirst.

The river of women
  penetrates boulders, climbs
    crags jagged as hate,
      weaves through clawing thorns
      to depths parched, shriveled
      offers ripples of hope.

Río de mujeres,
  soften our valley,
    braid through its silence
    carving your freedom
      to the song you learn
        on your winding way.

River of women,
   stream on in this valley,
      gather all spirits,
         deepen and rise,
            sustaining your daughters
              who dream in the sun.

CUENTISTA

She carries a green river
in her arms, a rolling play of light.
"En tiempos pasados" she whispers,
"waves of the old sea crested, rose
on these stern mountains. Over this sand,
fish and stars swim."

Ripples and fins stream
silver on and in our skin. Our bones sway.
"The land dried. Crawl into caves,
dark,
damp as owlmouth.
Still, agua santa echoes."

At night, fish stream
through her hair, water fronds.
The whisper of scales,
a muted song, vanishes in sunlight,
like the stars.

She carries a green river,
heavy, but it hums.
In any desert, she can bow her head
and sip from her own arms.

Gary Paul Nabhan

THE SEED OF A SONG

When I was young, my uncle brought me seeds
he had sequestered in a cool dark place, saying,
"Now these are yours for sowing; as you plant,
speak some kind of prayer, sing to the germ
so that its stock will rise to be replenished."

As I went out to the garden to kneel there
next to the opened earth, at first I felt awkward talking,
my mouth dry next to the wetted soil where
I was to put the seeds in place. And so I whispered,
"May you find . . . enough moisture . . . to express yourself . . .
may your growth be . . . long enough to . . . ripen,"
and soon my whisper turned into my uncle's song.

It was not until many years had gone by,
as I prepared my son and daughter
for the passing down of family stock:
I finally came to understand how the seeds
passed from hand to hand had spoken back to me
how the place most fertile for planting
is where generations upon generations find a way
to string the seeds together with their singing.

THE VILLAGE ON THE OTHER SIDE OF WHITE HORSE PASS

for Ofelia Zepeda

We walked before dawn over White Horse Pass.
"There," she nodded toward it, "my heart rests."

A few adobe homes, once scattered by storms
then left in place when the winds finally ceased,
six weeks grama grass dying in-between.

Within the shade of the ocotillo *vatto*
her mother was already cooking for us.

"Even before we turned the final corner,"
she inhaled, "it smelled like home:
where rain arouses its greasewood scent."

Gogogs wagged their way up to meet us, tails
sweeping a path clean to the east-facing door.

Barbara ("Barney") Nelson

TERRITORIES

On the Chihuahuan desert, grass is short, bunched, and dust colored. Passers-through sometimes can't see it. Visibility improves at sundown when the cool late evening light bathes the land in fuzzy gold. Except for the grass, this desert is like all deserts: hot, dry, and washed with muted color. Here green is not garish like '50s neon, but sophisticated and low-key. Blue is not royal but powdered like faded denim. No lipstick company would copy desert reds unless their customers wanted dignity instead of attention. Desert colors are not aggressive. They don't compete, don't shout—just whisper.

The ground is rocky, rainfall sporadic, water sources tiny—the grass desert's greatest assets. If any one of these factors were changed, this country would be filled with something else: farms, industry, cities. Wide fifty-mile flats are broken by mountains but not mountain ranges. Even mountains in this country prefer to be scattered. Sometimes one, sometimes two, no more than four or five are bunched together. A local lion trapper calls them "islands." He says they keep the lion population viable by causing sometimes 200-mile territories and extremely long migrations for dispersing kittens. Time, heat, and distance frustrate the efforts of trappers. Time, heat, and distance bring in new blood.

Mountain lions are territorial. Where mountains appear in belts of high, wide ranges, lion territories are much smaller. Lions don't seem to like open country, so a mountain island becomes home to sometimes only one lion. Passers-through, smelling the territory markers, keep loping unless the smell tells them that the occupant is weak or old or in heat. Studies done in Big Bend National Park show that one lion family will claim the same territory sometimes for generations, sometimes until the patriarch or matriarch becomes sterile unless a kitten kills and replaces an aging mother or challenges and beats an aging male.

Food sources are precious. When survival depends upon limited supplies, mothers kill kittens, females kill males, and kittens or old lions who want to survive hit the trail. Dispersing kittens and ragged grands sometimes end up in town, living for a while on pets, until someone looks up from morning coffee and spots tawny fur in the apple tree. One enterprising kitten followed a dog through a pet-door entrance, killed it in the kitchen, dragged it back out the pet door and into the rocks to eat and cover with litter for later. But few end up on the open flats except when passing through. Local ranchers have capitalized on this knowledge by raising colts—a lion delicacy—in the flats. One border country rancher, who likes to test boundaries, has started a small band of sheep—just to prove he can attract eagles by feeding them—and defy environmentalists. He blames the current lack of eagles on their "protection."

There are few mountain lion stories in Native American collections, but in the modern grass desert, my territory for the past twenty-five years, everyone has a lion story. We call them our ghost cat. Except for trappers, one must believe in them rather than see them. Trappers have shown me their tracks, their scat, their scrapings, but I can't read them or even see them without a trapper. I have never seen a lion in the wild. We also call our mountains ghost mountains and say at night they go away to play with other mountains, but I can see the mountains even at night.

Cows in my country also become very territorial. But their tastes in country seem opposite from lion tastes. Ideal country to a cow is flat; climbing rocks makes their feet hurt. And cows, although they seldom kill one another, are just as cruel when defending their spot. Old cows, young cows, lame cows, cows who are weak for any reason, are pushed out of the group according to the law of survival of the fittest.

I have lived and worked on the big ranches of the ghost mountains all of my adult life. We were classified as migrant workers. The house I raised my baby daughter in has been plowed off the face of the earth since I moved out, deemed unfit for human habitation because of yellowjackets in the walls and rattlesnakes denning under the porch. My next home still stands, but unoccupied, again found unfit for humans because frogs live in the toilet. My territories were easy to keep because no one else wanted them.

For thirteen years I lived on a big ghost mountain ranch whose markers enclosed over 220 square miles, most of it fenced only by rimrock and canyon. When gathering cattle in this country, we found the same cow in the same place, year after year. We raised horned Herefords, and although they never drew blood, they hooked and horned each other until some kind of status quo was reached, even inside corrals. The cows who held the territory along the streams that ran through the flats were the most aggressive, but I always liked best the ones who ranged on the rocky points with the lions. Seems like they always had the best calves and the longest horns, but maybe I just wanted that to be true.

I prefer horned cattle, but I once knew an old one-eyed muley who gained my respect.

Ranchers sometimes discover a piece of country within their territories where water dries up too often, where cow teeth wear out too fast, or where calf numbers are low because bulls can't handle the steep terrain well enough to get around and breed. Sometimes when country never makes a profit and honest, hard-working young people who want to put together something of their own come along, a benevolent rancher might lease that poor land. Bankers will also sometimes lend money to young, hard-working people whose pride will make them somehow pay back a loan even if the venture doesn't work. But gambling sometimes works.

So a partner and I leased Dry Canyon and put down our scent markers. Young healthy heifers were too expensive and Dry Canyon too remote to husband them through their first calf; prime cows were impossible to buy at any price, so we bought grannies. Ranchers sell old cows when the cows don't look like they'll make it through another winter. Dry Canyon was remote, rough, and had only one dependable water source. But we had a plan.

We had a good holding pasture with good grass where we could keep the grannies until cool fall weather, where they could regain strength now that their calves had been shipped, then we'd drive them horseback into Dry Canyon. We knew the long drive would be hard on them, but a level place above the canyon, where they could rest, had caught water. We planned to ride in and move them through the lease as the water dried up, ending at the permanent water and grass at the bottom of the canyon where they could calve and be in the best shape to climb back out the next spring.

It was a good plan. We carefully bought twenty cows, all preg checked by a vet to ensure a spring calf. We wouldn't need a bull. If the venture worked, we'd have the old cows to sell at a better price than we gave for them, and calves too, without the drain of bank interest.

All the cows were horned Herefords, except one. She came from a ranch we neighbored and seemed in good shape except for being horn-less and one-eyed. She had evidently had cancer-eye back when cattle-men still thought a cow was worth an eye operation—which consisted of digging out the bad eye with a pocketknife and sewing the bloody wound closed. Today most cattlemen just ship a cow to market at the first sign of cancer-eye. Bad eyes are a common problem in white-faced Herefords, especially those who live in desert country, where sunlight is intense. Because she had a defect, the horned cattle hooked her unmercifully.

The trail to Dry Canyon is only one cow wide. Steep canyon cliffs rise and fall on each side, making cowboying difficult. Four riders took on the job. One rode ahead, hoping the cattle would follow and to keep the lead cattle on the right trail. The most patient rider, my little daugh-ter, rode at the rear, using just enough pressure to keep the last animal walking. Some people like a wide herd, but cows don't get as hot or as tired when allowed to "trail" one another in single file. The other two riders were going to fight the cliffs and brush to try to keep the middle of the herd walking and trailing. But we soon discovered that two riders could ride along in front and chat and two could ride along in the rear and chat. The old one-eyed cow, because the others picked on her, struck the lead and never stopped. The others simply followed.

One-eye's habits became more interesting as the winter wore on. When we gathered the grannies to move on to the next water hole, the old one-eyed cow was already there. She had new water trails well marked for the followers. As the herd moved in, she moved out, and sometimes one or two went with her. By the end of February, when we rode in to make the final push to the last water before we moved the cows to the bottom of the canyon, we watched old one-eye slip quietly onto a deer trail, disappear over the edge and down. We marked the spot.

We didn't make it. We ran out of water long before we ran out of grass. The country was too rough for grannie cows. Some died from eating plants we didn't know would kill them. One died black with lice, still nursing her calf, but seemed to be the only one affected. Perhaps as Barry Lopez hints in his "conversation with death" theory, she sacrificed herself for the herd. By spring, only ten cows and fifteen calves remained alive, but one of them was the one-eyed muley. She had a good calf and she led us back out. We cut our losses and finally, years later, repaid the debt.

I've never looked at a one-eyed muley quite the same way since, a lesson my more expensive college education never taught. Today I have a young dispersal-aged kitten who is dating poor young cowboys. Jobs are scarce, cowboy habitat shrinking, but my daughter knows Dry Canyon, its water, and its trails. And I'm too old to fight her for it.

Naomi Shihab Nye

PAUSE

The boy needed
to stop by the road.
What pleasure to let
the engine quit droning
inside the long heat,
to feel where they were.
Sometimes
she was struck by this,
as if a plank had slapped
the back of her head.

They were thirsty
as grasses
leaning sideways
in the ditch,
friendly Big Bluestem
and Little Barley,
Texas Cupgrass,
Hairy Crabgrass,
Green Sprangletop.
She could stop at a store
selling only grass names
and be happy.

They would pause
and the pause

seep into them,
fence post,
twisted wire,
brick chimney
without its house,
pollen taking flight
toward the cities.

Something would gather
back into place.
Take the word "home"
for example,
often considered
to have an address.
How it could sweep across you
miles beyond the last
neat packages of ice
and nothing be wider
than its pulse.
Out here,
everywhere,
the boy looking away from her
across the fields.

MUCHAS GRACIAS POR TODO

This plane has landed thanks to God and his mercy.
That's what they say in Jordan when the plane sets down.

What do they say in our country? *Don't stand up till we tell you.*
Stay in your seats. Things may have shifted.

This river has not disappeared thanks to that one big storm
when the water was almost finished.

We used to say thanks to the springs
but the springs dried up so we changed it.

This newspaper tells no truth thanks to people.
This river walk used to be better when no one came.

What about the grapes? Thanks to the grapes
we have more than one story to tell.

Thanks to a soft place in the middle of the evening.
Thanks to three secret hours before dawn.

These deer are seldom seen because of their shyness.
If you see one you count yourself among the lucky on the earth.

Your eyes get quieter.
These deer have nothing to say to us.

Thanks to the fan we are still breathing.
Thanks to the small toad that lives in cool mud at the base of the zinnias.

Simon J. Ortiz

LAND AND STARS, THE ONLY KNOWLEDGE

North, West, South, and East.
Above and Below and All Around.
Within knowledge of the land,
we are existent.
Within knowledge of the stars,
we are existent.

Coldness and wind and the snow, northward.
Mildness and mountain and the rain, westward.
Hotness and desert and the hail, southward.
Warmness and mesa and the sun, eastward.
Starshine and sky and the darkness, upward.
Earthsource and stone and the light, downward.

By this Northern Mountain, we live.
On this Western Peak, we live.
In this Southern Canyon, we live.
Upon this Eastern Mesa, we live.
Below this Sky Above, we live.
Above this Earth Below, we live.

We are Existent within knowledge of land.
We are Existent within knowledge of stars.
All Around and Below and Above.
East, South, West, and North.
This is our prayer. This is our knowledge.
This is our source. This is our existence.

Always the land is with us.
Always the stars are with us.
With our hands, we know the sacred earth.
With our spirits, we know the sacred sky.
We are with the land and stars.
We are with the stars and land.

With offering, all around outside.
With offering, all around inside.
This is the knowledge we have.
This is the existence we have.
In thankfulness, we give and we know.
In thankfulness, we receive and we know.

CULTURE AND THE UNIVERSE

Two nights ago
in the canyon darkness,
only the half-moon and stars,
only mere men.
Prayers, faith, love,
existence.
                    We are measured
by vastness beyond ourselves.
The dark is light.
The stone is rising.

I don't know
if mankind understands
his culture: the act
of being human
is not easy knowledge.

In the canyon
with painted sticks
and feathers,
we journey toward stone,
a massive presence
in midwinter.
We stop.
                Lean into me.

           The universe
in song, in quiet meditation.
We are wordless:
           I am in you.

Without knowing why
culture needs our knowledge,
we are one self in the canyon.
And the stone wall
I lean upon spins me
wordless and silent
to the reach of stars,
to the heavens within.

It's not mankind after all
nor is it culture
that limits us.
It's the vastness
we don't enter.
It's the stars
we don't let own us.

GETTING READY

Split piñon and cottonwood logs this morning.
See Lloyd taking the stones out of the pit.
Watch Jesse bring the wheelbarrow over.
Split some more piñon logs.

        We are here.
        The blue mountains are over there.
        Lloyd asks, "What are those
        mountains called?"
        "Sangre de Cristo," I tell him.

Call to James to help Jesse.
See Jesse limping back to the sweat lodge.
See James K. start to lay logs for the stones.
Think I've split enough wood.

        We are everywhere.
        The acts of Creation are everywhere.
        Stone, wood, fire, and water:
        These are the elements.

Walk to the fire pit and help.
Wad up newspapers and push them between logs.
Study the wind a moment and light the paper.
Hope the fire will catch quickly.

We have only this place.
It's always been like this.
One time, one place at once.
Nothing but ourselves, the nearby mountains,
our voices, our preparation to become.

Alberto Ríos

THE CURES OF GREEN AND NIGHT

Evening. The medicinal smells
Rise in the steam of the chamomile tea,

The steam's white arms
Reaching to me as I remember being reached for

By the arms of a nurse when I was five
Asleep in the hospital.

Those weeks and always after when I was sick
My grandmother made me the tea, very hot.

And from that tea her own white steam arms rose,
From inside the tea itself, some hand,

An arm and some fingers, reaching out.
This hand of hers was an open hand

But also an entertainment, the hand in the steam
Wobbling like a puppet's.

It made me laugh. I let the hand touch me,
Tickle me as it reached and held me,

Its long fingers circling around my head
Holding me a moment to an invisible shoulder,

This hand and this arm from the tea, this hand
The hand that had made the tea,

That had struck the match
And had wiped itself on my grandmother's apron.

It was her, her hand, I knew it even like this,
My grandmother's third hand.

Drink, she would say, and nothing more.
Chamomile, my grandmother's medicine

For children, and we were all children
In the luxuries and excesses of her kitchen

Whose smells and tastes were as much garden
Her bread made from leaves and blossoms

After rain. I have walked and I walk even now
Through this garden so filled with its mulch

I am above the ground walking on it.
At night, asleep, when sleep has come,

I have walked the hard walk
On the easy ground of this old wood.

The cure is like that, in that place
Green with the eyes open, green with the eyes closed.

Its green is chamomile with mint leaf,
Its particular fragrance a smell different

Like trees remarkable for the sounds of a bird
You cannot see, its sound

A song coming from the inside of the leaves.
The cure has always been that

And nothing more. It is still
These counsels of the small world:

Break open a leaf and a song comes out,
A song in the leaf in the hand.

A PHYSICS OF SUDDEN LIGHT

This is just about light, how suddenly
One comes upon it sometimes, and is surprised.

In light something is lifted.
That is the property of light,

And in it one weighs less.
A broad and wide leap of light,

Encountered suddenly for a moment—
You are not where you were

But you have not moved: it's the moment
That startles you up out of dream

But the other way around: it's the moment instead
That startles you into dream, makes you

Close your eyes, that kind of light, the moment
For which in our language we have only

The word *surprise,* maybe a few others,
But not enough. The moment regular

But with a knowledge that electricity exists
Somewhere inside the walls;

Tonight that the moon in some fashion will come out;
That cold water is good to drink.

The way taste slows a thing
On its way into the body,

Light, widened and slowed, so much of it: it
Cannot be swallowed into the mouth of the eye,

Into the throat of the pupil, there is
So much of it. But we let it in anyway,

Something in us knowing
The appropriate mechanism, the moment's lever.

Light, the slow moment of everything fast:
Like hills, those slowest waves, light

That slowest fire, all
Confusion, confusion here

One more part of clarity: in this light,
You are not where you were but you have not moved.

Wendy Rose

THE ENDANGERED ROOTS OF A PERSON

I remember lying awake
in a Phoenix motel. Like that
I remember coming apart accidentally
like an isolated hunk of campfire soot
cornered by time into a cave.
I live even now
in an archaeological way.

    Becoming strong on this earth is a lesson
    in not floating, in becoming less transparent,
    in becoming an animal shape against the sky.

We were born
to lose our eyes in the Sun Dance
and send out lengths of fishline
for the clouds, reel them in
and smooth away all the droughts
of the world.

    Sometimes Medicine People shake their hands
    over you and it is this; to drop your bones
    into the sand, to view yourself
    bursting through the city
    like a brown flash flood.
    The healing of the roots
    is that thunderhead-reeling;

they change and pale
but they are not in danger now.

That same morning
I went for coffee down the street
and held it, blowing dreams
through the steam, watching silver words
bead up on my skin. The Hand-trembler said
I belong here. I fit in this world
as the red porcelain mug
merges in the heat of my hand.

On some future dig
they'll find me like this
uncovered where I knelt
piecing together the flesh
that was scattered in the mesa wind
at my twisted-twin birth.

Benjamin Alire Sáenz

CEBOLLEROS

1959

The little boy and his father walked out of the barber shop on Picacho Street into the light of a summer evening. The boy thought the shadows were alive, speaking to him, whispering in his ears. He stared at the faded blues and reds of the barbershop pole winding forever down. The street was quiet, and the passing cars said things to the street, secrets the boy wanted to know, to touch. And for a moment, he imagined he was a car with tires talking to the streets in a language only the asphalt and the shadows understood.

The west side of town was dying. The hotels, peeling like sunburned skin, no longer attracted overnight tourists on their way to California. Music floated out of the rooms, music, Mexican music, from another country. The boy liked the music, and he tapped his foot to the rhythm and heard his mother singing as she did the laundry. Somewhere inside of him she was smiling. He wanted to dance but didn't know how. No one had ever taught him. He was a tire; he was dancing on the street to the music, the Mexican music, and the street melted with his secrets. The shadows of the evening were dreaming of another country, and the boy was the heart of the country, a new country.

An old truck with the same sunburned skin as the hotels drove slowly down the street. The truck had a long bed full of migrants and a railing; the people looked as if they were surrounded by a fence. They were colored in sweat, shiny and smooth, and their smell mingled with the shadows and the onions they picked. Early evening air and summer onions. The boy wanted to know, wanted to be the sweat and the smells, wanted to be the deep blue in the sky that would be turning pink and orange in a matter of minutes, wanted to be the magic.

"*¡Cebolleros!*" his father yelled as the truck drove past them. His voice was deep and harsh. He laughed and yelled it again. "*¡Cebolleros!*" The sound echoed in the boy's ears. Cebolleros. Cebolleros. The boy stared up at his father's moustache. He didn't like the sound of the words, but the people didn't seem to mind. He watched the people in the truck, and his eyes caught the face of a sunbrowned woman who smiled at him. He wanted to ask his father why the people were fenced in, but his father didn't like questions. The boy looked at his father's moustache and then smiled back at the woman. She blew him a soft kiss and laughed.

The truck came to a complete stop. The boy stared at the tires and wanted to be the truck. If he were the truck he would let the people out of the fence. Some of the men jumped off the truck holding their sweaty shirts in their hands. The boy stared at the shirtless men, the muscles, the strong backs. Maybe someday he would be strong like them. The men were laughing and saying things to each other: "*Ahora sí, unas cuantas cervecitas.*" The men laughed and went inside the hotel where the music was coming from. The little boy knew they were going inside to dance because they seemed happy. He glanced at the woman who had thrown him a kiss. He wanted to tell her she was good and beautiful. He couldn't take his eyes off her. "*¡Cebolleros!*" his father yelled again. The little boy didn't like the sound of it.

The truck drove away, the truck with the woman and the people and the fence around them. The boy watched them all disappear. "I wish I were a truck," he whispered. "*Pobres pendejos,*" his father said. The boy looked up at his father and wondered what he would look like without his moustache. When he grew up, he didn't want to have hair growing over his lip.

1967

My father lost his job that spring. That was the way of the construction business. That spring, no one was building. I heard my parents talking in the kitchen. I could hear them always—I could hear everything from everywhere. No one had any secrets. I was sitting in our room trying to read a book. I used to get lost in books, but that evening I wasn't lost. My parents were talking about what had to be done. The money my mother was making at the factory where she inspected pantyhose wasn't enough. It wouldn't be much of a summer without money. No swimming, no movies. No money, no summer. "I'll have to keep looking," my father said, *"tiene que haber trabajo."* And then he said that my older brother had to find a job to help out. I tried to imagine my brother working, the brother I always fought with, the brother who slept in the same bed I did, my brother who was only one year older than me. Fifteen wasn't old enough to get a job. "He's too young," I heard my mother say, *"no quiero que se salga a trabajar tan joven."*

"He can lie about his age," my father said. But I knew no one would believe he was old enough to work. He couldn't even grow a moustache. After a long silence my father said there might not be a job for him anyway, maybe a job for no one.

I heard my two younger brothers arguing over what they should watch on television. They were always fighting, but they were always happy. School would be out in another week. They would laugh and fight all summer. I walked out of our room and told them both to stop arguing or I'd turn off the television. They made faces at me—then laughed. Julian, the youngest, told me he wanted a television that showed things in color. "Just pretend," I told him. "It's more fun that way." I walked into the kitchen where my parents were drinking coffee. My father kept combing his hair with his fingers, always working. He had big hands, rough, strong like his voice. I stared at his moustache that covered his whole face. I wanted to say something but didn't know what, so I said nothing. I looked at my mother and smiled. She smiled back—we had secrets. I remember that spring.

There wasn't much to do after school let out. My father was home all the time, so we had to ask him for permission to do everything. It was better when he was working—when he was working, we could go anywhere we wanted. We couldn't even have a good fight because it made my father nervous. My brother and I kept wishing Dad would find a job before everyone exploded.

I was always reading books. Library books; long books about English people, novels about men and women falling in love in London or in the country. I remember thinking that where they lived was not like New Mexico. It was green, not like the desert. I imagined their rivers were blue, and they probably had boats, and the people in all those books didn't need to work. But I knew they were just books, and people didn't want to read books about people's work—so they kept the work out of it. I kept an eye on my younger brothers as I read, and every day it was my job to make lunch. Mostly I warmed up the food my mother left for us. My father was very quiet when we ate.

After two weeks, I heard my father tell my mother that we were going to pick onions. "Not much pay," he said, *"pero siquiera no me vuelvo loco."* That Sunday, my father told us that the onions were ready. He had spoken to a man he knew, and the man told him to come to the fields. "We're all going," he said. My brother and I looked at each other, but said nothing. "The kids too?" my older brother asked. "They can't stay here," my father said, "there's no one to take care of them. They can help us out."

Monday morning, when it was still dark, my mother woke us up with her whispers. She sounded like the rain. Everyone was too sleepy to say anything at breakfast, so we sat and heard each other eat. I watched my mother make the burritos, watched her hands move quietly. I watched her wide-awake face and the lines around her eyes. I wondered what she was thinking.

My father came into the kitchen and said it was time to go to the fields. I thought of the fields in the book I was reading, green and full of trees, English trees. My father reminded me and my brother that this was serious business. "We're here to work—not play. *No anden jugando.*" We nodded and looked at each other. As we walked outside, the sky was already turning blue. The morning, cool and soft, reminded me of my grandfather. In the morning, his chocolate eyes had been almost blue, showing me everything I ever wanted to see.

My father had collected plastic buckets for the onions—empty five gallon paint buckets that had been washed out. I looked at the scissors and turned them over in my hands. "I don't know how to use them," I told my brother. "Dad will show us," he said, "it'll be easy." He thought everything was easy. To me everything seemed hard like the cement driveway my father had poured last year.

We reached the fields as the sun lifted itself into the sky, turning the sky dusty blue. The people in the fields, wearing reds and pinks and blues, began claiming their rows. My father claimed some rows, and we followed him. My younger brothers were excited, and they kept running up and down the rows like it was a playground. The onions had been turned up by a machine and were lying on the ground waiting to be picked up. The smell of earth and onions dug into my skin, and I wanted to be an onion. I wanted to be the earth.

Everyone was talking. No one spoke English. I liked the sound of Spanish—it made me happy like the songs of my grandfather. My father went to talk to some of the men and then returned to the rows we had claimed and said we had to get to work. He looked at my brother and me and showed us how to clip the roots and the wilting tops. "We should have bought some gloves," he said, "but we can't be spending money on them right now. Maybe next week. You'll get blisters." He laughed. "It's all right, men's hands should have blisters."

I thought of the English novels where the men had no blisters on their hands, smooth, white hands—not like my father's. Dad rubbed my hair, and that made me smile. We got to work. I bent down and scooped up a smooth onion and cut it with my scissors, just the way my father had taught me. The snip sounded tinny as I cut the roots and the stems. Cutting. One onion, then another, then another. I was careful not to cut too close, because if I cut too close to the onion I'd ruin it, and we didn't get paid for ruining good onions. I watched myself cut the onions, cut them, and toss them carefully into my bucket until it was full. I pretended I was filling a basket with Easter eggs, yellow eggs, but it was hard to pretend because my hands were already getting blisters. The eggs were growing on my hands. "My hands are too soft," I mumbled, "they're not a man's hands." I stood straight, unbent my back, and showed my hands to my brother. He grinned and showed me his. Onions, yellow onions the color of my grandfather's teeth.

In the next row two women were talking as they worked. They were fast, much better than me and my brother. I thought of a man I had once seen drawing a church—he did it fast, perfect—perfect like the women in the next row. I heard them talking, voices like guitars singing serious songs: *"Bueno, mi esposo es muy bueno pero toma mucho. Y mis hijos salieron peor. Dios mío, no sé que voy hacer con esos hijos que tengo—pero son muy trabajadores."*

My youngest brother came to take the bucket to empty it into a gunny sack. It was too heavy for him. I picked him up and threw him in the air—he was so small and happy. "Do it again," he yelled, "do it again." My other brother showed up, and together they carried the bucket of onions away. "This is fun," they yelled. But it wasn't. My back was beginning to feel bent and crooked. I arched myself as far back as I could—my neck stretching away from the ground. The woman in the next row smiled at me: *"Qué muchachito tan bonito."* I bowed my head, bent my back toward the earth again—toward the earth and the onions.

By the end of the day I did not know how many sacks of onions we had picked. My brother asked my father. "Thirty," he said. Thirty, I thought, maybe a world record. My brother and I looked at each other and smiled. "Your nose is sunburned," my brother said. "So is yours." We fell to the ground wrestling and laughing. I heard my father talking to the men. They were laughing about something, too.

We walked back to my father's Studebaker, and my brother kept saying it was a dumb truck and that we needed a new one. He kept talking all the way home, but I wasn't listening. My nose was hurting; my back felt as if I had been carrying someone all day; my blisters were stinging. I wanted to go home and sleep. I didn't care how bad I smelled; I wanted to sleep or die or wake up in the fields of my novels. When we got home, my mother had dinner ready. She took my youngest brother in her arms and laughed. She looked so clean. She kissed me on the cheek and told me to take a shower.

I felt the hot water hit my body—I was a candle. I was melting into nothing. I ate the warm dinner but couldn't taste it. I was too tired to talk. My father told my mother we were going to have to work harder: "Only thirty sacks. *A veinte y cinco centavos al costal nunca la vamos hacer.* Tomorrow we'll work harder."

I went to bed and did not read my English novel. My brother told me he was glad I wasn't going to read because he hated for the light to be on while he was trying to sleep. "You read too damn much anyway." I looked at him and wanted to stick my fist through his face. I threw my book across the room and turned off the light. I dreamed I had a horse and lived in a house where they played only Mexican music, a house where I could dance in every room.

The second day was the same as the first, only we worked harder, and wore hats. By the end of the day, we had picked fifty-five sacks. It was better, but it still wasn't enough. I dreamed I was standing on a hill made of onions. There was a huge crowd of English people yelling at me: *"¡Cebollero! ¡Cebollero!"* I woke up and smelled the onions and the dry earth. I walked into the bathroom and threw up. I didn't read any more books that summer.

The whole week was the same. We worked, we ate, we slept. The second week was better. I was getting used to the work, and we were up to seventy sacks of onions a day. I started hating the sun and the earth and the onions, but the voices of the people played over and over in my mind, the music. The music kept me working.

We moved to another field in the middle of the second week. When we left the old field I felt I was leaving something behind, but when I searched with my eyes, I saw nothing but graying earth and sacks of onions waiting to be picked up by other workers who would sort them. I half-thought that if I looked in each sack, I would find people hiding.

The first day of the third week was the same —until the afternoon. The sun was hotter than usual—white, blinding, everything feeling as if it were touched by flames. My father made sure we were drinking plenty of water. The afternoon was too hot for talking, and everyone worked quietly. In the silence all I could hear was the onions being dumped into gunny sacks and scissors snipping at roots and stems, but the sounds were distant—almost as if the sun were swallowing all the sounds we made with our work. The fields were strange. We were in another country, a country I didn't know.

"I'm an onion," I said out loud, "but I don't want to be one." My brother looked at me and told me I was saying dumb things. "If you say something like that one more time, I'm going to tell Dad you've had too much sun." "I am an onion," I said, "and so are you." He shook his head and kept working.

In the heat I heard a voice yelling, and some of the people working

in the fields ran and hid in a nearby ditch. Other people just kept working. I didn't know why people were hiding, and the woman in the next
row told me not to say anything to the *Migra*. *"Nomas no digas nada,
mijo."* I nodded, but I wasn't sure what she was talking about. I was
keeping a secret but I didn't know the secret. I looked at my brother and
again I knew I was an onion.

The Border Patrol van stopped at the side of the road, and some
men dressed in green uniforms got out and walked into the fields. They
looked like soldiers. The men stopped and asked people questions.
Some of the workers showed them pieces of paper and others showed
them their wallets. One of the men in green came closer to our row. He
asked the women in the row next to ours a strange question: *"¿Tienen
papeles? ¿Permisos?"* I smiled at his Spanish, not like music, not even like
a language. The women spoke to him in fragmented English. "I don't
need paper," one woman told one of the men in green. Her voice was
angry like a knife. She showed him a driver's license and what I thought
was a birth certificate. The officer reached for the document. She
pulled it away. "I'll hold," she said, "don't touch." He nodded, and
walked away. *"Muchachos,"* he said to my brother and me, *"¿tienen papeles?"* Neither one of us said anything. I moved closer to my brother.
He asked his question again. "I don't know what that is," I said. He
smiled. "You're a U.S. citizen, are you?" "Yes, sir," we both said. "Who
was the first president?" he asked. "That's easy," I said, "George Washington." He winked at us and kept walking down the row. I didn't go
back to work until I knew my father was safe.

1970

The boy had grown up, looked almost like a man, but his eyes were still
those of a child. These days were different for him: days of black arm-
bands to protest the war that had lasted as long as the boy could remember; days of draft cards and draft numbers; days of putting up posters on
his walls and making his father angry; days of examining his face in the
mirror looking for signs of manhood; days of joining sit-down strikes to
change the dress code at school. The boy was still listening to music,
still in love with sound: Three Dog Night, Grand Funk Railroad,
Crosby, Stills, Nash, and Young. In his spare time, the boy stared at the

posters that surrounded him: Jimi Hendrix and Janis Joplin and Che Guevara. There were farm worker boycotts, but the boy did not think of the boycotts: he was in love with Joan Baez, dreamed of the barefoot madonna. He wanted to grow his hair long, but his father would not let him. He got angry but said nothing. Sometimes he was happy and angry at the same time, though he didn't know why. This was the year he was going to graduate. This was going to be *the* year, he told himself, the best year of his life.

Some nights he wrote to his brother who was in the war, and when he signed the letters he hated the whole world for taking his brother away.

His last semester in high school, the boy was confused, but he tried not to think about the chaos in his mind. Words swam up there like fish at the edge of a lake trying to flap themselves into the water, back into life. He tried not to think about the future since his father had already decided he would go to the local college, but he knew it wasn't just his father—it was money, no money, no money to go to a school far away. But the boy blamed his father. He tried to focus his attention on the enemy at hand: the high school. He fought his final days at school as if everything were a protest song—a stubborn song being banged out on a guitar.

He was getting good grades in everything except chemistry. If he didn't pass, he'd have to go to summer school because it was a required course. All those good grades, and it had come down to this. He was a borderline student in that class and he knew it, but there wasn't any time. There wasn't any time. And the teacher hated him. He could feel the teacher's hatred, the blue-eyed wrestling coach who favored athletes and nice-looking white girls. His brother wrote and told him to calm down, told him everything would be all right: "Just graduate and go to college. Do whatever it takes, just don't join the army."

His father had been sick, had been taken to the hospital where the doctors discovered he'd had a stroke. He was recovering at home, slowly, and the boy's mother signed up to work longer hours at the factory. The boy came home after school, made dinner for his younger brothers and his father. Afterwards, he went to work at a hamburger joint. He studied late at night, and he was too tired for chemistry.

Sometimes, he would stay home from school and keep his father company, even though his father didn't say much. Talking didn't matter to
his father—he just hated being alone. The boy wanted to speak, to say
something, but there was little to talk about when he tried. He sometimes looked at his father's face, his graying moustache, and wondered if
he would die, but then put the thoughts away like dirty clothes in a
hamper. He thought instead of the chemistry teacher. He might have a
better chance of passing the class if he took off the armband he wore
every day to school, but his father was happy his son was wearing it.
The boy and the father were together on the subject of the war.

The boy had missed too many days of school when his father had
been unable to care for himself, but when he improved, the boy started
getting back to his studies, back to his chemistry. "I have to pass this
course," he told himself, "I have to. This can't keep me down. *This
won't keep me down."* He thought of all the work he'd done, all the A's
he'd made for his father, and now this—this because the old man had
gotten sick. "He had to get sick," he mumbled. He clenched his jaw,
did not say a word to anyone.

His father mentioned to him that the Brown Berets were coming
to town. The boy laughed when his father told him his uncle had said
they were just a bunch of punks. "Yeah," the boy answered, "Uncle
Nacho also says that the peace sign is the footprint of the American
chicken." They both laughed. The boy was happy when his father
laughed.

"Chicano Power," the boy repeated to himself. The words
sounded strange. The movement, the movement, it had come, had finally reached his hometown. It would change everything. Would it
change everything? Anything? Anything at all? He read a poster calling
for an all-out student strike, and music played in his head, music like
he'd heard floating out of a forgotten hotel from his childhood. His father said they had the right idea but growled that they needed haircuts.
The boy shook his head.

The Chicanos were going to strike. The boy wanted to be with them,
wanted it, wanted to march. He was afraid, and he was angry with himself for being afraid. He kept studying. The students were asked to walk
out of their classrooms, and the blue-eyed coach kept talking about what

chemicals, when combined with others, caused an explosion. The boy smiled. He could hear the Chicanos coming down the hall: ". . . Chicano!" a voice yelled. "POWER!" the voices shouted back. MUSIC, the boy thought, music. "Chicano . . . POWER . . . Chicano . . . POWER . . . Chicano . . . POWER . . ." The voices grew louder. The sound of marching feet echoed down the hall. They're dancing, the boy thought, and his feet shuffled under his desk. "Chicano . . ."

The wrestling coach stared at his class as the voices came closer. "No one is to leave this classroom—no one."

". . . POWER! . . ."

"I don't like my class being interrupted. This is a school, not a playground for idiots." The boy listened to the sound of his teacher's voice. It sounded as if it were made of cardboard—nothing at all original in what he said, nothing interesting, just a voice, a voice addicted to the attention of his students.

". . . POWER . . ."

The boy's friend looked at him, and words were written in his eyes: "The hell with him, come on . . ." The boy looked at his friend, and his eyes nodded. He wanted to dance, he wanted to sing, he wanted to answer: "The hell with him."

"If anyone leaves this classroom, I'm suspending them." The coach shut the door, his eyes bulged at his students. His eyes erased the color of most of his students. "We're all equal here—nobody's better than anybody else. They're just noise. This is the age of noise. No need for any of you to get involved. This is not the place . . ."

The boy's friend looked at him again.

The boy looked back, his brown eyes speaking: "I can't. He'll flunk me. Do you understand that I can't?"

"Chicano . . ." They were marching past the classroom. Hundreds of them. *Millions of us, millions.* The boy's heart shook. He thought it would shake forever.

". . . POWER . . ."

His friend stared at him: "Now. Let's go. Now!"

I'll suspend anyone who leaves this class. The boy looked toward the door; he heard every footstep.

He looked at his friend and shook his head.

One of the marchers opened the door—raised a fist at the students sitting at their desks.

The boy's friend raised a fist, too. A salute; he held his fist high like a man reaching for something.

The wrestling coach glared at him.

The boy's friend glared back. He kept his fist up, then put it down—slowly. Deliberately. He smiled at the teacher.

The boy smiled, too. He didn't march. He passed the course. He graduated.

September 16, 1970

Dear Javier,

Well, I started college two weeks ago, and so far it seems to be OK. Nothing special. The old man's already on my case about studying, as if I was always messing around. I swear I don't understand that man. I don't think anyone does. And he never lets up.

School doesn't seem very hard, but I didn't think it would be. I guess you already know I didn't want to go to school here. I wanted to go to a better school—anywhere—just not here. I didn't want to live at home, but I guess I'll just have to deal with it. Anyway, Dad's happy about it. He's always talking about how he built those buildings and how they belong to us. Try telling that to the State!

I'm still working on weekends and even during the week some-times. If I'm not working, I'm studying or going to class. I even find time to go to movies sometimes with our little brothers (who are now bigger than you and me). Somehow, they don't seem to ever change—they still think everything is funny. They have Mom's sense of humor. (Thank God!) And speaking of Mom, she's doing great. She looks a lit-tle tired sometimes, but she's alright. I think she worries about you a lot. She has your picture beneath the statue of the Virgin, and has a can-dle lit for you (of course!). The kids call it the eternal flame. Clowns! Mom says you look very handsome in a uniform. Personally, I think you look better in jeans.

Mom says Dad's taken to dreaming about you, but she says she can't get much out of him. I swear he gets more uncommunicative every day (if that's possible). He's so damn stubborn, and he's sick all the time. I think it's because he keeps everything in—it just eats at him. Anyway, enough of all that.

I don't have much time right now—I'm in between classes, but I at least wanted to drop you a note to let you know I think of you and miss you. It's strange. I sometimes think you'll come walking through the door any minute. Take care of yourself, OK? Watch out for Charlie. Write when you get a chance—your last letter was great (even though your penmanship sucks!).

Un abrazo,
Luis

1974

I graduated from college yesterday—from the university my father wanted me to attend. Somehow it was a letdown, but it was a letdown from the very beginning. This is not what I wanted. This is what my father wanted. I never said a word. He never lived to see me graduate. Right after the ceremony I wanted to rush to the cemetery and throw my diploma on his grave and yell: "Goddamn you, there it is! There it is!" I couldn't quite bring myself to do it. Yelling at the dead seemed like such a stupid thing to do. I did go to the cemetery. I placed the diploma on my father's gravestone and said nothing. It was like he was still alive and I was simply giving him something he wanted, something he needed.

Looking at Dad's grave, I thought of the summer when he picked onions in the fields. For whatever reason, it was the only summer I remembered. I remembered him mocking the migrants when we came out of a barbershop one time—a vague memory, but I know it happened. And yet, when he was working in the fields, he seemed alive, a part of everything. Everyone liked him because he was so rebellious, and he made jokes about the gringos. Everyone would laugh. A man from that summer even went to my father's funeral. He told me my father was a good man. Yes, he was a good man, but that didn't make him any easier to love. I wish love had come as easy to him as work.

Standing there in the cemetery I suddenly remembered being afraid when the Border Patrol came looking for "wetbacks," and I couldn't go back to work until I knew my father was safe. Safe from what? I cut the weeds around the graves, and it made me think of the stems of the onions. I looked at the graves—my grandfather's, my father's, my brother's. "Remember, Javier, how I told you that we were all onions?" There was no answer. His voice was buried somewhere deep—in the land of the dumb. He was gone. They were all gone. I knew someday there would be a place for me next to them—in the company of men who did not speak.

1985

The young man in his early thirties drove into the parking lot of the grocery store. Lines were forming around his eyes, and his hair was prematurely graying. He checked his coat pocket for the list his wife had made for him that morning. The afternoon sun was so hot it seemed to be melting everything, but the man did not seem to be bothered by the heat. He had a sort of lazy walk, and he was singing to himself in Spanish, a song, a Mexican song that was always sticking in his mind, and he swayed his body to the internal rhythm.

Inside the grocery store, he grabbed a cart and pretended he was driving a car in a race. He laughed to himself. He had given up trying to change—now he just enjoyed the games he played. He looked over the list and headed for the fresh vegetables. He felt the heads of lettuce and talked to them. He found just the right one and tossed it in his basket as though it were a ball going through a hoop. He smiled. He picked out fresh cilantro, tomatoes, jalapeños. He tore a plastic bag from the roll hanging above the vegetables and waited behind two women who were standing above the onion bin.

"God," one of them said, "these onions are absolutely beautiful. What would we do without onions?"

"Eat boring food, I suppose," the other answered. "Who invented them anyway?"

The other lady laughed. "No one invented them—the farmers grow them. It's amazing how farmers can grow things, isn't it?"

"And the nice thing about onions is that they're so cheap."

The man with the moustache nodded to himself. For a moment he did not seem like the happy young man who had skipped into the gro-cery store. He looked like a lost child, fenced in, a little boy who was lost in the fields of a summer in a country he had left but still dreamed of—a country that had claimed him forever, a country he would never understand. "Onions *are* cheap," he said aloud, "dirt cheap."

Luci Tapahonso

THE MOTION OF SONGS RISING

The October night is warm and clear.
We are standing on a small hill and in all directions,
around us, the flat land listens to the songs rising.
The holy ones are here dancing.
The Yeis are here.

In the west, Shiprock looms above the desert.
Tsé bit'a'í, old bird-shaped rock. She watches us.
Tsé bit'a'í, our mother who brought the people here on her back.
Our refuge from the floods long ago. It was worlds and centuries ago,
yet she remains here. Nihimá, our mother.

This is the center of the night
and right in front of us, the holy ones dance.
They dance, surrounded by hundreds of Navajos.

          Diné t'óó àhayóí.
          Diné t'óó àhayóí.

We listen and watch the holy ones dance.

          Yeibicheii.
          Yeibicheii.
          Grandfather of the holy ones.

They dance, moving back and forth.
Their bodies are covered with white clay
and they wave evergreen branches.
They wear hides of varying colors,

their coyote tails swinging as they sway back and forth.
All of them dancing ancient steps.
They dance precise steps, our own emergence onto this land.
They dance again, the formation of this world.
They dance for us now—one precise swaying motion.
They dance back and forth, back and forth.
As they are singing, we watch ourselves recreated.

Éé álts'íísígíí shił nizhóní. The little clown must be about six years
old. He skips lightly about waving his branches around. He teases
people in the audience, tickling their faces if they look too serious or
too sleepy. At the beginning of each dance, when the woman walks by to
bless the Yeis, he runs from her. Finally, after the third time, she
sprinkles him with corn pollen and he skips off happily. 'éí shił nizhóní.

The Yeis are dancing again, each step, our own strong bodies.
They are dancing the same dance, thousands of years old. They are here
for us now, grateful for another harvest and our own good health.

> The roasted corn I had this morning was fresh,
> cooked all night and taken out of the ground this
> morning. It was steamed and browned just right.

They are dancing and in the motion of songs rising,
our breathing becomes the morning moonlit air.
The fires are burning below as always.

> We are restored.
> We are restored.

Peter Wild

HAVASU CITY

Over there in California
      where everything happens,
   cars are swerving off bridges,
        their drivers madly fighting the wheel,
    or still placidly steering
         as they arc through space,
  while other people, as corporate buildings
      sway and twist, up that high in pinnacles
are now convinced there really is
      a pit beneath their lives.
But hundreds of miles away
      out in the desert,
   over here in Havasu City,
     closer to the center of the universe,
   there's only the serene movement
        of the earth's waterbed around us,
     while a few glass trinkets crash to the floor,
and the tourists in the curio shop
      not knowing what to say
    for once in their lives, but feeling
       the ground rolling beneath them,
   experience something most of them
         won't see in a lifetime,
   up on the shelf the kachina dolls,
      those little gods of beneficence

who've stood there so long
                           they're mad about it,
        at last begin to flap their wings.

Ofelia Zepeda

WIND

The wind was whipping my clothes harshly around me,
slapping me,
hurting me with the roughness.
The wind was strong that evening.
It succeeded in blowing my clothes all around me.
Unlike others I revel in it.
I open my mouth and breathe it in.
It is new air,
air, coming from faraway places.
From skies untouched,
from clouds not yet formed.
I breathe in big gasps of this wind.
I think I know a secret, this is only the opening act
of what is yet to come.
I see it coming from a long distance away.
A brown wall of dust and dirt,
moving debris that is only moments old,
debris that is hundreds of years old.
All picked up in a chaotic dance.
The dust settles in my nostrils.
It clings to the moisture in my mouth.
It settles on my skin and fine hairs.

Memories of father and how he sat in front of the house
watching the wind come.
First he would smell it, then he would see it.

He would say, "Here he comes,"
much in the same way as if he saw a person on the horizon.
He would sit.
Letting the wind do with him what it will,
hitting him with pieces of sand.
Creating a fine layer all over him.
Finally when he could not stand it any longer
he would run into the house, his eyes shut,
shut against the tears getting ready to cleanse his eyes.
We all laughed at his strange appearance.
He also reveled in this wind.
This was as close as he could get to it,
to join it, to know it, to know what the wind brings.
My father would say, "Just watch, when the wind stops,
the rain will fall."

The story goes.
Wind got in trouble with the villagers.
His punishment was that he should leave the village forever.
When he received his sentence of exile
Wind went home and packed his things.
He packed his blue winds.
He packed his red winds.
He packed his black winds.
He packed his white winds.
He packed the dry winds.
He packed the wet winds.
And in doing this he took by the hand
his friend who happened to be blind.
Rain.
Together they left.
Very shortly after, the villagers found their crops began to die.
The animals disappeared,
and they were suffering from hunger and thirst.
To their horror the people realized they were wrong
in sending Wind away.

And like all epic mistakes it took epic events
to try to bring Wind back.

In the end it was a tiny tuft of down
that gave the signal that Wind was coming back.
With him was his friend, Rain.
He brought back the dry wind,
the cold wind,
the wet wind,
the cool wind,
but in his haste,
he forgot
the blue wind,
the white wind,
the red wind,
and the black wind.

MORNING AIR

The early morning air,
enveloped in heavy moisture.
I go outside and it lays on my shoulders.
I go about my business,
carrying the morning air
for the rest of the day.

PART IV

Taking a Stand

VOICES OF CONSERVATION

AND RESTORATION

Rudolfo Anaya

DEVIL DEER

At night, frost settled like glass dust on the peaks of the Jemez Mountains, but when the sun came up the cold dissolved. The falling leaves of the aspen were showers of gold coins. Deer sniffed the air and moved silently along the edges of the meadows in the high country. Clean and sharp and well defined, autumn had come to the mountain.

In the pueblo the red ristras hung against brown adobe walls, and large ears of corn filled kitchen corners. The harvest of the valley had been brought in, and the people rested. A haze of piñon smoke clung like a veil over the valley.

Late at night the men polished their rifles and told hunting stories. Neighbors on the way to work met in front of the post office or in the pueblo center to stop and talk. It was deer season, a ritual shared since immemorial time. Friends made plans to go together, to stay maybe three or four days, to plan supplies. The women kidded the men: "You better bring me a good one this time, a big buck who maybe got a lot of does pregnant in his life. Bring a good one."

Cruz heard the sound of laughter as neighbors talked. In the night he made love to his wife with renewed energy, just as the big buck he was dreaming about. "That was good," his young wife whispered in the dark, under the covers, as she too dreamed of the buck her husband would bring. Deer meat to make jerky, to cook with red chile all winter.

These were the dreams and planning that made the pueblo happy when deer season came. The men were excited. The old men talked of hunts long ago, told stories of the deer they had seen in the high country, sometimes meeting deer with special powers, or remembering an accident that happened long ago. Maybe a friend or brother had been shot. There were many stories to tell, and the old men talked far into the night.

The young men grew eager. They didn't want stories, they wanted the first day of deer season to come quickly so they could get up there and bag a buck. Maybe they had already scouted an area, and they knew some good meadows where a herd of does came down to browse in the evening. Or maybe they had hunted there the year before, and they had seen deer signs.

Everyone knew the deer population was growing scarce. It was harder and harder to get a buck. Too many hunters, maybe. Over the years there were fewer bucks. You had to go deeper into the forest, higher, maybe find new places, maybe have strong medicine.

Cruz thought of this as he planned. This time he and his friend Joe were going up to a place they called Black Ridge. They called it Black Ridge because there the pine trees were thick and dark. Part of the ridge was fenced in by the Los Alamos Laboratory, and few hunters wandered near the chain-link fence.

The place was difficult to get to, hard to hunt, and there were rumors that the fence carried electricity. Or there were electric sensors and if they went off maybe a helicopter would swoop down and the Lab guards would arrest you. Nobody hunted near the fence; the ridge lay silent and ominous on the side of the mountain.

All month Cruz and Joe planned, but a few days before the season started Joe was unloading lumber at work and the pile slipped and crashed down to break his leg.

"Don't go alone," Joe told Cruz. "You don't want to be up there alone. Go with your cousin, they're going up to the brown bear area. . . ."

"There's no deer there," Cruz complained. "Too many hunters." He wanted to go high, up to Black Ridge where few hunters went. Something was telling him that he was going to get a big buck this year.

So on the night before the season opened he drove his truck up to Black Ridge. He found an old road that had been cut when the Los Alamos fence had been put in, and he followed it as high as it went. That night he slept in his truck, not bothering to make a fire or set up camp. He was going to get a buck early, he was sure, maybe be back at the pueblo by afternoon.

Cruz awoke from a dream and clutched the leather bag tied at his belt. The fetish of stone, a black bear, was in the bag. He had talked to the bear before he fell asleep, and the bear had come in his dreams, standing upright like a man, walking towards Cruz, words in its mouth as if it was about to speak.

Cruz stood frozen. The bear was deformed. One paw was twisted like an old tree root, the other was missing. The legs were gnarled, and the huge animal walked like an old man with arthritis. The face was deformed, the mouth dripping with saliva. Only the eyes were clear as it looked at Cruz. Go away, it said, go away from this place. Not even the medicine of your grandfathers can help you here.

What did the dream mean, Cruz wondered and rolled down the truck window. The thick forest around him was dark. A sound came and receded from the trees, like the moaning of wind, like a restless spirit breathing, there just beyond the Tech Area fence of the laboratories. There was a blue glow in the dark forest, but it was too early for it to be the glow of dawn.

Cruz listened intently. Someone or something was dying in the forest, and breathing in agony. The breath of life was going out of the mountain; the mountain was dying. The eerie, blue glow filled the night. In the old stories, when time was new, the earth had opened and bled its red, hot blood. But that was the coming to life of the mountain; now the glow was the emanation of death. The earth was dying, and the black bear had come to warn him.

Cruz slumped against the steering wheel. His body ached; he stretched. It wasn't good to hunt alone, he thought, then instantly tried to erase the thought. He stepped out to urinate, then he turned to pray as the dawn came over the east rim of the ridge. He held the medicine bag which contained his bear. Give me strength, he thought, to take a deer to my family. Let me not be afraid.

It was the first time that he had even thought of being afraid on the mountain, and he found the thought disturbing.

He ate the beef sandwich his wife had packed for him, and drank coffee from the thermos. Then he checked his rifle and began to walk, following the old ruts of the road along the fence, looking for deer sign, looking for movement in thick forest. When the sun came over the volcanic peaks of the Jemez, the frost disappeared. There were no clouds to the west, no sign of storm.

Cruz had walked a short distance; a shadow in the pine trees made him stop and freeze. Something was moving off to his right. He listened intently and heard the wheezing sound he had heard earlier. The sound was a slow inhaling and exhaling of breath. It's a buck, he thought, and drew up his rifle.

As he stood looking for the outline of the buck in the trees he felt a vibration of the earth, as if the entire ridge was moving. The sound and the movement frightened him. He knew the mountain, he had hunted its peaks since he was a boy, and he had never felt anything like this. He saw movement again, and turned to see the huge rack of the deer, dark antlers moving through the trees.

The buck was inside the fence, about fifty yards away. Cruz would have to go in for the deer. The dark pines were too thick to get a clear shot. Cruz walked quietly along the fence. At any moment he expected the buck to startle and run; instead the buck seemed to follow him.

When Cruz stopped, the buck stopped, and it blended into the trees so Cruz wasn't sure if it was a deer or if he only was imagining it. He knew excitement sometimes made the hunter see things. Tree branches became antlers, and hunters sometimes fired at movement in the brush. That's how accidents happened.

Cruz moved again and the shadow of the buck moved with him, still partially hidden by the thick trees. Cruz stopped and lifted his rifle, but the form of the deer was gone. The deer was stalking him, Cruz thought. Well, this happened. A hunter would be following a deer and the buck would circle around and follow the hunter. There were lots of stories. A buck would appear between two hunting parties and the hunters would fire at each other while the buck slipped away.

Cruz sat on a log and looked into the forest. There it was, the outline of the buck in the shadows. Cruz opened his leather bag and took out the small, stone bear. What he saw made him shudder. There was a crack along the length of the bear. A crack in his medicine. He looked up and the blank eyes of the buck in the trees were staring at him.

Cruz fired from the hip, cursing the buck as he did. The report of the rifle echoed down the ridge. Nearby a black crow cried in surprise and rose into the air. The wind moaned in the treetops. The chill in the air made Cruz shiver. Why did I do that, he thought. He looked for the buck; it was still there. It had not moved.

Cruz rose and walked until he came to a place where someone had ripped a large hole in the fence. He stepped through the opening, knowing he shouldn't enter the area, but he wasn't going to lose the buck. The big bucks had been thinned out of the mountain. There weren't many left. This one had probably escaped by living inside the fenced area.

I'm going to get me a pampered Los Alamos buck, Cruz thought. *Sonofabitch* is not going to get away from me. The buck moved and Cruz followed. He knew that he had come a long way from the truck. If he got the buck he would have to quarter it, and it would take two days to get it back. I'll find a way, he thought, not wanting to give up the buck which led him forward. I can drive the truck up close to the fence.

But why didn't the buck spook when he fired at it? And why did he continue to hear the sound in the forest? And the vibration beneath his feet? What kind of devil machines were they running over in the labs that made the earth tremble? Accelerators. Plutonium. Atom smashers. What do I know, Cruz thought. I only know I want my brother to return to the pueblo with me. Feed my family. Venison steaks with fried potatoes and onions.

As he followed the buck, Cruz began to feel better. They had gone up to the top of the ridge and started back down. The buck was heading back toward the truck. Good, Cruz thought.

Now the buck stopped, and Cruz could clearly see the thick antlers for the first time. They were thick with velvet and lichen cling-ing to them. A pine branch clung to the antlers, Cruz thought, or patches of old velvet. But when he looked close he saw it was patches of hair that grew on the antlers.

"God Almighty," Cruz mumbled. He had never seen anything like that. He said a prayer and fired. The buck gave a grunt, Cruz fired again. The buck fell to its knees.

"Fall you *sonofabitch!*" Cruz cursed and fired again. He knew he had placed three bullets right in the heart.

The buck toppled on its side and Cruz rushed forward to cut its throat and drain its blood. When he knelt down to lift the animal's head he stopped. The deer was deformed. The hide was torn and bleeding in places, and a green bile seeped from the holes the bullets had made. The hair on the antlers looked like mangy, human hair, and the eyes were two white stones mottled with blood. The buck was blind.

Cruz felt his stomach heave. He turned and vomited, the sandwich and coffee of the morning meal splashed at his feet. He turned and looked at the buck again. Its legs were bent and gnarled. That's why it didn't bound away. The tail was long, like a donkey tail.

Cruz stood and looked at the deer, and he looked into the dark pine forest. On the other side of the ridge lay Los Alamos, the laboratories, and nobody knew what in the hell went on there. But whatever it was, it was seeping into the earth, seeping into the animals of the forest. To live within the fence was deadly, and now there were holes in the fence.

Cruz felt no celebration in taking the life of the buck. He could not raise the buck's head and offer the breath of life to his people. He couldn't offer the corn meal. He was afraid to touch the buck, but something told him he couldn't leave the deer on the mountainside. He had to get it back to the pueblo; he had to let the old men see it.

He gathered his resolve and began dragging the buck down the ridge toward the truck. Patches of skin caught in the branches of fallen trees and ripped away. Cruz sweated and cursed. Why did this deer come to haunt me? he thought. The bear in the dream had warned him, and he had not paid attention to the vision. It was not a good sign, but he had to get the deformed deer to the old men.

It was dark when he drove into the pueblo. When he came over the hill and saw the lighted windows, his spirits raised. This was home, a safe circle. But in his soul Cruz didn't feel well. Going into he fenced area for the deer had sapped his strength.

He turned down the dirt road to his home. Dogs came out to bark, people peered from windows. They knew his truck had come in. He parked in front of his home, but he sat in the truck. His wife came out, and sensing his mood, she said nothing. Joe appeared in the dark, a flashlight in his hand.

"What happened?" Joe asked. Cruz motioned to the back of the truck. Joe flashed the light on the buck. It was an ugly sight which made him recoil. "Oh God," he whispered. He whistled, and other shadows appeared in the dark, neighbors who had seen Cruz's truck drive in. The men looked at the buck and shook their heads.

"I got him inside the fence," Cruz said.

"Take Cruz in the house," one of the men told Joe. They would get rid of the animal.

"Come inside," Joe said. His friend had been up on the mountain all day, and he had killed this devil deer. Cruz's voice and vacant stare told the rest.

Cruz followed Joe and his wife into the house. He sat at the kitchen table and his wife poured him a cup of coffee. Cruz drank, thankful that the rich taste washed away the bitterness he felt in his mouth.

Joe said nothing. Outside the men were taking the deformed buck away. Probably burn it, he thought. How in the hell did something like that happen. We've never seen a deer like this, the old men would say later. A new story would grow up around Cruz, the man who killed the devil deer. Even his grandchildren would hear the story in the future.

And Cruz? What was to become of Cruz? He had gone into the forbidden land, into the mountain area surrounded by the laboratory fence. There where the forest glowed at night and the earth vibrated to the hum of atom smashers, lasers, and radioactivity.

The medicine men would perform a cleansing ceremony; they would pray for Cruz. But did they have enough good medicine to wash away the evil the young man had touched?

Jimmy Santiago Baca

SPARTON INDUSTRY

Manufactured electronic computer boards.
Out of business now, the cinder block building
broods with a dark menacing abandonment
on Coors Road—barbwire gnarls the dusty tumbleweed property.
NO TRESPASSING and crossbone skulls
click
    click
       click
          in the silence.
Once, wild west outlaws, more heroes than criminals,
inspired ballads and campfire tales.
But as happiness arcs its lightning
into scorched tragedy, the romantic villains
have become executive murderers.
       How do you assess the crime
of businessmen who lock shop and flee,
who for years dumped chemicals into the ground,
so toxic a cup of water from the city reservoir can kill you?
It's not as easy to erase as graffiti on walls
sprayed by municipal workers with high-powered wands.
       What crimes do we charge them,
       what penalties do we levy,
       how do we classify this lethal threat to existence?
How do we interpret other crimes, or those who glut our prison
system, the kid doing time for stealing a tire or smoking crack?
       In the human journey, sorrows have created poems and
       songs,

and what of human wisdom is born from what Sparton
Industries has done?
Making life itself cease and gasp and choke and rot,
murdering all who breathe in the microscopic
particles of blackened dirt,
and while corporations hire Milkens and Boeskys
of the world,
next to my children at night at my kitchen table,
helping them with their homework,
how do I explain why we must drink bottled water,
that there are no rivers safe to wade or fish to
eat or air to breathe,
how do I tell them I am as guilty
as the genocidal engineers who created death
for innocent children and future generations,
how do I admit even to myself, much less tell my

children,

I could have changed it and didn't
(I could have tried at least),
that I am sorry
the world they live in is uninhabitable?
What do we do?

Charles Bowden

FROM DESIERTO:
MEMORIES OF THE FUTURE

He is sitting on the wall smoking a cigarette and telling of the thorn forest and his village. The home place seems strange down there on the border of Sonora and Sinaloa. When he was a boy he would walk the almost forty miles into town, but now he has prospered and owns shoes. He has a good house, a pool, and does not go to the nearby fiesta for the Virgin of Balvanera—that is for Indios, for the dark-skinned people, the *borrachos.* Long ago, when the Americans had their First World War, two gringos from Texas fled the draft and came to the village and now their descendants flood the area. "Imagine," he says, "a pueblo of blue-eyed, fair-skinned Mexicans."

His brothers stayed in the village but in recent years it has gotten very bad there, many shootings and killings. *Las drogas.* He has had to bring his mother into town for her own safety. But that is not what he speaks of now. It is evening, we have been drinking, the Mexican sky bleeds stars. In a while, he will go to visit his girlfriend, then home to the wife, and a good night's sleep. He is explaining the uses of the forest, the various barks, herbs, fruits, roots, remedies, the lore of *brujas,* and *curanderas.* And, of course, the cats. There is the *león,* the lion, and ocelot, and the *onza,* yes, yes, Señor, it truly exists. And the *tigre,* the jaguar.

I quicken. The cats always seduce us, the grace, the silence, the dreams of giant purrs rolling off their bloody mouths. We find their tracks, stumble on their scat, smell the strength of their urine, but as for the animals themselves, we seldom catch even a glimpse, a few brief flashes in an entire lifetime. We look down at the paw print in the soft, moist ground and imagine the claws. A few months back, a *tigre* swept through his ranch, slaughtered a calf, and the man and his vaqueros took up a kind of pursuit. Of course, they failed. Without dogs, a man has almost no chance of treeing such an animal.

But his brother, his brother had better luck recently. He is still living back in that crazy village of blue-eyed Mexicans, and he hired some Tarahumara Indians from the sierra to help out. The Tarahumara are famous in Mexico for their foot races of a hundred or two hundred miles, for their refusal to become Mexicans—some still live in caves— and for their keenness out on the land. When a jaguar started killing his brother's stock, the Tarahumaras took up the pursuit. And they were successful. This is the interesting part, the man says. Mexicans, he explains, will eat mountain lions. You see, he instructs me, the lion eats cattle and deer and so is sound meat. But the jaguar, the jaguar eats anything, including men, and therefore it is not clean. But these Indians, they cut up the jaguar and made jerky, and then they pounded that jerky into powder and mixed it with spices and made *machaca*. And then, they ate it.

He looks over at me with a smile and shakes his head at the imagined horror of such an act. I say nothing. I imagine the Indians eating the cat, putting the power of the beast inside their own bodies. I become hungry.

Storm clouds scud low off Tonto Rim and the air rushes raw with cold fingers across the desert. The men walk slowly into the Gila County courthouse, the Levis worn, the fingers scarred, hands big, guts hanging over their belts, their shirts all with metal snaps. The faces are well creased by memories of sun and wind, the hats, they are different here, deliberately out of fashion, crown high and barely dented, brim pulled down fiercely in front and back. They nod to each other and barely speak. There is little need, the blood goes back three, four, five generations. The men under the hats share these things: they hate lions, they kill lions. And they love lions. These matters will never be spoken, but in the Rim country most of what is, is never said. Or it will not be at all.

They have killed hundreds, lassoed them, shot them, tracked them with hounds up the rock and into the trees. Shot down the mothers, brought home the kittens and raised them in cages. Crossed their yards each morning, the cats standing up, the blank green eyes reaching through the bars.

"You wonder what they're about," one rancher says. "You watch your ten-year-old kid walk past the cage and then look into those eyes."

I am sitting in the back of the room and do not speak but watch. I have driven up here in order to listen to the lion world. To consider nature, that fine word we feel more than understand. Ignore drugs, ignore them absolutely. Forget development, Charlie, finance, wine in goblets with fine stems, the voices on the phone with whispers of deals, testimony, fissures of bankruptcy streaking across the country club faces. Of course, there is no Mexico in this part of the desert, it is safely kept out of sight and mind. There is also the matter of love. And I have come to meet Harley Shaw, the one man in the state paid to think about lions.

My interest goes back to a time I cannot remember, perhaps when as a boy I hunted all day in the desert for deer and then as light began to fail turned back toward camp and followed my tracks. For more than a mile, I saw the dusty print of a lion in the outlined tread of my boots. Probably it started at that moment, realizing something I had never seen had followed me and watched me for hours. It may have been the Yaqui barrio that clung near the freeway in the city. I would go down there as a boy and stay all night to watch the dances. The Yaquis have songs, songs I did not understand until decades later, but songs that I heard and that seeped somehow into my imagination.

The Yaquis have a lot of songs and there is one about a female mountain lion. No one sings this song much up on Tonto Rim.

> Flower lion, flower lion,
>   walking in the wilderness, flower lion.
> Flower lion, flower lion,
>   walking in the wilderness, flower lion.

There are also songs about deaf mountain lions. And mad lions. But that is the flower world.

When I was a kid I sat in the Yaqui village late one night in the house of a man who talked in Spanish or Yaqui, neither of which I understood. His face was pleasant and blank to my eyes. The house was bare and simple, naked light bulbs hanging from the ceiling, a white porcelain sink standing free and gleaming like a treasure in the corner. The hours crawled by. After a while the man, he was the village head-man with a secure job on a highway crew, offered me a jar of *chiltepíns,* small red balls of explosive pepper. I did not know what they were and threw a fistful into my mouth. The man laughed silently as I bolted for the faucet.

Later, I sat under the ramada of an old man in his eighties. He swept out the church for the priest. When he smoked a cigarette, the end was soaked from his hungry lips. As a young man he had been a warrior in the Yaqui wars that raked Sonora until the '30s. Now he made flutes from cane. I still have one.

There is a place that is the desert—except that it is the desert made perfect. The deer are there, as they are here, and the flowers. This place is called Sea Ania, there the people are called Surem. The Yaqui learned of this place when a man who herded sheep and goats began to envy the hunters he saw decked out in the hides of many animals. He made a bow, fashioned an arrow, and went into the forest. He saw two large antlered deer rasping their horns together and a third, a smaller deer, moving around them. Then he understood: the large deer were making the music and singing, the small deer was dancing. He learned the songs and from that moment on the wall fell between this world and the flower world, the Sea Ania.

They say, for those who know the way, it lies to the east beneath the dawn.

One night at the dances I see this man. He is crawling across the dirt plaza toward the big wooden cross. It is black, mesquite smoke drifts on the March winds, the ground shakes with the stomping of the dance. The Yaquis huddle in a village of shacks less than a mile from the freeway. They are surrounded by the night moans of the city, a pudding of cement and tract houses that has flowed across the desert floor and trapped a half-million Americans in its grid of streets. The dancers do not hear the city, the man crawling does not hear the dance. He is drunk, he is a disgrace, he has, I suppose, violated the sacred rituals of the tribe's Easter. The dancers are in the flower world, the other reality where deer explain the nature of life to Yaquis.

They can do this but I cannot. The village has these problems, the heroin dealers, the lack of money, and of course the drunks. These matters cannot enter the flower world. The drunk has crawled on another ten years, he is covered with dust and strange grunts and cries pour out of his foamy mouth. No one says anything to him. No one tries to stop him. He does not exist in the flower world. So he does not exist.

Men who are not dancing sit on benches and smoke cigarettes. They wear deer heads. The drunk is struggling to his feet now, he is at the big cross that dominates the plaza. He cannot keep his head erect, he weaves and staggers forward. I am the only human being in the village who will look at him, but then he and I are not in the flower world. He lunges forward, drapes his outstretched arms on the cross. There, the silhouette against the fire: crucifixion.

Before the Spaniards arrived, all the people divided into two groups—the Surem and the Yoemem. A young Surem girl listened to a talking tree and when her people heard the tree's prophecies they decided to hold a dance. When it ended the Surem went into the earth. They are enchanted. Some argue that they became ants or dolphins, others say they still look human—they are just magical. To this day, a Yoemem will stumble on a Surem, a visitor from the enchanted world, the flower world. Such a meeting may kill the Yoemem. This is the way Felipe Molina reports the matter in a book. He is a Yaqui living near Tucson. He also notes, "for that reason, my grandfather and especially my grandmother disapproved of me going into the desert alone."

Perhaps, that is where the interest in lions began. For years, decades, I find their tracks, their dung, their lairs. But I never see one. I look for almost twenty-five years before I so much as catch a glimpse, the green eyes burning in the night.

Harley Shaw stands up in the Gila County courthouse and explains some new rules on killing lions and reporting the killing of lions and the how and the why of it. He is the bridge in this room between the men out on the land and the people who never see the land but make the rules for it. The walls of the room are decorator-selected soft tones and there is no clue within this chamber that this is the ground that spawned fables of the West. Zane Grey, a dentist, sought out this place to hunt and fish and pump the memories of local people for tales, odd yarns that he could stretch into short books for insurance salesmen bored with their jobs and their women back in Pittsburgh. The Pleasant Valley War left blood just to the north, the grizzly staged a last stand here. Just on top of the Rim in the town of Young with Moon's Saloon on the main dirt drag, the village hugging the edge of Pleasant Valley. In the '50s a woman tells me the boys were lounging out in front knocking back some cool ones when the first motorcycle to ever beat its way out of Tonto Basin came rolling down the street. They shot its tires out so as to have a better look.

The lions have never left, never given ground.

When Harley Shaw went to college, he wrote a paper in his freshman English class on Ben Lilly, a legendary hunter who died in 1936. Lilly started in Alabama and worked his way west slaughtering bears, coyotes, wolves, and lions. Once he guided for Theodore Roosevelt. He married twice, but these ventures did not work out. His first wife went insane, his second wife he abandoned. He was a solitary man, a religious man, who followed his hounds on foot six days a week subsisting on a little parched corn. At sundown on Saturday, he tied his dogs—Ben Lilly would not hunt on the Sabbath. If a dog failed to perform up to his standards, he beat it to death. He ended up in Arizona's Blue River country exterminating the last holdouts among the grizzlies and wolves. His name still conjures up tales in that region. For hunters, Ben Lilly is truly a legend—Texas folklorist J. Frank Dobie once wrote a book stating just that in the title, *The Ben Lilly Legend*. Shaw as a boy was fascinated by wildlife and so Lilly, the premier killer, was a link to the natural world for a boy growing up in the valley east of Phoenix.

Now Shaw is older and he is Arizona's expert on mountain lions. He remembers his fascination with Lilly and a soft grin graces his face. Harley Shaw has spent eighteen years following the lions on foot, on horseback, behind dogs, from airplanes.

He has never killed one.

Like us, lions kill. In the Southwest, their house occupies about 150 square miles on the average, and they move patiently through its many rooms. They are 5.5 to 7.5 feet long, the weight ranging from 75 to 190 pounds. We seldom see them: perhaps if lucky, once in a lifetime. But they always see us. They like to watch, they will follow us at that slow walk for hours. They almost never attack—in Arizona perhaps once a decade according to our records. They seem not to regard us as a suitable source of food. But the kill is the thing and what they like is something around a hundred pounds and alive. Studies in Arizona find about one out of every five kills is a calf. They eat what they kill, not what others have killed. We have studied this matter and we have numbers to comfort us. Every ten and a half days, an adult will kill. Or, if a mother, every 6.8 days. In certain regions, at certain times, under certain conditions. Because we really know very little about them, very, very little. Our major contact with them has always been on bloody ground, the kill.

I am standing in a patch of chaparral on the edge of Salt River north of Globe and the rancher is angry in that slow, hard way that ranchers vent their emotions. The voice is flat, almost monotone, the face placid. In one month he has lost thirty-four calves to them with calves worth hundreds of dollars apiece. But it is more than the money. It is the kill, the neck punctured by those large teeth, the small animal ripped open like an envelope. It is logical to argue that he was merely going to raise the calves to a certain weight and then ship them off to eventual slaughter. But this fact does not abate a rancher's anger. The calves were under his care, *his care,* and he has been violated by a force he never sees but whose presence he constantly suspects. He calls in the expert hunters and has seven of them taken off his land. That was months ago, but still he is not at peace. The fury of finding those dead calves in the morning light will not leave his eyes. He reaches the conclusion that many others have who stumble into their country: they like the killing.

And perhaps they do.

We will never find out.

We do not know how to ask.

It is just before Christmas. A mountain lion workshop clogs the lobby of a fine old hotel with 150 biologists, guides, animal control folk (trackers, trappers, poisoners, and hunters), plus a handful of conservationists, all tossing down drinks during the get-acquainted cocktail hour. A rumor floats through the room, one brought here by a government hunter from California. A woman, about fifty-one, has been found. The skull said to be punctured by a large tooth mark. The other whispered signs offer unmistakable evidence of a kill. The autopsy, well, that's the kicker, the autopsy, according to the rumor, suggests that the woman was alive while being eaten.

The kill.

I have come here with my simple question. What is it like to kill with your mouth? The biologists turn away when I ask. There are things about the wilds, we are not supposed to say.

And this brings us down to perhaps the fundamental fault line between us and lions. Our basic contact with mountain lions is the kill and yet what little we know suggests this is not the major portion of a mountain lion's life. Harley Shaw has studied lions in Arizona for eighteen years and he is the host of this big workshop. He is fifty-one now, the hair and trimmed beard silver, a bearlike man who is not tall, the eyes and voice very alert and deliberate. At times, he can be a bundle of statistics and graphs and scat samples and radio-collared plottings of lions. But now he is sitting down and just talking.

"Lions," he says, "more than other animals, have time for contemplation. They lay up, seek high places and vistas. So you wonder what goes through their minds."

You certainly do.

As soon as we knew they were around, we tried to kill them. When the Jesuit priests hit Baja at the end of the seventeenth century, they ran into a culture, one now vanished which we recall as the Pericue, that refused to slay lions. Imagine it is three hundred years ago and Father Ugarte, a large man and a strong man, wants the lion dead. The cat comes in the night, slaughters the mission stock at his outpost in southern Baja, then vanishes. The Indians will not kill the beast—if they do, they say they too will die. The priest is riding his mule on a narrow path, he sees a lion, throws the stone, the animal dies. He places the warm body across his mule, rides back to the mission, and shows off his trophy. The Indians watch, the priest does not die. See, he says, now you are free, now you can kill the lions.

We have not stopped since that moment. As a people, we've had a hard time abiding lions because they want what we want: meat, especially venison, lamb, and beef. Take Arizona. Between 1918 and 1947, 2,400 lions were killed in Arizona. Mainly, they were taken out for killing stock. Legendary men emerged like Uncle Jim Owens of the Grand Canyon country who is said to have bagged 1,100 cats in his life-time. A man named Jack Butler is reported around 1929 to have killed fifty-eight in eighteen months in the Sowats and Kanab Wash area around the Canyon. Government animal control people tried poison, traps, dogs, bullets—everything in their arsenal. In 1947, the state legis-lature took a look at the situation and decided to offer a bounty, one that floated between $50 and $100 for the next twenty-two years. They were moved to add this incentive because decades of lion killing had not seemed to dent the lion population. When the bounty finally be-came dormant in 1969 (it is still technically on the books ready to come to life if desired) another 5,400 lions had been knocked down.

All over the West (with the exception of Texas) attitudes about lions began to change in the sixties, and first one state and then another shifted them from varmints to game animals, started issuing hunting tags, and generally tried to manage them just like deer, bighorn sheep, elk, and antelope. Arizona made this shift in 1970 when it allowed one lion per hunter per year, stopped funding the bounty system, and gave control of the beast to the Game and Fish Department. Stock-killing lions could still be taken out by ranchers if they contacted the government.

What is the net result? No one's really sure. There are somewhere between two thousand and three thousand lions in Arizona—nobody has any good way to count them. The hunt has now been limited to six months a year, and Game and Fish is busily studying their new charges. Each twelve months between two hundred and four hundred of the cats are killed (the state figures run around two hundred, but some critics figuring in estimates of unreported rancher kills tend toward the high end). And after a century or more of slaughter they are still out there. In the American West there is no place where lions are endangered. They have survived without our help, they have survived in the face of our hatred.

David James Duncan

FROM "LAKE OF THE STONE MOTHER"

Three Thousand Wagons, Nine Hundred Graves

On January 14, 1844, Captain John C. Frémont and twenty-four other white men were searching the deserts of western Nevada for a river reputed to flow east to west from the Rocky Mountains to San Francisco Bay—a river reputedly large enough to be navigable, at least by large canoes. What Frémont found instead, at the terminus of the unnavigably small, swift river now known as the Truckee, was a huge, landlocked, saline lake. On this lake's eastern shore, miles away across the water, Frémont spotted a four-hundred-foot triangular rock that reminded him of an Egyptian pyramid. In his journal he wrote:

> We've encamped on the shore, opposite a very remarkable rock in the lake, which had attracted our attention for many miles. This striking feature suggested a name for the lake, and I called it Pyramid Lake.

There is just one problem with Frémont's journal entry: the lake already possessed a name. Resident Paiutes had long ago named it after a little tufa-rock formation just behind Frémont's grand pyramid, a formation called Tupepeaha, which translates "Stone Mother." Unprepossessing though she was, the Stone Mother's legend was the Paiute people's origin myth—their three-dimensional Book of Genesis, if you will—and for centuries the tribe had told stories and sung songs that gave her real presence in their lives. It was her tears that had created the lake and its life-giving bounty (and when you taste the water, sure enough, it's salty). According to Joe Ely, the tribe's ex-chairman, the Stone Mother and her legend "set our identity, and forever fix the components that make up our way of life." In the tradition of Great White Explorers the world over, however, Captain Frémont was not interested in indigenous tongues, mythic names, or mysterious presences. Frémont desired a navigable east-to-west river, not a navigable inner life. And most of our forebears have inherited, by choice or by force, the tongue and mindset of Frémont, not that of the Paiutes. So the Stone Mother continues to be an ignored matriarch of knowledge lost or forgotten. And the lake continues to bear a trivial name.

How important is this loss of meaning? Does it matter who names a lake, or any other body of water? Does it matter *what* they name it?

I believe that it may. It rains an average of five inches a year in west-central Nevada. The wettest year on record here is nine inches, and the dry year's record is no measurable rain at all. In a land this arid, H_2O ought to be measured in karats, not acre-feet. Water here is the essence of life, the only possibility of it. And to be careless in the way one handles life's essence can be fatal.

Four years after Captain Frémont "discovered," denamed, and re-named Pyramid Lake, gold was discovered in California. In the ensuing cross-continental rush of "forty-niners," an estimated 45,000 would-be millionaires crossed, or attempted to cross, the nameless forty-mile-wide soft-sand desert just south and east of Pyramid Lake. By the end of that year (see George B. Stewart, *The California Trail,* McGraw-Hill, 1962), that little no-name desert contained 9,771 dead domestic animals; 3,000 abandoned wagons; and 963 fresh human graves. Yes, there were precious metals in California. But on the trail through Nevada, water proved even more precious.

Nevada is a strange state for many reasons. High on the list of strangenesses is the fact that 82 percent of the state isn't even the possession of the state: it's public land owned by every single person of the United States. Equally high on the strange list is the legal gambling, which has created a multi-billion-dollar tourist business, which has in turn created Las Vegas, Reno, Tahoe, and other casino cities, which have in turn created dire water shortages, extinct species, traffic gridlocks, foul air, high crime, mafia corruption, environmental devastation, and all the other urban amenities. But even stranger, and more crucial, than either of these things—especially juxtaposed to these two things—is that five annual inches of rain. A "Fun Nevada Fact": there are more than twice as many people employed full-time by the Mirage Casino in Las Vegas as by every farm and ranch in the entire state. An UnFun Nevada Fact: the Mirage Casino, the 800,000 residents of greater Las Vegas, and the city's 20 million annual casino-bound visitors are dependent not on Nevada's own rivers, rainfall, or mountain runoff, but on the state's entire portion of Colorado River water, *and* on the eons-old, nonreplenishable underground reserves the city is sucking at a no-tomorrow pace.

In "Living Dry"—his definitive essay on the American understanding, and misunderstanding, of the arid inland West—Wallace Stegner pointed out that the syllable *pah,* in the Great Basin's Shoshonean tongues, means "water, or water hole." This is why so many Shoshone place-names (Tonopah, Ivanpah, Pahrump, Paria) contain this syllable. It's also why the region's prevalent tribe are called Paiutes: Pah-Ute means, literally, "Water Ute."

The Paiutes of Nevada, accordingly, lived in small, highly specialized, lake-dwelling, marsh-dwelling, or river-dwelling bands, most of which were named after the prevalent food of their small ecosystems. The Paiute word for cattails, for instance, is *toi,* and the word for eating is *dokado,* so the band that lived on Stillwater Marsh was known as the Toidokado—the cattail eaters. Trout, similarly, are *agai,* so the trout-eaters of the Walker River region were the Agaidokado. And the endemic (and now endangered) food fish of Pyramid Lake were the *cui-ui* (pronounced "kwee-wee"), so the band that lived here were the Kuyuidokado—cui-ui eaters. Cattails, trout, cui-ui—pah foods, water gifts, all.

Stegner wrote:

> The West is defined by inadequate rainfall [and] a general deficiency of water. . . . We can't create water or increase the supply. We can only hold back and redistribute what there is. . . . Aridity first brought settlement to a halt at the edge of the dry country and then forced changes in the patterns of settlement. . . . It altered

farming methods, weapons, and tools [and] bent water law and the structure of land ownership. . . . In the view of some, it also helped to create a large, spacious, independent, sunburned, self-reliant western character. . . . Of that, despite a wistful desire to believe, I am less than confident.

Sipping scotch on the rocks in an air-conditioned casino while pumping one's paycheck into a slot, one feels infinitely removed from the natural laws of the desert. But the fact remains—sorry, gamblers—that the rocks in those scotches come to us compliments of the pah, a place of water. This is why, minor or moot as the point may seem, I'm serious about my refusal to accept Frémont's offhanded renaming of the Kuyuidokado's desert lake. Four inches of rain per annum is not a viable climate, it's a perennial crisis; 963 graves just south of the Stone Mother demonstrate that to be careless in the face of this crisis is fatal. And a cavalier naming of a desert body of water is a form of carelessness.

There was a culture that lived with quiet grace beside these waters for tens of centuries. There is another culture that's left devastation, dreck, and dead bodies strewn all along the path of its half-cocked arrival. The Kuyuidokado, the Agaidokado, the culture that considered water to be the Stone Mother's tears, has nearly vanished. The culture of the gold rush and the Mirage has begun to feel the desert heat. In this land of constant, critical aridity, who can we trust to properly name and care for the precious springs, hidden seeps, and rare bodies of water? What should the inland sea known as Pyramid really be called? I don't pretend to know. But I do know that we must soon find out; that we must ask the water questions unselfishly; that we must dig deep, and listen to the earth, and each other, very closely.

Where, exactly, to begin?

Were it up to me, I'd ask the Stone Mother.

Fly-fishing Atlantis

On April 28, 1993, a battered American pickup empties an expedition of four white guys—me; a sculptor friend, Frank Boyden; The Nature Conservancy's Graham Chisholm; and the Paiute tribe's fisheries biologist, Paul Wagner—onto the shore of a large saline lake at the terminus of the Truckee River. Maps, road signs, countless books, and the local populace all refer to this body of water as "Pyramid Lake." But scattered along the beach upon which we've parked are fishermen—fly-fishermen, most of them; eighteen, at a quick count. And each of them has carried an aluminum stepladder out into the lake, which they are now using as casting platforms as they ply the wide waters for trout. Watching them cast—and still obsessing on Captain Frémont—I pop open a beer, reach for my pen, and make a journal entry of my own. I write:

> We've encamped on the shore, opposite a very remarkable row of men in the lake, which row had attracted our attention for many miles. This striking feature suggested a name for the lake. I have therefore decided to hell with the maps, road-signs, books and native populace, and have renamed the whole shit-a-ree "Aluminum Stepladder Lake."

This beach has a name. It's called "The Nets." And it was not, I am happy to say, named by Captain Frémont. It was christened just recently, Paul tells me, by the local Paiutes, after a failed attempt to raise Lahontan cutthroat trout in net-pens right off the beach here.

Graham has fixed us chips and salsa. He's watching birds now. And he's spotted two kinds of warblers I could have added to my life list if I'd been looking. But—typical fly-fisherman—I was watching a cloud of mayflies hovering over the hood of the pickup.

We've seen five or six hundred white pelicans, many at close range, a few still in sight on the lake. Also mallards, great blue herons, coots, grebes, many doves, Graham's warblers. My favorite sighting was a raven, alone on a big tufa formation over near the Stone Mother, madly croaking at the jet trails in the sky above. Low-flying black god calling out to high-flying white ones. Be careful who you worship, Raven. (But maybe he was cursing . . .)

The hills are pale pink, the sagebrush pale green, the lichen on the rocks brilliant yellow. The white snow patches high up on the Pah Rah Mountains seem precious in this clime: next month's water. If we stayed on this beach and kept eating these chips for a couple of decades, perhaps we'd become known to local Paiutes as the Chips&Salsadokado.

Maybe the Stone Mother would begin to speak to us. Hope so. My wife sure wouldn't.

In digging out my notebook I found a tourist brochure about the lake. Not the sort of thing I normally read, but it's amusing, with the lake right here, to compare the purple brochural rhetoric to the bright blue evidence before my eyes. Pyramid, the brochure assures us, is "a magnificent lake; a lake remarkably different from any you've ever seen. It's enchanting, a primeval lake where the weathering forces of wind and water have carved one of nature's bold statements: timelessness."

Something about this "timeless" prose makes me want to glance at my watch and note that it is 5:30 P.M. But I do agree that the lake is a "bold statement" of some kind. It's twenty-six miles long, four to ten miles wide, up to three hundred feet deep, and its waters range, as the brochure promises, from turquoise to copper green to deepest blue. The wide beach upon which we've parked is one of "more than 70 miles of sandy beaches that make picnicking and camping ideal." A beach-feature the brochure neglects to mention, though, is the cow pies. We had to displace an entire herd of impending hamburger in order to park our trucks, and there are cow calling cards everywhere. Not that I'm complaining. It's an occasion for added sport, actually: the desert air dries the pies so fast that I find (after my second beer) that I can take a little run, hop onto the dried top of a pie, and "skimboard" three or four feet along the beach, leaving a fragrant green streak (another "one of nature's bold statements"?) on the sand behind me.

Swallows dip low over the pelican-tracked and tire-tracked sand. Sound of waves, sound of gulls, sound of fly-reels cranking. But the predominant sound here at the Nets is the human voice: deep male voices, most of them; calm for the most part, and conversational; but now and then broken by the weird grunts, hoots, and laughter of men hooking and playing trout. . . .

We've left The Nets behind, driven to a quieter, much more beautiful beach, and as the sun drops behind the Pah Rahs I'm wading out, rod in hand, intent on experiencing the "something."

Paul's name for this quiet cove is "Atlantis." Back in the eighties, his explanatory story goes, the boosters of Reno and Washoe County decided to sink some money into a campground in hopes of luring more spendthrift fishermen to the lake. To that end they built eight concrete picnic tables with permanent metal sunshades, several deluxe outhouses, and a large, all-weather concession building to purvey hot food and drink. Demonstrating the booster's unwavering fondness for both anachronism and cliché, they dubbed the place "Warrior Point." But happily, almost the day the job was finished the record rains of the mid-eighties began, the lake rose twenty feet, the concession, outhouses, and tables were flooded, and Warrior Point, for Paul anyway, became "Atlantis."

In the drought of the past seven years the waters dropped and the campground reappeared. But the risen Atlantis seems to have been discovered by no one but the ubiquitous cows, who, judging by the ample evidence, are experiencing serious confusion about the respective functions of the picnic area and the outhouses. Graham's begun making barbecued veggies and chicken while the rest of us fish. I'm happy to report that he's cooking on the beach, not in the picnic area.

Lahontan cutthroat are famous for feeding right on the bottom, so I'm a little surprised, after a few fruitless casts, to see a fish rise nearby. I point out the rise-form. "Tui chub," Paul speculates. A trash fish. But I cast to it anyway—with a no-name nymph a friend sent in the mail. It's covered with peacock feathers, like a dancer in an MGM floor show—feathers that imitate no insect known to man but do sometimes generate the same iridescent confusions in trout that the dancers do in humans. The nymph hits the water while the rise-form rings are still expanding. I start it strutting across the sandy bottom. The fish takes it. I set the hook. But as the rod bends hard I know before I see it that this is no kind of chub: it's one of Paul's Lahontan pets. It's not a leaping fish, but it makes several strong runs. Its fighting tactics remind me more of brown trout than of the cutthroats I'm used to catching on the Oregon coast.

All through the long dusk and into the darkness the cutthroat keep rising. And casting to those rises I hook, and further educate, eight of Paul's bright pupils. Fourteen to nineteen inches, if anyone's wondering. All rock-hard, moon-silver swimmers, reluctant to let me touch them in order to let them go. No trout I take compares to the two bloodied lunkers Clark Gable was holding in the photo. But—no political innuendo intended—I didn't get my ass Coolidged, either. And every trout with whom I danced at Atlantis is still living in this once-ruined lake, slowly growing—if we're careful, and lucky—back into something wonderful.

I am, however, a fly-fisherman. And "It is not fly-fishing," wrote my neighbor, Norman Maclean, "if you are not looking for answers to questions." So let me ask: *how wonderful?* How wonderful can a manufactured lake fishery ever really be? Isn't this lake, divorced by dam from its river, a bit like a body divorced from its head? I come from the Pacific Northwest—land of migrating salmon—and I've felt the wonder that passes, at the salmon's annual coming, between the fish people and the two-leggeds. Something crucial, two mysterious messages—one from mountains, rain, and snowmelt, another from the sea—crisscross in the heart of a waiting human when the great salmon runs pour in each fall. So I can't help but remember the Lahontan trout's ancient spawning runs. Will the big cutthroats ever again climb the Truckee to Lake Tahoe and beyond? Am I being absurdly neolithic to even consider such a question? Or is there something worth yearning for here? I have lived my life on the shores of little rivers where, each fall, enormous ocean-fattened, exotic-colored creatures suddenly appear on beds of gravel to circle, dig, and dance their species to life even as they batter their own bodies to death. That's the biological truth of the salmon's life-cycle—but also a spiritual example that changes the way a lot of us Northwesterners choose to live. So what about the cutthroat? Will the guardians and users of this small inland sea and river one day yearn to see their trout set the same beautiful example?

I don't pretend to know. In the climate of our time it's just a dream to me, or prayer. Were I ever to require an answer, though, you'd find me rod in hand on the vast, salty lake there, close by the Stone Mother.

Lisa Gerber

WITNESS

The San Rafael Swell is a geologic wonder in southern Utah. My partner and I make the pilgrimage there at least twice a year, traveling from
the narrow valleys of western Montana to the vast expanse of southern
Utah. He is a geologist and satiates himself in the exposed open rock,
while I absorb the openness of a high desert that is like the landscape of
my childhood.

The Swell is a held breath, a kidney-shaped geologic dome eighty
kilometers long and fifty kilometers wide. Open and exposed, a place
where everything is distinct. Each piñon, juniper, saltbrush, and Mormon tea asserts its life from the other plants around them. Exposed bare
rock marks high cliffs and deep canyons. Our camp is at the head of
Wild Horse Canyon. I read history by looking up at the pattern of
rocks. The Navajo is on the top, its white rounded cliffs speaking of
sand dunes in an arid Sahara-type desert 200 million years ago. Below
that is the Kayenta formation. It is horizontal and interlayered, alternat-
ing siltstone and sandstone. Below that is the majestic Windgate, more
large sand dunes from an arid desert. The rock is usually pale orange to
red, but here in the Swell it is a tannish white.

These formations are the staples of the Swell. They are friends
greeting me as I travel throughout the region. This is how I connect
myself to the history of a land covered with sand dunes or silt deposited
by a water bed. It is a tenuous connection and stretches my mind to its
furthest limits as I imagine how this place may have looked millions of
years ago.

Humans are small in this landscape, moving specks near the high
cliffs and open desert. Perception is changed out of necessity. You can

look at a butte and imagine it is close, a few hours' walk, when in reality the journey could take a whole day. We make tiny footsteps in the landscape. This environment, unlike cities, is not adjusted to human scale. Buildings are not proportioned to the human figure; doorways do not complement our height. Walls are 250-meter cliffs stretching up; the ceiling is an infinity-touching dark space. Our breath swirling up.

Northeast of our camp is Temple Mountain. It was named after a Mormon Temple in Manti, Utah. Similar in appearance, the worship is different. Temple Mountain was one of the largest uranium producers in the entire San Rafael region. Mines, dark holes with rock slides below them, circle the mountain. The chain of holes is evidence of the people who blasted and drilled deep into the crust. The mining activity was focused in the Chinle formation, which fans out under the Windgate. A green band in the Chinle, the Moss Back Member, hosts the uranium.

Temple Mountain was busy in the 1950s. There was a grocery store, and miners' trailers were scattered throughout the piñons and junipers. People drove their cars up the graded roads, bulldozers worked the land, water and gas trucks gave life to machines and people. Proof of the mining boom is revealed by abandoned cars, cement foundations, and a few rock houses. Pieces of drill bit and dynamite boxes dot the landscape like desert flowers. Mountain bikers, hikers, horseback riders, and dirt bikers replace the workers who once used the mining roads.

It is easy to hike up Temple Mountain. There are two main mining roads encircling the mountain. One above the other. Many other roads shoot off the main roads, switching back and forth until they reach a mine. Some of these roads are eroded away. Large boulders, rock slides, and saltbrush have come to reclaim the mountain.

I imagine a dragon curled up inside Temple Mountain. Angry. Her eyes gleaming and alert. Nostrils flared, her breath an acrid smoke. But she is sleeping now, settled. It has been forty years since she gave us a warning. Even in her anger her warning was only a hint, a small fraction of her power.

My dad watched thirteen nuclear explosions. He was participating in Operation Redwing in the Marshall Islands. He says that he watched the "big boys," meaning he witnessed the hydrogen bombs, bombs tenfold larger than the atomic bombs exploded over Hiroshima and Nagasaki. These were fusion bombs that relied on a fission uranium bomb as their trigger. My dad sometimes says that if it weren't for nuclear bombs, I wouldn't be here. His short time with the navy had given him an opportunity to turn his life around; on the ship he studied, revisioning his life from small-town boy to man with a Ph.D. in plasma physics. So I am a child of nuclear bombs.

My dad had to search his memory when I asked him about the tests. He was twenty-two at the time. Young and on a short stint with the navy. Most of his memories were excruciatingly human. He said the Marshall Islands were hot—hot climate and hot water. He and the other men would go to the island for shore leave. Wearing shorts, the men simply hung out. They drank beer that was laced with formaldehyde so it wouldn't spoil. My dad slid down coconut trees. Other men swam in the hot water. In their isolation and ingenuity, the men set up a phone so they could talk with family and friends via a ham operator.

When I asked my dad about his work on the ship, he said he worked in electronics. A relic perhaps of living with Uncle Max, who tinkers with everything in his basement. On the ship my dad would fix and calibrate Geiger counters. While I have never seen a Geiger counter, I can hear the clicks and whirls that spoke to my dad about the intensity of radiation.

The Geiger counter was also a tool of choice in the San Rafael Swell. Prospectors would walk down washes and up cliffs holding Geiger counters in front of them, like blind men with a walking stick. From 1948 to 1958, many claims were found and many fortunes made with the help of this instrument. Vernon Pick discovered the Delta Mine in the southwestern part of the Swell. He made ten million dollars on the uranium and the eventual sale of his mine.

All kinds of people went prospecting in the Swell—schoolteachers, businessmen, sheepherders, farmers, high school students. They were all a part of the rush for uranium. Mines sprang up everywhere; among them were the Copper Globe, the Lucky Strike, the Cancer Cure, and the Dirty Devil. At the time uranium was the most critical material in America. The federal government wanted it, was willing to pay for it, and by law was the only buyer for it. Geiger counters helped find the mines but weren't used much when it came to mining. This was a lethal oversight. The radiation released during mining was toxic. Uranium has all the members of the radioactive family. Blasting and drilling operations instigate the process of decay. Radon gas is released into the atmosphere. This gas has a half-life of four days, then it further decays into the radon daughters, which are deadly. They can be inhaled and absorbed into the body. Many miners, twenty years after their first exposure, died from being radiated from the inside out.

That's the thing with radiation. It doesn't kill you instantly. It often is not apparent for years. Sadako Sasaki was two years old when the atomic bomb exploded over Hiroshima. The processed uranium released in Japan was not from America. It was ripped from the earth in the Belgian Congo, brought to America for processing, then exploded in Hiroshima one kilometer from Sadako's house on Kusunogi Street. Ten years later Sadako lay in the children's ward, racked by severe pain. Even with blisters over her whole body, she refused all painkillers. Instead, she had taken a Japanese idea to heart. She believed that if she folded a thousand paper cranes, she would be brought good fortune. In her hospital room she carefully folded medicine and candy wrappers into tiny cranes. They were so small she needed a needle to fold them. She died after folding 645 cranes.

Only five pictures were taken on the day that the bomb exploded over Hiroshima. In the pictures the sky is covered with a gray cloud, buildings are fallen, glass is blown through window frames. Yet all five pictures show survivors of the atomic blast—the photographer's wife putting something in a drawer, female high school students on a street, a policeman giving out bread certificates, a group of people, a man walking by a window. Yosito Matsushiga, the photographer, says, "Before I became a professional cameraman, I had been just an ordinary person, so when I was faced with a terrible scene like this, I found it difficult to press the shutter."

Sitting under the hot sun on Temple Mountain, I cannot make sense out of the madness. I sit here where rock was blasted out of the mountain. All of it is crazy—the splitting of rock from earth, the splitting of an atom, the splitting of limbs from bodies, and the splitting of links in the genetic chain; splitting ourselves from nature and trying to control power that is unfathomable in its destruction and proclivity for death. We threaten each other with annihilation as if it were our role.

Now I am somewhat afraid of this landscape I love. It's not the fear that comes with awe and care. It's more the fear of contracting a contagious disease. I look at a rock that lies to the left of me. It is a green-banded sandstone, beautiful in its markings, yet the color is a bright green, almost fluorescent. I wonder about the surrounding piñons and junipers; many of them were alive during the mining boom. Were they covered with the yellow dust that blew out of the mines? Years ago would a Geiger counter go off the dial when it came near them? And what about the lizards, coyotes, snakes, and bobcats? I lie back on the rocky ground and search the sky for a bird; perhaps I'll see one of the ravens who play in the updrafts along the cliffs. I long to follow her path and break free of this hard-rock confusion. I see no birds.

Bikini Atoll, March 1, 1954. It was the lack of birds following one of the first hydrogen bomb explosions that really holds my mind. This bomb was over twenty megatons, many times more powerful than the Hiroshima bomb. After the giant explosion—after the blast, ground shock, and air shock—there were no other noises. No singing birds that would ordinarily be flying around the atoll. The Bravo test was a Zen act of destruction. Everything falling into one moment. Any bird or animal that survived the blast was soon sick from the radiation.

The radioactive fallout was immense. A huge cloud of debris filled the air; as it moved with the air currents, it fell as gray ash, the particles getting larger and larger until they fell like hailstones. The test specialists, hiding in a reinforced concrete bunker with all their sophisticated instruments, knew they were safe in the bunker but wouldn't be safe if they were outside for more than eight minutes. Others, without the forewarning or instrumentation, were not so lucky.

The radioactive cloud originating at Bikini blew eastward. All eighty-two inhabitants on Rongelap Island 120 miles downwind were directly in the radioactive path. No one thought to warn them beforehand. Eventually they were evacuated to Hawaii and within two days grew sick from radiation. Their skin burned and many developed sores.

Each person vomited, but none of them died. They returned home three years later.

Closer to the explosion, seventy-five miles east, was the Japanese fishing boat *Fakurya Maru,* the *Lucky Dragon.* The twenty-three men were trawling for tuna. Early in the morning one man exclaimed that he could see the sun rising in the west. The sky turned from whitish yellow to orange. After the shock wave, a gray dust fell on them and the *Lucky Dragon.* After two weeks they had made it back to Japan, all sick from radiation, some of their fish contaminated. The radio operator, Aiticki Kuboyama, soon died, another Japanese killed nine years after Hiroshima.

The tests my dad watched were two years after the Bravo test. The military was testing a cleaner bomb. Bravo was a fission, fusion, fission bomb. The bombs my dad watched probably had the outer layer of uranium removed to cut back on radioactive fallout. But they still used a fission bomb as trigger. Two of the largest bombs were 3,800 and 4,500 kilotons. The bomb dropped over Hiroshima was 22 kilotons, small in comparison to the hydrogen bombs. In an official statement Admiral Strauss claimed these tests were successful, citing greatly reduced fallout. He concluded that the tests "have produced much of importance not only from a military point of view but from a humanitarian standpoint." I say humanitarian only in an insane world view.

The 3,800- and 4,500-kiloton bombs are real. I must constantly remind myself of this. I tend to abstract them, thinking of them as evil or death, symbols of our separation from nature, but these bombs are real entities. My dad tells me the blast was so bright that he could see his bones through his hands. I see him on his small carrier, the USS *Badoeng Strait.* Young, thin, healthy, standing tall. There is sweat dripping from his brown hair, and his eyes, brown eyes like mine, are covered with thin dark glasses. Arm outstretched, he holds his hand out in front of his face. A crash like a thunderbolt, then all the men hurry and go below deck before the water wave hits. The ship, twenty miles away, would encounter a wave powerful enough to tip the ship forty-five degrees. When the men came up later, the ocean would be gray, no sun getting through the debris cloud.

I think about my dad on this ship. Especially I think of those flimsy black glasses, almost the same as the ones I wear after having my eyes dilated at the optometrist. What kind of protection is this from an atomic blast? My dad has a swollen eye, his left one, and Dr. Stinchcomb cannot figure out what is wrong. Once when my dad and I were talking about health risks, he caught me staring at his eye. "Don't make me sick," he said.

I need to leave the mines. They are so big in my mind right now, overtaking all of Temple Mountain. I get up and walk down the road. Once more the landscape unfolds itself. The canyons call to me invitingly, and I leave the road to hike down a wash. The wash is dry, and I take off my boots to walk on the sandy soil. The tan cliffs rise above me, protecting me. They are thin, sometimes overhanging. I flow across the sand like water.

When I get to South Temple Wash, the Windgate is high above me. I raise my head and gaze at the figures painted long ago. I wonder how people got up there to create the pictographs. I see a tiny ledge, but it looks too dangerous to climb. I sit down on the sandy soil and gaze at the figures. Two human figures stand tall, rectangular. One is holding a snake. Both have missing heads. There are animals near these figures; one has a curled tail much like Terra's, my Siberian husky. Farther to the left is another figure. A warrior, exposing strength, stamina, will. He stands firm, a triangular body, wide at the top; his arms are thin lines coming down, an asterisk for his five fingers. There is a long line across his forehead; above that, his horned head.

I look at him, wondering about the circles that cover his body: one, two, . . . thirteen altogether. It takes me a while to recognize them for what they are—pellet scars from shotgun blasts. His arms, once defiant, hang in shock; his fingers clench in pain.

Another door slams. Why must we desecrate everything? I remember that the nuclear tests my dad watched were named after Indian tribes: Cherokee, Yuma, Erie, Flathead, Blackfoot, Kickapoo, Osage, Inca, Dakota, Mohawk, Apache, Navajo, Huron. Thirteen of them also. Each one exploding on the rock art, each one destroying the fragile islands, each one dragging a name across the ocean. I came here to make sense of something, but I have found no sense, only clarity.

I sleep away from other people tonight, farther down Wild Horse

Canyon. I ask Terra, my husky, to join me. Together we lie nestled against the cliffs of the canyon, watching the constellations turn around the northern star. I pray for all tonight—juniper, piñons, people, salt-brush, rocks, dragon, my dad, and Sadako, the air and sun. On and on. I cannot stop.

Joy Harjo

EAGLE POEM

To pray you open your whole self
To sky, to earth, to sun, to moon
To one whole voice that is you.
And know there is more
That you can't see, can't hear,
Can't know except in moments
Steadily growing, and in languages
That aren't always sound but other
Circles of motion.
Like eagle that Sunday morning
Over Salt River. Circled in blue sky
In wind, swept our hearts clean
With sacred wings.
We see you, see ourselves and know
That we must take the utmost care
And kindness in all things.
Breathe in, knowing we are made of
All this, and breathe, knowing
We are truly blessed because we
Were born, and die soon within a
True circle of motion,
Like eagle rounding out the morning
Inside us.
We pray that it will be done
In beauty.
In beauty.

Linda Hogan

WHAT HOLDS THE WATER, WHAT HOLDS THE LIGHT

Walking up the damp hill in the hot sun, there were signs of the recent heavy rains. The land smelled fresh, shaded plants still held moisture in their green clustered leaves, and fresh deer tracks pointed uphill like arrows in the dark, moist soil.

Along our way, my friend and I stopped at a cluster of large boulders to drink fresh rain collected in a hollow bowl that had been worn into stone over slow centuries. Bending over the stone, smelling earth up close, we drank sky off the surface of water. Mosses and ancient lichens lived there. And swimming in another stone cup were slender orange newts, alive and vibrant with the rains.

Drinking the water, I thought how earth and sky are generous with their gifts, and how good it is to receive them. Most of us are taught, somehow, about giving and accepting human gifts, but not about opening ourselves and our bodies to welcome the sun, the land, the visions of sky and dreaming, not about standing in the rain ecstatic with what is offered.

One time, visiting friends, I found they had placed a Mexican water jar on the sink and filled it for me. It was a thin clay that smelled of dank earth, the unfired and unshaped land it had once been. In it was rain come from dark sky. A cool breeze lived inside the container, the way wind blows from a well that is held in cupped hands of earth, fed with underground springs and rivers.

The jar was made in Mexico City, once called Iztapalapa, the place where Montezuma lived during the time Cortés and his Spanish soldiers were colonizing the indigenous people and the land. Writer Barry

Lopez has written about the aviaries of Iztapalapa that were burned by the Spanish, fires that burned the green hummingbirds and nesting blue herons, burned even the sound of wings and the white songs of egrets. It was not only the birds that died in those fires, but also the people and their records, the stories of human lives.

De Soto also had this disregard for life. He once captured an indigenous woman because she carried a large pearl. His intention was, when they were far from her homeland, to kill the woman and steal the pearl, but one morning along their journey she managed to escape. De Soto's anger was enormous. It was as if the woman had taken something from him, and that fierce anger resulted in the killing of people and a relentless, ongoing war against land.

Humans colonizing and conquering others have a propensity for this, for burning behind them what they cannot possess or control, as if their conflicts are not with themselves and their own way of being, but with the land itself.

In the 1930s, looters found the Spiro burial mounds of Oklahoma and sold to collectors artifacts that they removed from the dead. When caught and forbidden to continue their thefts, the men dynamited two of the mounds the way a wolverine sprays food so that nothing else will take possession of it.

It seems, looking back, that these invasions amounted to a hatred of life itself, of fertility and generation. The conquerors and looters refused to participate in a reciprocal and balanced exchange with life. They were unable to receive the best gifts of land, not gold or pearls or ownership, but a welcome acceptance of what is offered. They did not understand that the earth is generous and that encounters with the land might have been sustaining, or that their meetings with other humans could have led to an enriched confluence of ways. But here is a smaller event, one we are more likely to witness as a daily, common occurrence. Last year, I was at the Colorado River with a friend when two men from the Department of Fish and Wildlife came to stock the water with rainbow trout. We wanted to watch the silver-sided fish find their way to freedom in the water, so we stood quietly by as the men climbed into the truck bed and opened the tank that held fish. To our dismay, the men did not use the nets they carried with them to unload the fish.

Instead they poured the fish into the bed of their truck, kicked them out and down the hill, and then into water. The fish that survived were motionless, shocked, gill slits barely moving, skin hanging off the wounds. At most, it would have taken only a few minutes longer for the men to have removed the fish carefully with their nets, to have treated the lives they handled with dignity and respect, with caretakers' hands.

These actions, all of them, must be what Bushman people mean when they say a person is far-hearted. This far-hearted kind of thinking is one we are especially prone to now, with our lives moving so quickly ahead, and it is one that sees life, other lives, as containers for our own uses and not as containers in a greater, holier sense.

Even wilderness is seen as having value only as it enhances and serves our human lives, our human world. While most of us agree that wilderness is necessary to our spiritual and psychological well-being, it is a container of far more, of mystery, of a life apart from ours. It is not only where we go to escape who we have become and what we have done, but it is also part of the natural laws, the workings of a world of beauty and depth we do not yet understand. It is something beyond us, something that does not need our hand in it. As one of our Indian elders has said, there are laws beyond our human laws, and ways above ours. We have no words for this in our language, or even for our experience of being there. Ours is a language of commerce and trade, of laws that can be bent in order that treaties might be broken, land wounded beyond healing. It is a language that is limited, emotionally and spiritually, as if it can't accommodate such magical strength and power. The ears of this language do not often hear the songs of the white egrets, the rain falling into stone bowls. So we make our own songs to contain these things, make ceremonies and poems, searching for a new way to speak, to say we want a new way to live in the world, to say that wilderness and water, blue herons and orange newts are invaluable not just to us, but in themselves, in the workings of the natural world that rules us whether we acknowledge it or not.

That clay water jar my friends filled with water might have been made of the same earth that housed the birds of Iztapalapa. It might have contained water the stunned trout once lived in. It was not only a bridge between the elements of earth, air, water, and fire but was also a bridge between people, a reservoir of love and friendship, the kind of care we need to offer back every day to the world as we begin to learn the land and its creatures, to know the world is the container for our lives, sometimes wild and untouched, sometimes moved by a caretaker's hands. Until we learn this, and learn our place at the bountiful table, how to be a guest here, this land will not support us, will not be hospitable, will turn on us.

That water jar was a reminder of how water and earth love each other the way they do, meeting at night, at the shore, being friends together, dissolving in each other, in the give and take that is where grace comes from.

Teresa Jordan

FROM "PLAYING GOD ON THE LAWNS OF THE LORD"

There are a thousand of us and three hundred of them. We are *Homo sapiens* and they are *Bison bison bison*. We have come to this spot in the Flint Hills of northern Oklahoma to watch them released onto five thousand acres of native tallgrass prairie. The prairie and the bison evolved together over thousands of years. They have been separated for well over a century. They are coming together now, some order is being restored, and we are in a celebratory mood.

Each of us feels honored to be here. This is an invitational event, open to members of the Osage Tribe, which owns the vast oil reserves under this ground but not the ground itself; to members and friends of The Nature Conservancy, which now owns the ground; to General Norman H. Schwarzkopf, Retired, of the U.S. Army, who has just a few hours before, at dawn, received his Osage name of Tzizho Kihekah, or Eagle Chief; and to a swarm of schoolchildren, who sit restlessly on the grass waiting for the bison to appear.

No one denies that we are part of a spectacle. CBS is here. NBC is here. CNN is here. The *New York Times* is here. They have the best seats in the house, on the elevated platform near the gate through which the bison will run. Excitement fills the air, something akin to what one feels at a homecoming game, and we all have our cameras in our hands. Now we see the bison in the distance, a bounding line of darkness above the tallgrass, heading the wrong way at a dead run.

The cowboys do not ride horseback, but in pickups and on four-wheel all-terrain vehicles. They turn the bison toward the gate; the animals turn back the other way. The cowboys turn the bison again; once more, they refuse. The cowboys try a third time, and this time the great shaggy beasts come through the gate on the run, three hundred head, a diversified herd, ranging from calves born only a few months earlier, in the spring, to massive bulls a dozen years old that weigh nearly a ton.

We have grown quiet, as we've been instructed to do in order not to startle the animals, and our silence turns quickly to awe. So it's true, what we have read in books and seen in movies. The sound of bison on the run really does travel over a long distance. This is a quintessential American sound, something we must carry in our genes, bred into Native Americans by thousands of years of hunting and eating and living side by side with the beasts; bred into Euro-Americans as a haunting legacy of what our ancestors annihilated in a few short years only slightly more than a century ago. This is the sound of history and valor and triumph and squalor and sorrow, and it really does sound like thunder. But thunder would be borne by the air. We would feel it in our chests, our diaphragms. This sound comes up from the ground, through the soles of our feet. The sensation increases as the bison near, and they move like a dark roiling sea, swift and high bounding, closely packed. The damp overcast of the sky brings out the full spectrum of gold in their shaggy roughs and darkens the burnt sienna of their atavistic forms. They pass and we are no longer members of a crowd of spectators. Each one of us is alone, watching as if from great distance something primal and real. And most of us are weeping. . . .

Some hours after the bison were released, after the barbecue had ended, the band had left and the hundreds of guests had gone back to Pawhuska, Bartlesville, Tulsa, and points beyond, I took a long walk. The bison had settled down and were contentedly grazing; one old bull had wandered off by himself. I enjoyed my own solitude, walking in grass that towered over my head.

After the bustle of the day, the sounds of the prairie were soothing: the buzz of cicadas and crickets, the dee-dee-dee of a blackcapped chickadee, the rustle of a rabbit I couldn't quite see, my own steps swishing through the grass.

John Madson once described the tallgrass prairie as the lawns of God, and it was easy to hear a prayer in the whispers around me. I topped a ridge and looked out over thousands of acres of gently rolling hills, a sea of grass turned auburn with autumn, interrupted here and there, along creeks and on rims of limestone, with dark lines of oak. The grasses seemed to stretch forever and yet there were variations— sagey green in wallows, brighter green on burns, darker greens and grays in gullies. The clouds broke for a moment and the grasses waved iridescent gold, eighteen karat; the sky closed back down and they turned smoky blue. I rubbed my eyes and everything was so rose-colored I couldn't imagine anything could ever be wrong.

The lawns of the Lord are different than the lawns we mortals have created, those greenswards of infinite sameness. When I sank down on my haunches, I could number a dozen plants within a single arm's reach, from the big bluestems that soared over eight feet tall to the low-growing violet wood sorrel. Biologists have counted over five hundred different plants on the acres around me and the names form a prayer of their own: jack-in-the-pulpit and fire-on-the-mountain, wild white indigo and soft golden aster, witchgrass and weeping love grass, switch-grass and twisted ladies' tresses, shepherd's purse and button blazing star. And that doesn't begin to name the more than three hundred birds and eighty mammals that thrive here as well. Surrounded by such riches and hidden from view, I could forget for a moment the power lines and roads and fences that delimit this prairie world. It was a pleasing fantasy, but passing. We live within such boundaries. The question is where we go from here.

"When we have something valuable in our hands, and deal with it without hindrance," wrote Pedro de Castañeda de Najera over 450 years ago, "we do not value or prize it as highly as if we understood how much we would miss it after we had lost it." A member of Coro-nado's expedition north from Mexico in search of the mythical Seven Cities of Cibola, Castañeda was among the first Europeans to set foot on the western prairies, and he presaged a sadness that many of us feel today. "The longer we continue to have it the less we value it," he wrote, "but after we have lost it and miss the advantages of it, we have a great pain in the heart, and we are all the time imagining and trying to find ways and means by which to get it back again."

Sometimes we notice in time, and we can go some lengths toward repair. There would be no bison at all without the work of conservationists nearly a century ago. When a census turned up fewer than 550 of the animals, Theodore Roosevelt, ammunition king William Hornaday, and Molly Goodnight, wife of Texas cattleman Charlie Goodnight, joined others to establish the American Bison Society and preserve a small herd through the New York Zoological Society. The bison that now roam the tallgrass in Oklahoma are direct descendants of those that once lived in the Bronx. With luck, the prairie ecosystem itself will enjoy a similar salvation.

The Indian tribes that Castañeda encountered lived within the arms of God. They gave thanks for the life of each bison that fed them. Modern agriculture, on the other hand, has given us the sense that we *are* God. Developed over thousands of years, it has been the enthusiasm and genius of many of the world's peoples, and it has led us to believe that the earth should bend to our will. Science made us arrogant; now, as we begin to understand the ways in which we have damaged the systems that sustain us, it is making us humble. Perhaps, just perhaps, it can pave the path of our redemption. We have tried to tell the earth what to do; maybe now we can learn how to listen.

Gregory McNamee

FROM "REGAINING PARADISE"

All life is animated water.—VLADIMIR VERNADSKY

San Juan Day, June 24, and once again the rains have not yet come. As they have for centuries, the Tohono O'odham have made their saguaro wine, drunk it, and called up the rain clouds, but the rain clouds have yet to materialize. Only a few years ago an elderly Tohono O'odham man confessed to ethnobiologist Gary Paul Nabhan, "I still believe in Jesus and the saints, but I know too that when we drink the wine and sing I'itoi's help, the rains always come." But I'itoi, Elder Brother, the creator god of this dry stretch of universe, seems to have overslept this year, fast in his cave in the heart of Baboquivari Mountain.

Summer has come to the desert, a season punctuated only by small changes in the intense heat of day, when the dawn brings a wall of glaring white light upon the land, washing out its colors, when human and animal life slows to torpor until night has fallen. Those foolish enough to stay willingly in the desert in summertime—the mark, folks say around here, of the true desert rat—eat bushels of fruit, seek shade and breezes, and keep abundant liquids within easy reach, knowing only that the next few months will bring the same heat, day after day, hour after hour. You dare not read Raymond Chandler's short story "Red Wind" for fear that this time, yes, the heat will prove too much for the murderer within.

But the season usually brings rain as well, often half the rain that will fall each year on the Sonoran Desert. The lightning-lashed rise of an afternoon storm in this season is enough to give birth to a new theology, as deserts have bred the world's great faiths. It is a fine and oppressive time. It makes one think of water, of the open sea, of ice cold beer.

As I have been writing this book I have been thinking of rivers. I have been thinking of the rivers I have seen: the Thames, the Potomac, the Danube, the Mississippi, the Tiber, the Lerma, the Rhine, the Black Warrior, the Seine. Even the Hudson. (Has there ever been a tribe to bestow an ugly name upon a river? Their appellations sing. Even Dry Beaver Creek, in central Arizona, has its charm.) And I have been thinking of rivers I have never seen but hope to stand alongside one day: the Lena, the Brahmaputra, the Blue Nile, the Mackenzie, the Volga, the Amazon, the Ganges, the Yangtze. And the Gila and its many tributaries.

For the most part we know the rivers of the desert only by their absence, only as tiny blue scratches, separated by ellipses, on highway maps, in the cartographic code for the dead. The desiccated beds of those once great rivers, spanned by unsteady bridges, mock their intended function, carrying runoff from the heavens only a few days of the year, effluent from sewage treatment plants with greater regularity. For the rest of the year, bone-dry, they serve as dragstrips for three-wheeled recreational vehicles, as dumping grounds for unwanted mattresses and house pets, for defaulting cocaine consumers. They are rivers in name only, an insult to the theory and practice of flowing water.

To bring back the old rivers is not an impossibility; to declare that time cannot be reversed is mere dogma. But to regain the Gila, the Colorado, the San Pedro—residents of any other town west of the hundredth meridian need only substitute appropriate names for the rivers they have lost—will require an absolute change in the politics and economics of the American West, away from the ceaseless rapacity that has characterized the last century and toward a more sustainable ethic, one that recognizes water as the best of all clean industries, the best, as Herakleitos says, of all things.

Neither is to bring back the rivers mere wishful thinking. Rivers run as they will, despite the tethers we place on them; so long as water flows on earth, it will somehow find its way to the sea. In 1992 and 1993, water flowed through the desert in abundance, thanks to the influence of the El Niño weather pattern, which rises in the western Pacific and directs winter storms northeastward to the Hawaiian Islands and thence to the coasts of California and Mexico.

The winter of 1992 brought El Niño storms crashing into the tall mountains where the Gila is born, swiftly filling the rivulets and creeks and main channels with cold surging water. During two months of rain I followed the river from its source to its confluence with the Colorado, watching with amazement and pleasure as the river flowed over man-made restraints and roared through its normally dry bed, past the vast orange groves and palm stands of then-inundated western Arizona. The winter of 1993 brought still more rain, causing $200 million in damage along the Gila's length. There were times in January when I could swear I saw the neighborhood animals lining up two by two.

The floods came as no surprise to longtime Southwesterners. The desert, they know, has its cycles: some years it rains, some years it doesn't. El Niño brought plentiful rain to mark the onset of the 1990s, with wet winters and comparatively dry summers, the supposed "monsoon season." For the second time in a decade, most of New Mexico's and Arizona's rivers surged to so-called hundred-year flood levels, which, as the name implies, should occur but once in a century. The Verde River, a major tributary of the middle Gila, did even better, cresting to the thousand-year mark.

The floods had their surprises nonetheless. The developers who chose to build apartment complexes and shopping centers on obvious floodplains wondered why their properties had gone sailing off to Mexico. The residents of Winkelman Flats seemed to be taken aback by the raging Gila, which made off with their horse trailers and tool sheds and homes. Yuma farmers were stunned by their waterlogged fields and damaged crops. And the engineers who continue to channelize and dam Arizona's streams and rivers, hoping to tame them, wondered why nature refused to submit to their will.

Dams, as has been proved in many places at many times, cannot permanently thwart nature. When the great rains of October 1983 came, the rusty floodgates at Coolidge Dam failed to open. Glen Canyon Dam, on the Colorado, shivered loose from its bedding in soft sandstone, and its operators sounded a warning that it might collapse at any minute—taking with it, in turn, Hoover Dam, Davis Dam, Parker Dam, and Imperial Dam. By some miracle it stood, but dozens of earthen check dams crumbled across the Southwest.

January 1993 brought worse news for the dam builders. By the eleventh the Gila was flowing at 30,000 cubic feet per second, twenty times its normal load; Coolidge Dam again failed to do its putative job, and it released a dozen times more water than it did in 1983. Throughout the Southwest buckled roadways and shorn bridges, inundated fields and waterlogged crops, dismantled apartments and mangled automobiles, silt-covered floors and shattered lives attested to weeks of rain.

The sight of so much flowing water, of a Gila running fast and, for all purposes, free, gave much hope as well to those who seek to put it in that condition permanently. The Gila watershed may have witnessed many extinctions, many instances of environmental and social degradation, but it also has given rise to a number of protectors, among them modern activists Dave Foreman, from the little headwaters town of Reserve, and M. H. Salmon, now of Silver City; both have been important advocates against damming and for wilderness. . . .

Taking the lead from the Utah Wilderness Coalition, Southwestern activists need not be modest. Dave Foreman's recent call for the establishment of multimillion-acre wilderness areas throughout Arizona and New Mexico, for instance, pales with the proposal Rutgers University geographers Frank Popper and Deborah Popper have advanced for the Great Plains. They have noted that the Ogallala Aquifer, which underlies 1,375,000 square miles of high prairie, is being overdrafted fifty times faster than it can be replenished, a rate steeper by five times than the worst current overdrafting in the Southwest. The twenty million acre feet of water annually pumped from the Ogallala Aquifer nourish 20 percent of the irrigated farmland in America, and those farms are sure to fail as this ancient source of water dries up. (The 1988 drought on the plains cut our national grain production by 40 percent.) In the early 1980s the farm and livestock lobbies petitioned President Ronald Reagan to authorize funds to build an irrigation canal from the Great Lakes—which contain the world's largest supply of freshwater— across the Great Plains, from Minnesota to Texas. Reagan's aides, noting the failure of irrigation projects in the West to pay for themselves, demanded proof that 35 percent of the construction costs could be guaranteed within twenty years, and when the lobbyists answered that such proof could not be mustered, the project died. For their part, the Poppers call for a turn in the opposite direction. They argue that as the

plains are necessarily abandoned, native ecosystems be allowed to return, replacing introduced grains with indigenous tallgrasses. In the
light of their proposal—which has many merits, among them its recognition of "natural nations" based on watersheds—the notion of adding
on a couple of million acres to the present Gila Wilderness seems modest indeed.

There is still more to be done. One of the first needs is to set about
reforesting the Gila highlands. Our model can be the Civilian Conservation Corps' (CCC) work in the West in the 1930s and 1940s . . . when
millions upon millions of trees were planted. (On average the CCC spent
$85.50 per capita in the Western states, as against $19.50 nationwide, so
bad was the problem of clearcutting.) The corps employed some fifteen
thousand Indians to restore reservation tracts, including great parcels on
the San Carlos and White Mountain Apache nations, and in its first
year of operation alone the CCC had improved millions of acres of public land.

Without reforestation, the tremendous erosion that has been taking place along the Gila watershed for a century and a half can only
grow worse in the coming years. Frank H. Olmstead warned nine decades ago, "It is up to the men of this generation to meet the situation
manfully and to utilize fully every resource at the command of the
Nation . . . if we are not to lose what we have so carelessly guarded
from the date of our possession in 1848 to this time." He was not
heeded, nor have his likeminded peers been heeded then or since.
Across the nation we are losing the most precious natural resource: its
topsoil. Now, only 11 percent of the surface of the earth is arable; a
great portion of that productive land lies within the United States. But
thanks to industrial agriculture, with its destructive demand for over-
production, its refusal to allow land to lie fallow, to plow along contours, to treat the soil as a living entity, and thanks to industrial logging
in the highlands, some 35 percent of the nation's topsoil—formed in
geological time, the result of weathering and the decay of dead plants
and animals, essentially nonrenewable—has been lost, washed, or blown
away. In the twisted language of the agroindustrialists, it has for a century been more "cost-effective" to allow that loss rather than conserve
the soil, the occasional dust bowl be damned. In the last two decades

more than four million acres of productive crop land annually have
been lost forever through erosion; every bushel of Iowa corn costs two
bushels of topsoil to produce, every calorie of food costs ten calories of
energy, an intolerably misguided economy of waste.

We need to found a modern analog to the CCC if our mountains
are not to suffer further damage. As the most casual observation will in-
dicate, mere gravity pulls down everything that can be pulled—rocks,
trees, water. Only a healthy cover of plants can hold mountain soil in
place, and only a concerted effort or the magical disappearance of humans and cattle will ever put that cover in place.

In reforesting we must also reeducate the U.S. Forest Service.
Gifford Pinchot's notion of the service as a body of economic advisors
who counsel industry on the use of trees needs to be discarded, the
doctrine of multiple use abandoned. That reeducation had better come
fast, for the agency is blind to the lessons of preservation, to the fact that
it directly subsidizes a marginal industry. Even as I write, the Forest Service is hurrying to build 43,000 miles of new roads—adding to the
360,000 already in our national forests—so that new areas cannot be
designated as wilderness and thus removed from the sawyers' blades.

It should be noted, although the lumber industry would not want
it widely known, that sustainable forestry is possible. Loggers can, if they
choose, remove some mature trees from a forest and not clear the underbrush in doing so, and the forest would very easily recover. Leaving a
few felled logs behind would further generate additional mycorrhizae
that allow other plants to grow. In forests where this method has been
tried new growth occurs far more quickly than in clearcut areas, and
both the presence of undergrowth and the habit of random logging help
to maintain the genetic diversity that is so often lacking in our national
forests, which resemble nothing so much as tree farms. That diversity is
critical. As ecologist Ramón Mergalef has remarked, late stages of succession in climax or old-growth forests are stable precisely because of
their diversity; they are resistant to diseases and ecological invaders, and
they restrain great increases in natural populations of all kinds. Henry
David Thoreau put it another way: "In a wood that has been left alone
for the longest period the greatest regularity and harmony in the dis-
position of the trees will be observed, while in our ordinary woods man

has often interfered and favored the growth of other kinds than are best fitted to grow there naturally."

The work of a few hands in a forest can yield wonders. In Auro-ville, India, near Pondicherry, an international religious community has planted over a million trees in the last twenty years on two thousand acres of dry plateau. Formerly barren and bereft of life, the plateau now teems with species that had abandoned the plateau when the old-growth forest was cleared for fuel, and the project has been so successful that the Indian government has commissioned Auroville to undertake tree-planting campaigns elsewhere in the country. Similarly, let us recall Jean Giono's famed account of shepherd Elzéard Bouffier's single-handed campaign in the Provence, *The Man Who Planted Trees.* By the end of the nineteenth century charcoal makers had deforested the land; the streams had died, and southern Provence looked much like the Sahel. Beginning in 1914, Bouffier planted hundreds of thousands of trees on the denuded hillsides, and a vast deciduous forest now stands to commemorate his work.

Another step in reclaiming the Gila watershed is to reeducate the Bureau of Land Management (BLM), whose critics have properly re-named it the Bureau of Livestock and Mining. The first step is to re-move most cattle from the public lands of the West, recognizing that in the end the land can simply not sustain this eminently marginal eco-nomic activity. When cattle are removed a place often recovers remark-ably swiftly. The Blue River tributary of the Gila, for instance, was so overgrazed by the 1920s that its basal soils had washed out, leaving only a succession of ghost towns and abandoned peach orchards to attest that humans had once been there. Cattle were removed from the lower Blue in the middle 1980s, and at the same time a great swath of tamarisk trees were uprooted. Only a few years later the cottonwood-willow-sycamore associations are beginning to return to the once-ravaged landscape, and there is every reason to believe that similar recoveries will be the norm on other parts of the river.

"The deserts should never be reclaimed," wrote the acclaimed des-ert rat John Van Dyke at the turn of the century. "They are the breathing-spaces of the west and should be preserved forever." For too long the BLM has been in the business precisely of reclaiming the lands under its jurisdiction for the benefit of the few. The agency manages 85,000 miles of streams and rivers and 164 million acres of public grazing lands, and the sorry state of land and water alike in this country is testimony to its corruption.

If we are to undertake Frank Olmstead's challenge to combat erosion, we will need to set an agricultural revolution in motion—on the Gila, and throughout America. Wendell Berry has observed in *The Unsettling of America* and elsewhere that as our agriculture becomes ever more industrialized, its destructive manifestations become more and more pronounced. One of them is the rise of monoculture, the production of but a few "scientifically" selected varieties of food crops and the loss of genetic diversity that has come with it. As a result of the demands of industrialized, standardized agriculture, for example, of the seven thousand varieties of apples that have been developed in the United States, only four are generally available today: the Delicious, McIntosh, Winesap, and Jonathan, a meager table indeed. (The journalist and food critic A. J. Liebling wrote half a century ago, "People who don't like food have made a triumph of the Delicious because it doesn't taste like an apple, and of the Golden Delicious because it doesn't taste like anything.") As with such machine-produced items as metal bolts and pencils, the rise of industrialization in food production has led directly to an impoverishment of forms, a loss of the necessary complexity that informs any art rightly practiced and a diminution of choice.

But appropriate agriculture, like appropriate forestry and appropriate ranching, is possible. In the arid Southwest, appropriate agriculture naturally means farming crops that do not require much water. While only a few dozen species of plants are fully utilized in the modern diet of industrialized societies—the most important being wheat, rice, maize, and potatoes—the Sonoran Desert alone boasts more than 2,500 native species of food plants. In a regime of appropriate agriculture many more of them can be utilized effectively both to increase the local menu of foodstuffs and to battle monoculture.

Some Gila-watershed farmers are already producing arid-land crops. On the lower Gila now lie vast fields of jojoba *(Simmondsia chinensis)*, a bushy plant whose bean yields an oil that is nearly identical in chemical composition to spermaceti, the oil produced by sperm whales. This imperishable oil is extremely versatile: it can be used for cooking, in shampoos and soaps and cars, in medicines and industrial lubricants. (In the last use another Gila native, lesquerella *[Lesquerella fendleri]* shows promise as well.) Jojoba may become a major cash crop in the Southwest, especially as the industrialized world continues to deplete the planet's supply of fossil fuels.

In his recent book *The Diversity of Life,* E. O. Wilson reports that a Mexican graduate student recently located in the state of Jalisco a small field of *Zea diploperennis,* a wild relative of corn that was once thought to be extinct. (This patch was doomed to be cleared, and had the student not been a gifted persuader it may well not have survived the season.) *Zea diploperennis* may be introduced into various strains of *Zea mays,* our common food corn, and with it production will surely rise; a hybrid would be both disease- and drought-resistant and, unlike most domesticated corn, would grow perennially. This, too, promises a new, appropriate crop for the Gila watershed.

Other native plants can readily supplant marginal exotic plants as cash crops. Buffalo gourd *(Cucurbita foetidissima),* for instance, produces edible oil and grows on land unsuitable for most agriculture; halophytes such as saltbush *(Atriplex)* and Palmer's saltgrass *(Distichlis palmeri),* which grow in salty and even oceanic water, can replace alfalfa as fodder—and yield twice as much produce an acre. And thanks to growing cosmopolitanism in culinary matters in this and other countries, crops like *chiltepín (Capsicum annuum aviculare),* a pepper that ethnobotanist Gary Paul Nabhan calls "the red-hot mother of all chiles," are in wide demand, only second in cash value to saffron.

Even introduced plants have prospects. One is the neem tree *(Azadirochta indica),* a native of India, drought-tolerant and apparently compatible with native American desert vegetation. One of its wonders is that it produces natural pesticides that can easily replace chemical ones, thus allowing for the continued health of Mexican free-tail bats and agaves, of white-winged sphinx moths and saguaro cacti. The neem tree has been called "the village pharmacy," too, for the medicines its bark yields, and Indians who use its twigs as toothbrushes reportedly suffer far fewer dental problems than does the general population of the subcontinent. Other wonders await us in arid lands elsewhere on the planet, and they need not be horrors like tamarisk, cheatgrass, and tumbleweed.

"Should trees have standing?" asked Christopher Stone, a legal scholar, in his book of that name. Answering affirmatively, Stone argued that nature be allowed its day in court and protected by law from further encroachment. Echoing Stone, we might ask, should rivers have rights?

Yes, they should.

In our time, while the Amazon is burning and America's grain belt is withering away and the Aral Sea is disappearing, our courts have ruled that keeping water in rivers for the health of fish populations is not beneficial use, but that overallocating it for farming is. In our time—in late August of 1992, to be precise—the Bureau of Land Management attempted to designate fourteen miles of the upper Gila River near Safford as a roadway, both so that drivers of off-road vehicles could tear around in the riverbed with impunity and so that the river and its nearby tributaries could be exempted from consideration as wild and scenic rivers under the recent congressional act of that name. Given such actions, we can do far worse than press for the rights of our waterways immediately.

There are reasons to be hopeful. One is the passage, after years of legislative debate, of the national Omnibus Water Act of 1992. Among other things, the act requires that Western cities reserve large amounts of water to repair the environmental damage their sources of water have sustained: 800,000 acre feet of the water previously allocated to farmers in central California, for example, now annually must go to recharge the rivers and streams of the Sacramento and San Joaquin valleys.

The work of the national Nature Conservancy offers hope as well. The private group has recently acquired a sixty-nine-acre tract of palustrine wetlands at the confluence of the San Pedro and Gila rivers called Cooks Lake, one of Arizona's few wooded swamps, and it plans to convert several hundred additional acres of adjoining land to mesquite bosques. (The area had supposedly been "protected" by the provisions of the Clean Water Act, but instead was full of mine tailings from the nearby ASARCO smelter.) The San Pedro is one of only four American rivers to harbor significant quantities of mesquite, and along its course lie extremely valuable wildlife refuges that shelter fifty-five species of endangered animals, among them the peregrine falcon *(Falco peregrinus);* the gray hawk *(Buteo nitidus),* of which only fifty-four nesting pairs are thought to exist in the United States; the yellow-billed cuckoo *(Coccyzus americanus);* the vermilion flycatcher *(Pyrocephalus rubinus);* Costa's hummingbird *(Archilochus costae);* Bell's vireo *(Vireo bellii);* and the last ocelots *(Felis pardalis),* a globally endangered cat, known to exist in the lowlands of the Gila watershed.

The preservation of the San Pedro, which the Nature Conservancy has deemed one of the world's "last great places," is especially important given the overall decline in riparian habitats and consequently in migratory bird populations throughout the Western Hemisphere. The black-crowned night-heron *(Nycticorax nycticorax),* for instance, once lived in huge colonies along watercourses throughout the Southwest, including the Gila and its tributaries. When these disappeared so did the bird, and a decade ago the species was threatened with extirpation. The restoration of rivers like the San Pedro, coupled with the recent increased rains through the El Niño weather system, has brought the bird back to the region; while the population is not yet thriving, it at least shows the promise of reestablishing itself over time. We can resuscitate other ghosts, ghosts the poet Vachel Lindsay once conjured up:

> *When Daniel Boone goes by, at night,*
> *The phantom deer arise,*
> *And all lost, wild America,*
> *Is burning in their eyes.*

The restoration of the San Pedro provides a key for ways in which other Southwestern rivers can be brought back to life. River otters now swim freely in the lower Verde tributary of the Gila, thanks to individual initiative within the Arizona Game and Fish Department. In Florida, the Bureau of Reclamation is now "unreclaiming" the Kissimmee River, destroying old canals that in their turn destroyed wildlife habitats, just as projected dams along the Verde would have obliterated the last nesting habitats of the bald eagle in the Southwest. There is no reason the bureau could not direct its efforts to "unchannelizing" the Gila, the Salt, the Colorado.

All this is work for individuals and government alike. A farmer from Eloy, Arizona, not long ago donated a hundred miles of PVC irrigation pipe to a restoration initiative after the Central Arizona project began to deliver water to her fields. The pipe was in turn used to irrigate a nascent cottonwood-willow-mesquite forest along fifteen miles of the Gila southwest of Buckeye, Arizona, on the middle Gila. Within our lifetime this may become a new analog to the famous New York Thicket that brought so much joy to the Akimel O'odham; may many more such places soon arise.

Finally, the dams that dot the rivers of the Southwest must be removed, one by one. To dam a river is only to pretend that risk can be minimized, and ours has been a risk-fearing age, to the great delight of insurance companies and cowards. Between 1962 and 1968 more than twelve hundred major dams were built throughout the United States, more than in any other single period in our history, and sixty thousand dams now dot the national landscape. Six hundred thousand miles of American rivers have been inundated by reservoirs, and millions of acres of land have been lost. But there is no way, in truth, to remove risk entirely from our lives, and to pretend otherwise is mere naivete. Wind eddies grow to be cyclones; rivulets swell to floods; and rivers, if they are rivers at all, will on occasion leave their banks for a sojourn on nearby floodplains. The time has come to dismantle the dams that choke the rivers of these arid lands. Southwesterners will have to make do without a few things in the process: the green lawns brought from points east as tokens of cooler Anglo-Saxon climes; golf courses that consume a million gallons of water a day; inexpensive winter vegetables and cheap abundant beef. It has been remarked that the earth can sustain billions of humans, but not 250 million Americans. In the Southwest, we can at least begin to effect changes that will make us better planetary citizens.

Wilderness is its own argument, E. O. Wilson has reminded us. So, too, are mountains. If self-interest must enter into our bargaining with nature, consider the role of mountains as a source of reverie. The great religions were born in the deserts of the world, but mountains provided their inspiration; as the psychologist Bernard S. Aaronson has observed, "The traditional association of mountain tops with the abode of Deity may be less because they are higher than the areas around them than because they make possible those experiences of expanded depth in which the self can invest itself in the world around it and expand across the valleys." Mountains have utilitarian value as well, as John Muir pointed out more than a century ago. "Thousands of tired, nerve-shaken, over-civilized people are beginning to find out that going to the mountains is going home."

So, too, are rivers their own argument. The lapping sound of their waters is the most primeval sound in the world, our Ur-song; small wonder that in India the insane are often tied to trees alongside a river-bank, where the water's music helps soothe the confusion within. Just as other cultures, as Claude Levi-Strauss has reminded us, provide a tuning fork against which to sound our own, so the health of other species, the health of our woods and mountains and rivers, affords us a gauge by which to measure our own well-being. By this measure we are not doing so well, but in our recognizing this lies the germ of recovery.

The delicately balanced chain of life and the habitats of these arid places require constant protection, since humans, the chief agents of environmental change, are unlikely to alter their quotidian habits such that nature can put itself back in order. Where humans are not often found as permanent residents—the high country abutting the Gila's headwaters, for instance—there is perhaps less work to do, but every-where the intramontane West offers ample opportunities to reduce the effects of industrial-age humans on natural populations. As Aldo Leopold observed, "We abuse land because we regard it as a com-modity belonging to us. When we see land as a community to which we belong, we may begin to use it with love and respect." We can start by coming to know some of the animals that make their homes here, by paying closer attention to the lay of the land and the ineluctable rhythms of nature, by assuming guardianship of the rivers and moun-tains on which our lives ultimately depend. We can start by tending to our own garden, which is the world.

The nature of human beings is to dream. The nature of writers is to spin tales. It is time that we turn to better stories and dreams than the ones we have now.

A flowing Gila would be a start.

John Nichols

A TRAFFIC VIOLATION

Any implausible story worth its salt begins with an alarm going off.
"Shit!"

Arise, ye prisoners of starvation.

I woke up in a panic and started running. I had probably already
slept through three ten-minute snooze alarms. Today was National Feline Leukemia Prevention Day, so I scrambled about madly, grabbing
cats and shoving them one atop another into my cardboard Cat Caddy.
Last one in (Noodles), whom I crammed atop Elroy, Oopboop, Ginger,
and Muffin, squirmed, mewed, hissed, and clawed defiantly. But a
pumped-up Chelsey McFarland is nothing if not determined when the
chips are down, so I stuffed Noodles in among the others with a con-
temptible lack of sympathy for their claustrophobic dilemma.

But on a morning like this would my beater Buick convertible
(circa 1967) start right up soon as those first chipper little sparks hit the
eight eager piston chambers—?

"Oh *oh*!"

Then "I *hate* you, God! I *really* hate you!"

I fumbled in the glove compartment, ripping, digging, prying,
tossing out, flipping aside, pawing, pinching, cursing—"Ah hah!" A can
of Carb-Zap. I yanked the hood-latch handle, climbed over the jammed
driver-side door, raised the front hood, twisted the wing nut off the top
of the air filter, lifted the pan, poked open the gas jet lever (or whatever
it's called), and shot a few (environmentally murderous) squirts down its
gullet, then hurriedly circled the car, climbed inside, flipped the igni-
tion key—ROAR! A radiator fan blade hit the can of ether, belting it halfway across the driveway into a cluster of bachelor buttons, cosmos, and
still-flowering nasturtiums.

I really hate automobiles. I despise technology. I detest all the pollution *any* vehicle causes: cancer in my lungs, tumors in my brain, holes in the ozone. I *love* riding my bike. So all I'm asking is, when will the rest of the world wake up, raze Detroit and Japan, and return to public transportation, foot power, and velocipedes?

I replaced the air filter, banged down the hood, and headed north on Willow Road, creating one pound of carbon dioxide for every mile traveled. I actually cringed as blue smoke billowed out behind me, mugging a flight of evening grosbeaks in a box elder tree, scorching the petals of wild sunflowers, and laying a thin film of poisonous fallout on the foreheads of two Appaloosas staring benignly at my junker wheels.

"I'm sorry!" I shouted miserably. "I don't have the bread for a catalytic converter!"

What I really felt sorry about, however, were the plans to eradicate my beloved Willow Road, the last relatively untrammeled artery (and land) in our valley. Come November, in the election (Bush-Dukakis, what a choice!), a local mill levy proposition on the ballot (Prop X), if passed, would tax all of us befuddled citizens in order to build a highway bypass, an industrial park, and other assorted travesties on bucolic Willow Road. Coincidentally, the bypass would flatten my part-time employer (and albatross), Lydia Arlington Babcock, and in the process demolish a rare and endangered (and *very* boring) butterfly, the Rocky Mountain Phistic Copper, which called Lydia's property (and the end of Willow Road) its home. Enraged *(comme d'habitude)* by this short-sighted, environmentally terracidal project, I had recently decided to form an organization whose purpose would be to derail Proposition X. Given the politics and economic situation of our all-American town, plus the Neanderthal sensibilities of the goons who governed us, my protest would likely get me killed. But of course, I've always been one of those suicidal bleeding hearts who'd rather die free on their feet than grovel on their knobby knees like slaves.

Get the picture—?

When I turned off Willow Road onto Bayview, the modern world—the *real* world—hit me full in the face like a gigantic lemon meringue pie traveling at ninety miles an hour: *Poomph! Splatter! Glub!* First, in the Clarence Fagerquist Mobile Court, hundreds of bloated double-wides were lined end to end in an orgasm of aluminum siding and Astroturf welcome mats. Then came the Poddubny Estates, hermetically sealed Monopoly houses with an air conditioner in every window (*love* those CFCs!) and an ornamental maple blazing golden in the middle of every Weed Free Lawn.

"I need blinders like a fucking horse!"

I think I actually whinnied, a pathetic cry flung haplessly out into the gaping maw of an impersonal universe.

Then I slammed on the brakes in order not to cause a forty-one-car pileup. The brakes went to the floor, but when I pumped rapidly (forty-three times in 1.2 seconds), something caught, and at least the vehicle slowed down. I crawled a final half mile east behind the usual constipation of morning traffic, and turned left at the highway, out of Dante's Inferno and into Hieronymus Boschville. Like, if Jan van Eyck had met Andy Warhol's social secretary, they would have invented this strip, which, on the surface, contained six 7-Elevens, four Tastee-Freezes, eight video rental stores, five Exxon stations, two auto wrecking yards, three gravel pits, one General Uglification Warehouse, and two cut-rate beauty salons per square mile.

"Neon and freon!" I gabbled insanely, squinting against the glare. On the radio, WPNX disc jockey Randy Featherstone screamed, "HERE COME THE STONES!" and before you could shake a stick or shit a brick, Mick Jagger was bellowing that he couldn't get no satisfaction.

I knew the feeling well.

Four two-story cattle vans (Auschwitz or Bust!) thundered by, shuddering air and pavement and spewing exhaust in black molten clouds. A gas tanker aimed in the other direction swerved to avoid clobbering a Darth Vader monkey in a fluorescent pink rap jumpsuit on a Yamaha motorcycle. Then it swerved back just in the nick of time, striking only a glancing blow against a Winnebago from Anadarko, Oklahoma, home of the annual Joe Carey Bass-O-Rama (according to all twelve of its garish bumper logos). The Winnebago, encapsulated by hi-tech Rock Hopper mountain bicycles, was hauling a 4x4 Subaru truck and two Yamasaki Evil Knievel model dirt bikes.

I gritted my teeth and snarled, beeped at all the confusion, and passed on the right, pebbles flying. The usual assholes honked back, fired the required birdies, and shook their fists. I told them all to blow it out their fannies. Of course, I couldn't *see* half of them because they were hidden behind darkly frosted windows, anonymous voyagers on the road to hell. In fact, I bet half the cars lacked drivers altogether; they were simply proceeding under remote control, the playthings of invisible sadistic giants.

Joggers on the shoulders coughed and choked, inhaling eleven pounds of carcinogens for every mile traveled. Father Benny Wombat, corpulent religious factotum of the Guadalupe Catholic Church, and his best buddy, Farragut Martinez, devious mouthpiece for my friend Lydia Babcock, were huffing and puffing along, both recently discharged from quintuple bypass surgery compliments of Dr. Roderick "The Zipper" Nugent at our blighted paean to overpriced understaffed health care in America, Holy Cross Hospital. Father Benny could have been mistaken for a gargantuan rubber ducky, whereas Farragut was a dead ringer for all the cartoon turkey vultures in all those Walt Disney animated nature terror classics that have ever petrified our hallowed kiddies—thin, angular, hunch-shouldered . . . and slick as a piece of oiled taffy. Obliviously, the joggers performed adroit little hopping maneuvers over flattened cats and last night's lumpy harvest of fresh skunks. I expected that an enormous mutant pterodactyl would flutter down through the haze and commence spearing cyclists, Toyotas, maybe even an occasional Ford Escort with its razor-sharp talons. Made sense, *qué no?* I had to keep reminding myself whenever I traveled about town that this scene was "normal." Picturesque Willow Road, my quaint house and my surrounding gardens, was the aberration.

You could hardly see the nearby mountains for the smog.

When traffic finally thinned out, I hit the gas to make up for lost time. Promptly, the Southern Rocky Mountains' answer to Starsky and Hutch, Johnny Batrus, tripped his siren button and pulled me over.

Even before his ridiculous self-important macho ball-bulging saunter had carried him (and his filthy, alienating, one-way Mercury shades) to my door, my motor mouth was off and running:

"Johnny, Johnny, Johnny, I'm sorry, I'm late, I'm so late, I'll get fired if I don't make it to work on time and today's the only day they can fit in the cats for shots, I didn't mean it, I promise I'll never speed again, my doggone snooze button didn't work and then the car wouldn't start, so I hadda take off the air filter and squirt in some of that canned ether, listen, I'll give you guys a donation to the PAL this summer so you can buy baseballs made in Haiti by kwashiorkor vic—"

Great spiel . . . but it cost me thirty bucks anyway. It always does.

"That's just for going twenty over the limit," Johnny said. "I shoulda gave you another fifty for no seatbelt. Does this piece of crap even *have* a seatbelt? Well, you better get one, and then you better buckle up, because next time I catch you, Chelsey, I'm gonna throw the book."

Duduh, duduh, duduh.

Well, it served me right for not figuring out how to transport the cats on my bike.

Before I could split, however, a mud-spattered dyspeptic Toyota pickup missing the right front fender pulled over behind Johnny's cruiser, and a scrawny pop-eyed female dingaling jumped out, camera in hand: *click!click!click!* Then she skipped toward us, a ballpoint clamped between her teeth, flipping the yellow pages of her notepad.

"Hiya gang," this quirky zealot piped cheerfully. "Am I in time for a salacious tidbit? Hey Chelsey, what do I hear about this Butterfly Coalition?"

Susan Delgado, *Sentinel-Argus* cub reporter and the least popular carcinogen in Mapleville, U.S.A. But I kind of liked her, in a demented way. Being one myself, I guess I've always had a soft spot in my heart for grotesques.

"Beat it, Susan," Johnny said, heading back to his squad car. "Or I'll bust you for arrested development."

To me, he added, "You and Lydia Babcock deserve each other!"

Susan sighed, "Aww, gee. . . ." Then she just stood there, pigeon-toed, inhaling our exhaust. I felt bad, but I was in a hurry. *Ciao, baby—gotta book.* Save the scuttlebutt for later.

And anyway, the Butterfly Coalition was still supposed to be sort of under wraps, and once Susan got on the case it would be like bloodhounds in Bangladesh, searching for disaster.

"Kick back, lighten up, mellow out!" yammered Randy Featherstone. "It's a great gettin'-up morning and here to prove it are the Robocops with their hit single, 'Scum!' "

Oh Goody!

Gary Short

TEST

"You people who live near Nevada Test Site are in a very real sense active participants in the Nation's atomic test program."—ATOMIC ENERGY BOOKLET, PAGE 2, MARCH, 1957

The sky brightens with a flash.

A rancher feels the earth shudder
beneath his red roan.
He shields his eyes—
flesh is transparent,
his hand a diagram of bones.
My God, he whispers.

The mare shies,
only the pressure of his boots
urges her
through Eagle Valley to a ridge where
the only boundary
is the sky.

In the sparse shade of a Joshua tree
the pink clouds hover
over the ranges of his retina.

He rubs his burning nostrils
& tries to spit out the bitterness,

the metallic taste.

TIDINGS

Bitterness will flow
The earth will burn
—FROM A MAYAN PROPHECY

The bloated carcass of a wild horse
is not abstraction
but a specific example—

the cyanide that seeps into the creek
from heaps of dirt leached for microscopic gold,
its residue. The death of a mustang,
wind bristling a fetlock's stiff hair,
is a political statement.

Bitterness will flow

There are well-funded scientists
in a lab in California who breed weapons
delivered & unleashed at the Test Site
near cloud-shadowed Yucca Mountain.
A clacking train shakes the dreams
of a child in Fernley, Nevada.

Waking, she looks out the window. Her breath,
a quivering cell on the cold glass,
grows & then shrinks.
The bow on her white-sheep nightgown

is tied to sign for infinity.
She hears the lurching

boxcars full of harm
now past her. She cannot see
the steel tracks glint on & off in moonlight,
silvery rills of a stream
that runs to the vanishing point . . .

the earth will burn

Rebecca Solnit

FROM "FROM HELL TO BREAKFAST"

Dawn was only a faint glow behind the black crests of Skull Mountain and the Specter Range when I swung off Highway 95 and arrived, ten hours hard driving away from home. It was still too dark to pitch a tent, so I bundled my sleeping bag around me and curled up on the car seat. An hour later, groggy and aching, sleeping bag strings imprinted upon my cheek, I gave up on sleep and ventured out with my tin cup in hope of coffee. Someone who'd seen my little brother up at the gates of the encampment sent me his way.

In the morning light everything looked familiar again, the hard pale ground paved with rocks and the roads kicked into dust, the evenly spaced tufts of thorny grasses and scrubby bushes—the almost ubiquitous texture of the Great Basin, the plateau between the Sierra and the Rockies. The explorer John C. Fremont named it the Great Basin in the 1840s, when he realized that this vast expanse doesn't drain into either side of the Continental Divide. For one thing, there's hardly anything to drain. The major river in this place, the Humboldt, doesn't go anywhere at all; after flowing most of the way across northern Nevada it fades away into an alkali flat. Range after range of mountains, each separated by a flat expanse like the one the camp was in, rise for hundreds of dry miles across the state of Nevada into Utah, stretching north into Oregon and Idaho, hemmed in on the south by the Colorado River. It was the lowest, hottest, driest southwest corner of the Basin that I woke up in, and across the Funeral Mountains to the west, the Basin ends, and California, Death Valley, and the Mojave Desert begin.

I remembered to be afraid of the dust, the dust that might be radioactive, the dust that over the next few days would powder everything to biscuit color, the dust that might be the dust of the hundreds of nuclear tests conducted somewhere across the highway I'd just driven in on. At first I hadn't been alarmed by the dust here, and later it became second nature to fear dust everywhere, but this dust didn't look like anything special to the naked eye. Most studies suggested that the background radiation at the Peace Camp wasn't any worse than that in Las Vegas, seventy miles to the south, since they were both upwind of most of the nuclear tests—though that wasn't comforting, especially if you lived in Las Vegas. It wasn't the background radiation but the fallout mixed into the fine, pale, silky powder that posed most threat, however. "I will show you fear in a handful of dust," said a poet.

But to see mortality in the dust by imagining in it the unstable isotopes of radioactive decay took an act of educated faith or perhaps of loss of faith in the government. It looked like ordinary dust, and perhaps it will be, so far as the health of most of those who camped here are concerned. And people were living in this dust I had driven into, in a place called the Peace Camp, the gathering place for thousands who came every spring to prepare to invade the Nevada Test Site. The particular basin we were in is sliced in half by Highway 95, and across the road, along with Skull Mountain and the Specter Range, is the Nevada Test Site, the place where the U.S. and Britain have been setting off nuclear bombs for four decades, more than 900 so far in the hot secret heart of the Arms Race.

The Nevada Test Site (NTS) is big on a scale possible in few parts of the world, and in a way that only the West of the United States is big. The Test Site hewn out of Nellis Air Force Range in 1951 is 1,350 square miles, which makes it bigger than Yosemite National Park or Rhode Island. Nellis is a little over four times as big—5,470 square miles— bigger than Connecticut, a place that approaches one of the world's smaller nations in size—Israel, say, or Belgium. And if an army were to depopulate Belgium for half a century and explode hundreds of nuclear bombs on it, people would probably notice. Yet this has happened in the Great Basin, and few Americans know it has.

Before the bombs had gone underground, the public had been more aware of the goings-on at the NTS. The flashes were many times brighter than the sun, and those who were out before dawn could see the light of atomic fission from as far away as the mountaintops of northern California and southern Idaho. Strangely colored clouds drifted east across Nevada and Utah from the predawn explosions, and pictures of mushroom clouds sometimes appeared in the news. Nearby, the bombs felt like earthquakes. Since 1963, all of the tests here have been underground, but they have still been colossal explosions and they still leak radiation into the atmosphere. Since 1963, even most anti-nuclear activists haven't paid much heed to the Test Site. Nuclear war, whether you are for or against it, is supposed to be a terrible thing that might happen someday, not something that has been going on all along.

Test is something of a misnomer when it comes to nuclear bombs. A test is controlled and contained, a preliminary to the thing itself, and though these nuclear bombs weren't being dropped on cities or strategic centers, they were full-scale explosions in the real world, with all the attendant effects. I think that rather than tests, the explosions at the Nevada Test Site were rehearsals, for a rehearsal may lack an audience but contains all the actions and actors. The physicists and bureaucrats managing the U.S. side of the Arms Race had been rehearsing the end of the world out here, over and over again.

Even those who didn't question the legitimacy of the Arms Race sometimes questioned the necessity of testing. There were other ways to ensure the efficacy of existing nuclear weapons, and tests were only necessary for developing new weapons. The bombs set off in Nevada seemed instead a way of making war by display and displacement, as some cultures and species do—demonstrating their ability to attack rather than actually doing so. For every bomb set off in Nevada was potentially a bomb dropped on Odessa or Tashkent, and every bomb signified the government's willingness to drop a bomb on such a place, to pursue such a policy. And even if the bombs were invisible to most people in the U.S., the Soviets watched and took warning.

Other nations besides the U.S. and the U.S.S.R. had tested nuclear bombs, but only these two were rehearsing the end of the world, for they alone had developed enough bombs to annihilate not specific targets, but possibly whole continents of people and with them the natural order, the weather, perhaps the genetic codes of most living things. The bomb at Hiroshima was the end of a war, but the bombs on Tashkent and Odessa would have been the beginning of one, and the beginning of the end. The rehearsals were largely invisible, and so was the damage. Radiation is invisible, and the effects of radiation are invisible too. Although many more people are born with defects and die of cancer and other metabolic disorders in places affected by atomic fallout, the effects can only be calibrated statistically, with exhaustive research. There are already atomic epidemics, previews of what would happen to those who didn't die in an atomic war. And genetic damage—the scrambling of the codes—is as invisible as cancer, and as hard to trace to a cause. Radiation can make cells lose their memory, and loss of memory seems to be one of the cultural effects of the bombs too, for Americans forgot that bomb after bomb was being exploded here. Or perhaps people never forgot we were testing bombs, rehearsing the end of the world, but learned it so well and so deeply that the bomb makers no longer needed to terrorize children with bomb drills, or adults with civil defense scenarios and mushroom clouds on TV. Perhaps the bomb came to affect us all as an invisible mutation in our dreams, a drama we could watch in our sleep instead of the Nevada skies.

The Test Site was a blank on many maps, a forgotten landscape, off limits to the public and swallowed up in a state which itself seemed sometimes to be overlooked by the rest of the country. Even though Nevada is growing rapidly, its population is still not much over a million, half of it in Las Vegas and most of the rest of it in the Reno–Carson City area. There aren't many people living in all that open space, and few artists and writers have celebrated its qualities. Not very many people were displaced when the land that became Nellis was sealed off in 1941, when the population of Nevada was around 110,000, and not many people objected, because this landscape is widely thought to be worthless already.

Space itself isn't an absolute, or at least the spaciousness of landscapes isn't. Up close, aridity means that even the plants grow far apart from each other; for people and animals, this sparseness means that they too have to spread out to make a living off the land. In the East, a cow can live off a few acres of grass; out here the land is often overgrazed at only a few cows per thousand acres, and where they overgraze the soil erodes back to dust and rock. It is rock—geology—that dominates this landscape. In lusher landscapes, it is as though the skin and bones of the earth are dressed in verdure; here the earth is naked, and geological processes are clearly visible. It is geological time and geological scale that dominate this landscape, dwarfing all the biological processes within the uplift of ranges, the accretion of basins. The very rocks on the ground have lain in place so long around the Test Site that their tops and bottoms are different colors, and any disturbance leaves a lasting scar. Every act out here has to be measured against this scale of change and scope. It is this apparent geology, this bare rock, that makes newcomers read the desert as a dead or barren landscape, though if you spend more time in it, you may come to see the earth itself lives, slowly and grandly, in the metamorphoses of geology.

T. H. Watkins

NOT BY HUMAN MEASURE

Stone time has a separate measure. There are no clocks to mark its passage, no lexicon of hours by which to define its parameters. We make a lot of guesses, though, as if our estimates somehow were required to invest these works of earth with meaning. Bravely, we try to measure the years out in the rocks. Call it Jurassic, we say, and wrap up a few dozen million years; this is Permian, we claim, and encompass a universe of time. If stones could laugh, they would. Maybe real time is too much of a terror to be embraced without the labels with which we try so hard to pin it down. And maybe we have been thinking about it all wrong to begin with. "Chaos is the law of nature," Henry Adams wrote. "Order is the dream of man." In the darkest portion of the night in this country, when the moon hides on the other side of the world and only the stars wink back at you with their ice-eyes, when the solid darkness of the unseen walls and the landscape all around you makes you feel as if you are floating in a void, you can, if you concentrate long enough, imagine that you are peering so deeply into the tunnel of space that you can discern that farthest distance where the universe starts to bend, one curve in the long ellipse that turns Creation back in on itself—and with it all that we think we know of time. So considered, time is chaos given order not by human measure but by the mute imperatives of the universe itself, and it possesses no beginning and no end, only process.

Any lizard knows this. Its eye looks out upon the world of sun and hard edges, sees there much of what we see; but the reptilian gaze turns inward, too, as ours does not, looks back down a corridor of time to that moment when some stones and all lizards were young, and humankind was as yet ungraced by the breath of Creation. Nevertheless, there never has been anything in a lizard's eye compelling enough, it seems, to stop us in the pursuit of blind convictions, and it does not stop us here in the land of stone time, either. We not only persuade ourselves that we can take the human measure of inhuman time, we go further, and scribe the bounds of exploitation. This much is ours to use, we say, and that, and that. Listen: are the stones laughing yet?

That which we do not deign to use and use up we leave for what we call wilderness. There are those whose job it is to find it, mark it, make it visible in a boundaried age. They check the maps, walk around the country, lay it all out in finely drawn schemata. Yet they often seem to want to get it wrong. How else explain the wildness that has vanished from their charts? Exactly where, on such pages, does wilderness begin and end? There are better ways to measure and to use, and none rely on what we think we know. Here is one: Find a hidden canyon twisting in the sun, walk into its coils and climb until it narrows to a slit. Rest against the rock. Put out a hand and push against the fabric of the stone until it hurts. Feel it then: feel the weight of stone time.

Difficult as it is to know, stone time is your time, too. Stone and sky and water speak the language of memory. You may not understand memory here, but you cannot escape it. You can escape the hours of your life counted out like pennies, find refuge from the temple of your measured days, but you cannot escape the oldest memories we have. They are all around you in the ancient library of the bare and scoured rock, the volumes stacked on edge, then twisted and carved and slashed and broken, incised by the rivers, cleansed and polished by the wind. Look long and closely enough and you will find fossil memories so distant from known human experience that only the double helix of life itself preserves them. There are closer memories to be found on the stone, too, the mute articulations of the people who have vanished, the Anasazi, the Ancient Ones. Cabalistic geometry, stick creatures, ancestral gods play upon your mind, while seductive neolithic whispers murmur in your blood, almost as loud as the clamoring of your heart as you test it against the meandering challenge of the canyon. You are alone, here in this narrow, secret place. You are not alone, here in this narrow, secret place.

Solitude, like poetry, like the West (as poet Archibald MacLeish

reminded us), is a country in the mind. God knows, you can be un-
speakably alone standing on a city street corner, the pedestrian river
parting around your body like rushing water being split by a rock, the
barking of automobiles, the growling of trucks a kind of natural force,
like the sound of white water rapids or a high wind. But that is an inter-
nalized solitude, a fearful and niggardly thing, cutting all connections,
hoarding your perceptions behind a shell of indifference. It is not even
solitude; it is the most genuine loneliness.

There is no room for such indulgences in the land of stone time.
Here, the solitude is replete with connections and the clamoring life all
around you, the wide sky behind the piled-cotton clouds pulsing with
the depthless indigo of the troposphere, the sculpted redrock walls
stained with desert varnish like the big, careless splashes of a large-
souled painter, the trembling rustle of cottonwood leaves, the incom-
parable perfume of big sage rubbed between the fingers, the chuckle of
river-sounds, the keening cry of an eagle, the tumbling-down notes of a
canyon wren's song—all this demands an acceptance of the possible. Everything here is expectation, the premonition that even the ordinary is
likely to be invested with such shining individuality that it takes on the
character of the remarkable, the rare, the awesome. Unless the potential
for surprise has been leached from you, you cannot be lonely here,
merely solitary in your humanness.

And sometimes you get a message. In your wanderings, perhaps
you are lucky enough to encounter a mule deer browsing in the shade
of an enormous old cottonwood—a big doe whose muted gray-brown
hide makes her almost invisible in the mottled light beneath the tree.
You slow your pace, as if you were moving under water, mesmerized
by the sight of this sleek wild thing. You get very close before she raises
her head and looks straight into your eyes for a long, tremulous moment before she bounds away, appearing and disappearing repeatedly
with each impossibly graceful leap through the brush until she is lost to
sight, a dream to be remembered.

Connections. Place defined human beings as two-legged animals
without feathers. Even in the swarm of the cities we reflect that animal
nature—even if we refuse to acknowledge it and at the same time per-
vert it with the peculiarly human instinct for conscious cruelty. Savag-

ery is, perhaps, a function of intelligence, but if so it is not something from which we should derive much gratification. In this wild country it is possible to encounter and truly experience the sweet reality of other kinds of intelligence, minds more precisely tuned to the knowledge that echoes through corridors of evolution, telling us that none of us is alone on this cooling cinder. If we allow ourselves to put aside our arrogance long enough, perhaps we can read the lesson written in the eyes of lizards and deer deep in the land of stone time: this world and its creatures were not presented to us; we were joined to them in the exquisite saraband of life. The arrangement was never meant to be a conquest, and it is more deeply complex than a responsibility. It is a sharing.

So speaks the world of stone time. Come listen.

Suggested Additional Readings

Abbey, Edward. *Desert Solitaire: A Season in the Wilderness.* 1968. New York: Bantam, 1985.

———. *The Journey Home: Some Words in Defense of the American West.* New York: NAL–Dutton, 1977.

———. *The Monkey Wrench Gang.* New York: Avon, 1975.

Austin, Mary *The Land of Little Rain.* Boston: Houghton Mifflin, 1903.

Banham, Peter Rayner. *Scenes in America Deserta.* Salt Lake City: Gibbs M. Smith, 1982.

Cabeza de Vaca, Alvar Nuñez. *Adventures in the Unknown Interior of America.* 1542. Trans. and ed. Cyclone Covey. Albuquerque: University of New Mexico Press, 1988.

Fox, William L. *The Void, The Grid, & The Sign: Traversing the Great Basin.* Salt Lake City: University of Utah Press, 2000.

Heyne, Eric, ed. *Desert, Garden, Margin, Range: Literature on the American Frontier.* New York: Twayne, 1992.

Kappel-Smith, Diana. *Desert Time: A Journey Through the American Southwest.* Tucson: University of Arizona Press, 1992.

Krutch, Joseph Wood. *The Desert Year.* 1952. Tucson: University of Arizona Press, 1985.

———. *Grand Canyon: Today and All Its Yesterdays.* 1957. Tucson: University of Arizona Press, 1989.

Limerick, Patricia Nelson. *Desert Passages: Encounters with the American Deserts.* Albuquerque: University of New Mexico Press, 1985.

Lopez, Barry. *Desert Notes: Reflections in the Eye of a Raven.* Kansas City: Sheed, Andrews and McMeel, 1976.

McNamee, Gregory, ed. *Named in Stone and Sky: An Arizona Anthology.* Tucson: University of Arizona Press, 1993.

——. *The Sierra Club Desert Reader: A Literary Companion.* San Francisco: Sierra Club Books, 1995.

McPhee, John. *Basin and Range.* New York: Farrar, Straus & Giroux, 1980.

Meloy, Ellen. *Raven's Exile: A Season on the Green River.* New York: Henry Holt, 1994.

Powell, John Wesley. *The Exploration of the Colorado River and Its Canyons.* 1895. New York: Penguin, 1987.

Reisner, Marc. *Cadillac Desert: The American West and Its Disappearing Water.* New York: Viking, 1986.

Robertson, David. *Photo and Word.* Western Writers Series, No. 128. Boise, ID: Boise State University, 1997.

——. *Real Matter.* Salt Lake City: University of Utah Press, 1997.

Silko, Leslie Marmon. *Ceremony.* New York: Viking Penguin, 1977.

Stegner, Wallace. *Where the Bluebird Sings to the Lemonade Springs: Living and Writing in the West.* New York: Random House, 1992.

Tweit, Susan. *Barren, Wild, and Worthless: Living in the Chihuahuan Desert.* Albuquerque: University of New Mexico Press, 1995.

Van Dyke, John C. *The Desert: Further Studies in Natural Appearances.* 1901. Intro. Peter Wild. Baltimore: Johns Hopkins University Press, 1999.

Waters, Frank. *The Woman at Otowi Crossing: A Novel.* Athens, OH: Swallow, 1987.

Wild, Peter. *Desert Literature: The Middle Period.* Western Writers Series, No. 138. Boise, ID: Boise State University, 1999.

——, ed. *The Desert Reader.* Salt Lake City: University of Utah Press, 1991.

——. *The Opal Desert: Explorations of Fantasy and Reality in the American Southwest.* Austin: University of Texas Press, 1999.

Wilkinson, Charles. *The Eagle Bird: Mapping a New West.* New York: Pantheon, 1992.

List of Credits

About the Contributors

John Alcock is Regents' Professor of Zoology at Arizona State University. In addition to *Animal Behavior: An Evolutionary Approach* (1975), the most widely used textbook in the field of animal behavior, he has written many articles on desert biology for *Natural History* and *Arizona Highways* and has published a number of books of literary natural history, including *Sonoran Desert Spring* (1985), *The Kookaburra's Song* (1988), and *Sonoran Desert Summer* (1990). His essay "A Natural History" comes from *The Masked Bobwhite Rides Again* (1993).

Rudolfo Anaya has been a prolific and prominent figure in the Chicano literary renaissance that began in the 1970s and continues to the present. A native of Pastura, New Mexico, he studied at the University of New Mexico and later taught in the English Department there from 1974 to 1994. His novel *Bless Me, Ultima* (1972) may well be the all-time best-selling work of Chicano literature. He has also published many other novels, collections of stories, and books of essays. Three books—*Anaya Short Story Collection, Shaman Winter (A Sonny Baca Mystery),* and *Farolitos for Abuelo*—appeared in 1999. "Devil Deer," first published in 1992, was collected in *The Anaya Reader* in 1995. He continues to live in Albuquerque, New Mexico.

Jimmy Santiago Baca spent his teenage years on the streets of Albuquerque, New Mexico, and in various juvenile detention centers. He earned his high school diploma while serving a six-year sentence for possession of a controlled substance at a maximum security prison in Florence, Arizona—at the same time, he began to read literature and taught himself to write poetry. He went on to hold poetry residencies at the University of California, Berkeley, in 1989 and a year later at Yale University. His collections of poetry include *Immigrants in Our Own Land* (1979), *What's Happening* (1982), *Poems Taken from My Yard* (1986), *Martín and Meditations on the South Valley* (1987), *Black Mesa Poems* (1989), and *In the Way of the Sun* (1998). He lives in Albuquerque. His poem "Sparton Industry" was written specifically for this anthology.

Rick Bass has published fifteen books of fiction and nonfiction, including, recently, *Brown Dog of the Yaak: Essays on Art and Activism* (1999) and *The New Wolves: The Return of the Mexican Wolf to the American Southwest* (1998). His first novel, *Where the Sea Used to Be,* appeared in 1998. A native of Texas, Bass was raised in Houston and in the Texas hill country but has lived in the Yaak Valley of northwest Montana since 1987.

Bruce Berger received the Western States Book Award for his 1990 volume of essays, *The Telling Distance* (1990). He has published two other books of nonfiction, *There Was a River* (1994) and *Almost an Island* (1998), and the poetry collection *Facing the Music* (1995). He divides his time between Aspen, Colorado, and Baja California. "Transition Zone" appeared in *There Was a River.*

Gloria Bird is a member of the Spokane tribe of the *slawtaws,* or Chewelah band, a Kalispel band of the Flathead. Her books include *Full Moon on the Reservation* (1994) and *The River of History* (1996). She and Joy Harjo coedited *Reinventing the Enemy's Language: North American Native Women's Writing* (1998). She currently lives in Nespelem, Washington, on the Colville Reservation.

Steve Bodio's books include *Querencia* (1990) and *On the Edge of the Wild* (1998), among others. He has been a book review editor for *Gray's Sporting Journal* and a resident member at Sterling College's Wildbranch Writing Workshop. He has lived in Magdalena, New Mexico, for the past eighteen years.

Charles Bowden began his writing career as an environmental journalist with such projects as *The Impact of Energy Development on Water Resources in Arid Lands* (1975) and *Killing the Hidden Waters* (1977) and has since developed a vivid, gonzo-like narrative style for writing about the desert Southwest in such books as *Blue Desert* (1986), *Frog Mountain Blues* (1987), *Mezcal* (1988), and *Blood Orchid: An Unnatural History of America* (1994). The selection in this anthology comes from *Desierto: Memories of the Future* (1991). He lives in Tucson, Arizona.

Janice Emily Bowers is a naturalist who lives on the outskirts of Tucson, Arizona. For the past eighteen years she has worked as a botanist for the U.S. Geological Survey. She has published such books as *The Mountains Next Door* (1991), *A Full Life in a Small Place and Other Essays from a Desert Garden* (1993), and *Fear Falls Away and Other Essays from Hard and Rocky Places* (1997). The essay that appears in this collection is the title piece from *Fear Falls Away.*

Karen Brennan earned her Ph.D. at the University of Arizona and currently teaches creative writing at the University of Utah. She is the author of *Here on Earth* (1988), a poetry collection, and *Wild Desire* (1991), a book of short stories from which "Infidelity" was taken for this anthology. *Wild Desire* received the Associated Writing Programs Award for fiction.

SueEllen Campbell is an English professor at Colorado State University. "The Elements" comes from her 1996 book, *Bringing the Mountain Home.* She is the president of the Association for the Study of Literature and Environment (ASLE).

John Daniel is the author of *The Trail Home* (1992) and *Looking After: A Son's Memoir* (1996), both winners of the Oregon Book Award for Literary Nonfiction. His books of poetry include *Common Ground* (1988) and *All Things Touched by Wind* (1994), and he is the editor of *Wild Song: Poems of the Natural World* (1998). He lives in the foothills of the Oregon coast range, west of Eugene.

David Darlington is a freelance writer based in Berkeley, California, whose work often focuses on controversial aspects of southwestern natural history and conservation, especially when there's a California connection. He published *In Condor Country* in 1987 (reprinted as *In Condor Country: A Portrait of a Landscape, Its Denizens, and Its Defenders* in 1991). *Angels' Visits: An Inquiry into the Mystery of Zinfandel* appeared in 1991, followed by *The Mojave: A Portrait of the Definitive American Desert* in 1996 and *Area 51: The Dreamland Chronicles* in 1997.

Alison Hawthorne Deming teaches at the University of Arizona, where she also served for a decade as director of the University of Arizona Poetry Center. She received the 1994 Walt Whitman Award for *Science and Other Poems*. In 1994 she also published the essay collection *Temporary Homelands*. She edited *Poems of the American West* (1996), and her most recent books are *The Monarchs: A Poem Sequence* (1997) and *The Edges of the Civilized World* (1998). Her book *Writing the Sacred into the Real* is forthcoming in the Credo Series from Milkweed Editions, and she is currently finishing a new poetry manuscript titled *Genius Loci*.

David James Duncan is a novelist, nonfiction writer, fly fisherman, father, river advocate, and the author of *River Teeth* (1995); *The River Why* (1983), winner of the Pacific Northwest Bookseller's Award; and *The Brothers K* (1996), winner of a Pacific Northwest Bookseller's Award and an American Library Association Best Books Award. His essay "Lake of the Stone Mother" first appeared in *Heart of the Land: Essays on Last Great Places* (1994), edited by Joseph Barbato and Lisa Weinerman. Duncan lives with his family on a river in Montana, where he is currently finishing a book of essays.

Deidre Elliott has served as the nonfiction editor for *The Senora Review,* and her own work has appeared in *Northern Lights, The South Dakota Review, High Country News, Crazyhorse, Puerto del Sol,* and other periodicals. She also wrote the script for the PBS television series *Wild America.* She lives in Tucson, Arizona.

Suzanne Freeman has published her poetry in *Wilderness* Magazine.

Her work in this anthology appeared first in the special nature issue of *Southwestern American Literature*. She lives in Ingram, Texas.

Lisa Gerber completed her Ph.D. in philosophy at the University of New Mexico and currently teaches at Southwest State University in Marshall, Minnesota. Her essay in this anthology appeared in the special nature issue of *Southwestern American Literature*.

Ray Gonzalez is the author of five books of poetry, including *The Heat of Arrivals* (1996) and *Cabato Sentora* (1998). He published the essay collection *Memory Fever: A Journey Beyond El Paso del Norte* in 1993; a new, expanded edition appeared in 1999 from the University of Arizona Press. His numerous anthologies include *Currents Beneath the Dancing River: A Contemporary Anthology of Latino Literature* (1994) and *Touching the Fire: Fifteen Poets of the Latino Renaissance* (1998). His many awards include the 1997 PEN–Oakland Josephine Miles Book Award for Excellence in Literature. He currently holds a McKnight I and Grant Professorship at the University of Minnesota.

Susan Hanson lives in San Marcos, Texas, where she teaches writing at Southwest Texas State University. For more than a decade she wrote two weekly columns for the *San Marcos Daily Record*. In 1994 she received the Associated Press award for best feature article in a Texas newspaper. Her essays and book reviews focus on natural history and gardening.

Joy Harjo taught for many years in the Creative Writing Program at the University of New Mexico and performed in the band Poetic Justice. Her books include *In Mad Love and War* (1990), *She Had Some Horses* (1983), and *What Moon Drove Me to This?* (1979). *A Map of the Next World* was published in 2000. The poem included in this volume comes from *In Mad Love and War*. She now lives in Hawaii.

Steven Harrigan is the author of three novels—*Aransas* (1980), *Jacob's Well* (1984), and *The Gates of the Alamo* (2000)—and three volumes of nonfiction—*A Natural State* (1988), *Water and Light: A Diver's Journey to* *a Coral Reef* (1992), and *Comanche Midnight* (1995). A former senior editor at *Texas Monthly,* he now works as a freelance journalist and screenwriter, based in Austin, Texas. His contribution to this collection comes from *Comanche Midnight.*

Linda Hogan, who teaches at the University of Colorado, Boulder, is the author of many books of poetry, fiction, and essays. Her publications include *Power* (1998), *Dwellings: A Spiritual History of the Living World* (1995), and *The Book of Medicines* (1993). *Intimate Nature: The Bond Between Women and Animals,* which she coedited with Deena Metzger and Brenda Peterson, appeared in 1998. Her essay in this anthology comes from *Dwellings.*

Teresa Jordan, born and raised on a ranch in the Iron Mountain region of southern Wyoming, is the author of *Cowgirls: Women of the American West* (1984) and *Riding the White Horse Home* (1993). She has also edited *Graining the Mare: The Poetry of Ranch Women* (1994) and *The Stories That Shape Us: Contemporary Women Write About the West* (1995). *Field Notes from the Grand Canyon: Raging River, Quiet Mind* was published in 2000. "Playing God on the Lawns of the Lord" first appeared in *Heart of the Land: Essays on Last Great Places* (1994), edited by Joseph Barbato and Lisa Weinerman. Jordan currently lives in Salt Lake City, Utah.

Barbara Kingsolver's latest book, *The Poisonwood Bible* (1999), was a national bestseller. Her other acclaimed works of fiction include *The Bean Trees* (1988), *Homeland and Other Stories* (1989), and *Animal Dreams* (1990). The excerpt from her essay "High Tide in Tucson" comes from her 1995 collection of essays with the same title. She lives in Tucson, Arizona.

Ken Lamberton completed his M.F.A. in creative writing at the University of Arizona. He has published his natural history essays and creative nonfiction in such periodicals as *Snowy Egret, Bird Watcher's Digest, New Mexico Wildlife, Cimarron Review,* and *Southwestern American Literature.* In 1999 he published *Wilderness and Razor Wire,* a collection of essays. He lives in Tucson, Arizona.

Edward Lueders was a member of the English faculty at the University of Utah for many years. His publications include *The Clam Lake Papers: A Winter in the North Woods* (1977) and *The Wake of the General Bliss* (1989), and he edited *Writing Natural History: Dialogues with Authors* (1989). He and Naoshi Koriyama have collaborated on *Like Underground Water: Poetry of Mid-20th-Century Japan* (1995). He divides his time between Salt Lake City and Torrey, Utah.

Gregory McNamee lives in Tucson, Arizona, and is the author or editor of more than ten books, including *The Sierra Club Desert Reader* (1995), *Named in Stone and Sky: An Arizona Anthology* (1993), and *A Desert Bestiary: Folklore, Literature, and Ecological Thought from the World's Dry Places* (1996). His 1994 book, *Gila: The Life and Death of an American River,* from which the selection for this anthology comes, received the Arizona Library Association's Adult Author Award for 1995. His environmental and literary journalism has appeared in numerous publications, such as *The Nation, Outside, Audubon,* and *The Bloomsbury Review.*

Pat Mora, a native of El Paso, Texas, writes poetry, essays, and children's books. Her many publications include *Agua Santa: Holy Water* (1995) and *Garden: Voces del Jardin* (1997). Her poems for this volume come from *Agua Santa: Holy Water.* She currently lives in Santa Fe, New Mexico.

Gary Paul Nabhan is a John Burroughs Medal–winning essayist, conservation biologist, founder of Native Seeds/SEARCH, and the recipient of a MacArthur Fellowship. His work explores links among indigenous cultures, plants, and animals. He has published numerous books, including *The Desert Smells Like Rain* (1982), *Gathering the Desert* (1986), *Desert Legends: Re-Storying the Sonoran Borderlands* (1994), *The Forgotten Pollinators* (1997), and *Cultures of Habitat* (1998). His contribution to this anthology comes from his 1998 poetry collection, *Creatures of Habitat,* published in a limited edition by Tangram. Nabhan lives in Flagstaff, Arizona.

Barbara ("Barney") Nelson is an assistant professor of English at Sul Ross State University in Alpine, Texas, and the author of several books and numerous articles on ranching and landscape in the American West. Her latest book is *The Wild and the Domestic: Animal Representation, Ecocriticism, and Western American Literature* (1999).

Kent Nelson is the author of several novels and collections of short stories, including *Language in the Blood,* which won the Edward Abbey Ecofiction Award from *Buzzworm* Magazine in 1992. He published *Discoveries: Short Stories of the San Juan Mountains* and *Toward the Sun: The Collected Sports Stories of Kent Nelson* in 1998. His contribution to this anthology appeared in the 1995 special issue of *Southwestern American Literature.* He lives in Ouray, Colorado.

John Nichols is one of the best-known contemporary novelists and essayists of the American Southwest. His many books include the New Mexico Trilogy (*The Milagro Beanfield War* [1974], *The Magic Journey* [1978], and *The Nirvana Blues* [1981]), *On the Mesa* (1986), *The Sky's the Limit* (1990), and *Keep It Simple* (1993). A new book, *Dancing on the Stones: Selected Essays,* appeared in 2000. He lives in Taos, New Mexico.

Naomi Shihab Nye, from San Antonio, Texas, has published many books of poetry, such as *Tattooed Feet* (1977), *Different Ways to Pray* (1980), *Hugging the Jukebox* (1982), *Yellow Glove* (1986), *Red Suitcase* (1994), and *Words under the Words: Selected Poems* (1995). Her latest collection is *Fuel* (1998).

Simon J. Ortiz was born and raised at Acoma Pueblo in New Mexico. He has taught at numerous colleges throughout the United States and is the author of several poetry collections and editor of *Earth Power Coming,* a collection of Native American fiction. Three of his earlier poetry volumes were reprinted in *Woven Stone* (1992). *After and Before the Lightning* appeared in 1994. He published *Men on the Moon: Collected Short Stories* in 1999. He currently lives in Tucson, Arizona.

Robert Michael Pyle lives in Washington State on a tributary of the Columbia River. Besides hundreds of magazine articles, his many books include *Wintergreen* (1986), winner of the John Burroughs Medal for natural history writing, *The Thunder Tree* (1993), *Where Bigfoot Walks: Crossing the Dark Divide* (1996), *Chasing Monarchs* (1999), and *Walking the High Ridge* (2000). He has also written a number of important butterfly guides, such as the *Audubon Society Field Guide to North American Butterflies* (1981). He coedited *Nabokov's Butterflies,* a collection of Vladimir Nabokov's butterfly writings. His contribution to this anthology is a transcription from his field notes during several trips to the Southwest in the 1990s.

Alberto Rios is a professor of English at Arizona State University. The author of many collections of poetry and short fiction, he received the Walt Whitman Award in 1981 for *Whispering to Fool the Wind* and the Western States Book Award in 1984 for *The Iguana Killer: Twelve Stories of the Heart.* In 1999 he published *The Curtain of Trees: Stories* and *Capirotada: A Nogales Memoir.* The poems in this book appeared earlier in the special issue of *Southwestern American Literature.*

Ann Ronald is the author of *The New West of Edward Abbey* (1982, reprinted in 2000) and editor of *Words for the Wild: The Sierra Club Trailside Reader* (1987). She is currently completing *GhostWest,* a book of narrative scholarship set in the American West. Her contribution to this anthology is from *Earthtones: A Nevada Album* (1995), which combines her essays with photographs by Stephen Trimble. She is a professor of English at the University of Nevada, Reno.

Wendy Rose, a native of Oakland, California, has been coordinator of and instructor in American Indian Studies at Fresno City College since 1984. Her tribal affiliations are Hopi and Miwok. She has published more than a dozen books of poetry, including *Bone Dance: New and Selected Poems, 1965–1993. Halfbreed Chronicles* appeared in 1996. Her poem in this anthology is from the collection *Home Places: Contemporary Native American Writing from Sun Tracks* (1995), edited by Larry Evers and Ofelia Zepeda.

Sharman Apt Russell was born at Edwards Air Force Base, California, and grew up mostly in Phoenix, Arizona. She earned a B.S. in conservation and natural resources at the University of California, Berkeley, and an M.F.A. in creative writing at the University of Montana. Her nonfiction books include *Songs of the Fluteplayer: Seasons of Life in the Southwest* (1991), *Kill the Cowboy: A Battle of Mythology in the New West* (1993), and *When the Land Was Young: Reflections on American Archeology* (1996). Her children's book *The Humpbacked Fluteplayer* (1994) imagines what the Sonoran Desert would be like without the presence of Phoenix. *The Last Matriarch,* a novel, appeared from the University of New Mexico Press in 2000. Her essay "Gila Wilderness" comes from *Songs of the Fluteplayer.* She teaches writing at Western New Mexico University in Silver City.

Leslie Ryan received her M.S. in environmental studies at the University of Montana and has taught field courses since 1994 for the Sierra Institute (University of California, Santa Cruz) in southern Colorado and southern Utah. When not teaching in the Southwest, she lives in rural Virginia. Her writing has appeared in several journals and anthologies, including *Northern Lights: A Selection of New Writing from the American West* (1995), edited by Deborah Clow. The short story included in this book is set in the mountains along the Colorado–New Mexico border, just along the Tierra Amarilla Land Grant.

Benjamin Alire Sáenz, a native of Las Cruces, New Mexico, teaches in the English Department at the University of Texas, El Paso. His first book of poetry, *Calendar of Dust,* won an American Book Award from the Before Columbus Association in 1991. A year later he published *Flowers for the Broken*—the essay "Cebolleros" comes from this book. Since then he has written such volumes as the poetry collection *Dark and Perfect Angels* (1995), winner of a Southwest Book Award, and two novels, *Carry Me Like Water* (1995) and *The House of Forgetting* (1997).

Reg Saner, a long-time Coloradan, recently retired from teaching writing at the University of Colorado in Boulder. His many awards include the first Walt Whitman Prize for poetry and an NEA Fellowship. His book *So This Is the Map* (1981) was selected by Derek Walcott for the national poetry series. He published *Reaching Keet Seel: Ruin's Echo* *and the Anasazi* in 1998. His essay "Chaco Night" comes from the 1993 book *The Four-Cornered Falcon: Essays on the Interior West and the Natural Scene.*

Richard Shelton is the author of nine books of poetry, including *The Bus to Veracruz* (1978) and *Selected Poems: 1969–1981* (1982). His memoir, *Going Back to Bisbee,* received the 1992 Western States Book Award for creative nonfiction. He is the Regents' Professor of English at the University of Arizona.

Gary Short has been a Stegner Fellow at Stanford University and a resident of the Fine Arts Work Center in Provincetown, Massachusetts. He is the author of *Theory of Twilight* (1994) and a second book of poems, *Flying Over Sonny Liston* (1996), which received the Western States Book Award. He is from Nevada and currently teaches in the M.F.A. program at Old Dominion University.

Rebecca Solnit is an independent art critic and journalist based in San Francisco, California. The recipient of a 1993 NEA Fellowship for creative nonfiction and a Guggenheim Fellowship in 2000, she has numerous publications, including *Savage Dreams: A Journey into the Landscape Wars of the American West* (1994), *A Book of Migrations: Some Passages in Ireland* (1997), *Wanderlust: A History of Walking* (1999), and *As Eve Said to the Serpent: Essays on the Contemporary Landscape* (2001). Her contribution to the anthology is from *Savage Dreams.*

Luci Tapahonso, a native of Shiprock, New Mexico, is a member of the Navajo Nation. She has published several books of poetry, including *One More Shiprock Night* (1981), *Seasonal Woman* (1981), *A Breeze Swept Through* (1987), *Sáanii Dahataal / The Women Are Singing: Poems and Stories* (1993), *Blue Horses Rush In: Poems and Stories* (1997), and also several children's books. She currently teaches at the University of Arizona.

Stephen Trimble lives in Salt Lake City, Utah, where he writes about and photographs western wild places and native peoples. His 1989 book, *The Sagebrush Ocean: A Natural History of the Great Basin,* won the Sierra Club's Ansel Adams Award and the High Desert Museum's Chiles Award. His other books include *The People: Indians of the American Southwest* (1993), *Words from the Land: Encounters with Natural History Writing* (2nd expanded edition, 1995), and *The Geography of Childhood: Why Children Need Wild Places* (1994), co-authored with Gary Paul Nabhan. Based on a novel in progress, "On the Back of the Dragon" won third place in the 1995 Frank Waters Southwest Writing Awards. It was published in *ISLE*: Interdisciplinary Studies in Literature and Environment. Catherine S. Fowler, from the University of Nevada, Reno, helped with the section of the story in Southern Paiute.

T. H. Watkins was the author of more than 300 articles and book reviews for some fifty journals, magazines, and newspapers and was the author, co-author, or editor of twenty-six books. *The Redrock Chronicles (Saving Wild Utah)* was published by Johns Hopkins University Press in 2000. His contribution to this anthology comes from the 1994 book *Stone Time: Southern Utah: A Portrait and a Meditation.* He was the Wallace Stegner Distinguished Professor at Montana State University before his death in 2000.

Peter Wild has published more than fifty books and monographs, ranging from literary criticism to poetry to a book about the life cycle of the saguaro cactus. He is also a prolific editor, and his anthologies include *The Desert Reader* (1991) and *Into the Wilderness Dream: Exploration Narratives of the American West 1500–1805* (1993). His contribution to this anthology comes from the 1994 poetry collection *Easy Victory.* He teaches in the English Department at the University of Arizona.

Terry Tempest Williams is the author of *Pieces of White Shell: A Journey through Navajoland* (1984), *Coyote's Canyon* (1989), *Refuge: An Unnatural History of Family and Place* (1991), *An Unspoken Hunger: Stories from the Field* (1994), *Desert Quartet: An Erotic Landscape* (1995), and two children's books. She received the Southwest Book Award for *Pieces of White Shell* in 1985, a fellowship from the Lannan Foundation in 1993, and a Guggenheim Fellowship in 1997. A lifelong resident of Utah, she recently moved from Salt Lake City to the desert outside Moab. *Leap,* her latest book, appeared in 2000. Her contribution to this book includes a transcript of her field notes that resulted in the writing of her essay "Homecoming" and the completed essay.

Ofelia Zepeda is a professor of linguistics and American Indian studies at the University of Arizona. She is the author of two collections of poetry, *Ocean Power* (1995) and *Jewed 'I-Hoi: Earth Movements* (1997), and numerous articles on the O'odham language. She edits the Sun Tracks series for the University of Arizona Press. Her poems in this anthology come from *Ocean Power.*

Ann Haymond Zwinger is the author of numerous books about the natural history of the American West. *Run, River, Run: A Naturalist's Journey Down One of the Great Rivers of the West* (1975) won the John Burroughs Medal for natural history writing in 1976. She received the Distinguished Achievement Award from the Western Literature Association in 1991. Her 1995 book, *Downcanyon: A Naturalist Explores the Colorado River through the Grand Canyon,* received the Western States Book Award for creative nonfiction. Her recent books include *The Nearsighted Naturalist* (1998) and *Shaped By Wind and Water* (2000). She lives in Colorado Springs, Colorado, and is an adjunct professor at Colorado College.

About the Editor

Scott Slovic is an associate professor of literature and the environment at the University of Nevada, Reno, where he directs the Center for Environmental Arts and Humanities. The author of numerous articles on environmental literature, he has also written or coedited seven books, including most recently *Reading the Earth: New Directions in the Study of Literature and the Environment* (1998) and *Literature and the Environment: Readings on Nature and Culture* (1999). He served as founding president of the Association for the Study of Literature and Environment (ASLE) from 1992 to 1995. Currently he edits ASLE's journal, *ISLE: Interdisciplinary Studies in Literature and Environment*.

Index